THREE KINGS

ALSO BY TODD BALF

The Last River: The Tragic Race for Shangri-la

The Darkest Jungle: The True Story of the Darién Expedition and America's Ill-Fated Race to Connect the Seas

Major: A Black Athlete, a White Era, and the Fight to Be the World's Fastest Human Being

Complications: The Diagnosis Was Bad. The Aftermath Was Calamitous. My New Life As a Medical Train Wreck.

HOW RECORD-SMASHING SWIMMERS JOHNNY WEISSMULLER, DUKE KAHANAMOKU, AND KATSUO TAKAISHI CHANGED THEIR SPORT AND EACH OTHER FOREVER

THREE KINGS

TODD BALF

BLACK STONE PUBLISHING

Blackstone Publishing
31 Mistletoe Rd.
Ashland, OR 97520

www.BlackstonePublishing.com

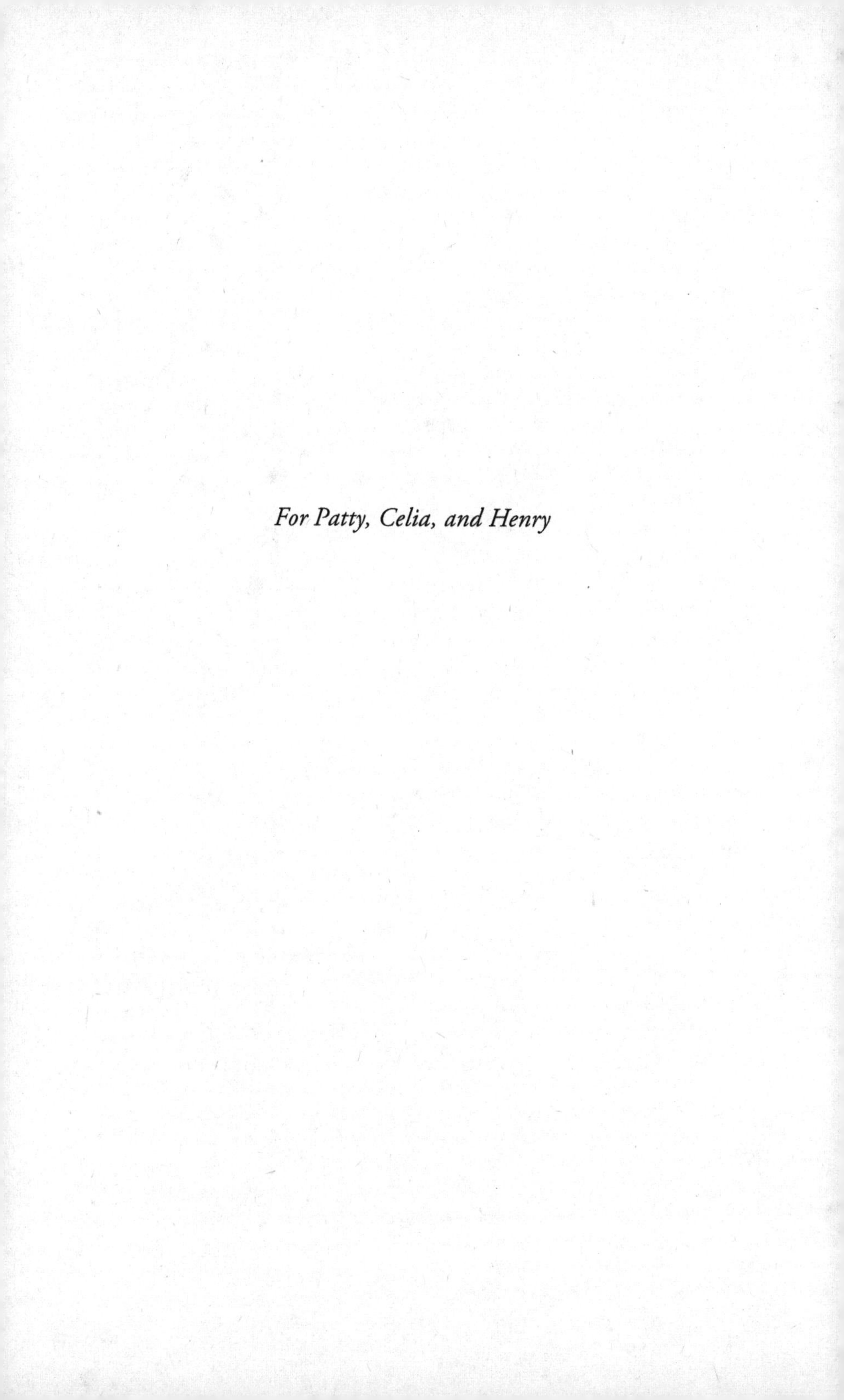

For Patty, Celia, and Henry

CONTENTS

1957
"DUKE KAHANAMOKU,
THIS IS YOUR LIFE!"

DUKE KAHANAMOKU is killing time on a Hawaiian-themed soundstage in Burbank, California, believing he is about to do an advertising shoot. He is wearing a loose-fitting aloha shirt and dark slacks, his long hands slid comfortably inside the deep pockets. His thick silver hair is slickly combed back as if he has just cracked the ocean surface after a swan dive. A veteran of waiting around for the cameras to start rolling, he's chatting amiably with a production assistant.

Then suddenly the lights come up, the famous television host Ralph Edwards steps forward out of nowhere, and the camera pans to reveal a studio audience cued to full roar. "Duke Kahanamoku . . . this is your life!" Edwards booms.

Those at home expecting a knee-buckled, jaw-dropped reaction from Kahanamoku will be disappointed. Instead, what they get is calm bemusement, his steady, agreeable gaze suggesting he is no more excited by the moment than if he'd just arrived at a cocktail party. There is a gentle, warm smile, though.

Edwards, host of the popular show that surprises celebrities with onstage retrospectives of their lives and careers, tells Kahanamoku that tonight's episode of *This Is Your Life* is about "a little Hawaiian boy who became the most famous swimmer in the world." He competed in four Olympic Games between 1912 and 1932, obliterated world records, and is now considered not only the father of modern swimming but of surfing, too. He is known worldwide as Hawaii's ambassador, the ever-welcoming face of aloha.

Today's date is February 20, 1957, thirty-three years since Duke's last Olympic podium appearance, alongside American teammates Johnny Weissmuller and his brother Sam Kahanamoku. *This Is Your Life* is a top-rated show, and no expense seems to have been spared. Just about everybody is on hand, short of the Duke of Windsor, whom Kahanamoku famously took surfing in 1920 when the former king was Prince of Wales. Kahanamoku's seven brothers and sisters come around the curtain, followed by Duke's former coach George "Dad" Center and Michael McDermott, a teammate from the 1912 and 1920 Games. Then three of the eight people Duke courageously rescued after their boat capsized in huge surf at Newport Harbor, California, in 1925. The anecdotes pile up as Duke smiles his placid smile.

Retelling his story — especially the turbulent early 1920s, when he shuttled between Waikiki and Los Angeles seemingly not sure where his future lay — has held little interest for Duke. Coaxed by his wife, Nadine, he recently described a few keystone events in longhand on three unlined sheets of pink mimeograph paper. As he had done his whole life, he left out the slights and struggles and betrayals, choosing frictionless occasions of triumph and joy. He would never publicly share stories of bigotry (though restaurants denied him service and he was unwelcome to race in the American South), but there was no hiding the unspoken narrative. At the same time the champion Black boxer

Jack Johnson was arrested in Chicago for transporting a white female companion across state lines, Duke was named as a co-respondent in a divorce suit in Hawaii, accused of having an affair with a beautiful British society woman who was white. The months prior to his arrival in Paris as captain of the 1924 U.S. swim team were even more fraught. He was investigated for violating amateur rules, which threatened his Olympic standing; sentenced to ten days in jail for speeding in Los Angeles; made headlines by competing in a white-only pool in Pasadena; and awaited judgment in a malice suit he brought against a white-owned Honolulu newspaper that had admonished him for skipping a race that the paper sponsored. The article called him a "slacker" and "quitter" who wasn't worthy of his people.

None of this is part of the show, of course. But those memories are stirred when the most famous person from Kahanamoku's past is introduced. Before he strides in, his disembodied voice consumes the studio: "This was my first Olympic meet and I was many years younger than Duke . . . ." Johnny Weissmuller, known primarily for his role as Tarzan on the silver screen, enters in a dark business suit, his shoulders as broad and angular as a carpenter's T square. Gregarious and ever playful, he grabs his former rival, pulling him close, brown eyes dancing.

Unlike Duke, Weissmuller had willingly lived his life in the celebrity spotlight, beginning as a young man in Paris in 1924. Like Duke, he represented peak human form — an Adonis, as he was described in 1920s parlance. Unlike Duke, he was white. Because of this, there had been little doubt that Weissmuller would be famous, but from the start, he proved himself to be infamous, too. During the ocean voyage to the Paris Games, he capped off a team talent show by swinging from a chandelier and letting out a jungle roar, a portent to his future as the Ape Man. He would only get more outrageous as a gold medal winner. In undated photos at the International Swimming Hall of Fame, he is surrounded by a smirking women's swim team, his white robe collected at his feet, his nude body resplendent.

Few knew Weissmuller was raised in racially violent Chicago, abandoned by an abusive, alcoholic father, and haunted by a lie that threatened each of the five Olympic gold medals he won in 1924 and 1928. At the height of his swimming fame, he paired with a famous doctor, John Harvey Kellogg, who founded and zealously led the Race Betterment Foundation, a eugenics organization that advocated for extreme methods to prevent the dissolution of the white race. As with horses, Kellogg hoped to advance a program of eugenic marriages and biological sanitation to breed more thoroughbreds just like Johnny.

Today's Weissmuller is heavy and jowly, privately worn down and struggling to stay financially afloat. But he can still charm, and he can still race. A few months later, a U.S. team swimmer training for the Olympics would encounter Weissmuller on the pool deck of the War Memorial Natatorium in Waikiki. To the swimmer's embarrassment, the "balding, overweight" Weissmuller stripped down to an "ancient racing brief," readying to demonstrate his famous freestyle sprint. But rather than creak forward, Weissmuller transformed into "a sleek torpedo that lunged out two body lengths, hit the water, and never looked back." His stroke was "poetry in motion," said the transfixed young Olympian. Weissmuller touched out at 27.1 seconds for fifty meters.

"Eh polu," Kahanamoku had muttered in Hawaiian when he first heard the familiar backstage voice. His brothers, situated around the set's centerpiece, a catamaran, nodded. In that moment, Duke was suddenly far away, thinking not about the aged man in front of him but his brash, record -breaking, twenty-year-old counterpart, the two of them in side-by-side lanes in a Paris pool, one man white the other dark, waiting for the starter's gun.

Ralph Edwards, having heard Duke's remark about Weissmuller, looked at him curiously. "What does that mean?" he asked. "Or perhaps you shouldn't tell me."

A WORLD AWAY, ANOTHER SWIMMER watches Kahanamoku and Weissmuller closely on his television. Their size is as imposing as ever — Katsuo Takaishi, still fit and trim, is a head shorter than his Paris adversaries, closer in stature to the program host, Edwards. Now a successful executive and founder of a swimming school in Osaka, Takaishi's stunning performance in that same 1924 race launched a revolution in Japan, leading to a national program that in a mere eight years supplanted the U.S. as the world's swimming powerhouse. When Takaishi left for Paris, there were few racing coaches in Japan and only two swimming pools, one of which he and his teenaged teammates had dug for themselves. He was not a high school dropout like Weissmuller and Kahanamoku but a full-time business student at Waseda, a prestigious if restive university in Tokyo. He was nineteen at the time of the 1924 Games, part of a tiny Japanese delegation of twenty-four athletes versus three hundred fifty Americans. As an Asian who was dismissed as just one more of the "little yellow men" by the French founder of the modern Games, Baron Pierre de Coubertin, Takaishi surely shared a sensibility with the Pacific Islander, Kahanamoku. He knew what it was like to be demeaned as less than.

But he also had the arrogance of Weissmuller. He was a handsome icon with a bright, camera-friendly smile, so popular in his own country that when he returned from a competition in Hawaii with a tight Navy cut, it launched a countrywide *mobo* (modern boy) hairstyle craze. He would go on to become the first Asian to medal in the Olympics in swimming, and from 1924 to 1928 was considered the leading challenger to Weissmuller's sprint crown.

The artificial construct of a fifty-meter pool with marked lanes built for sporting glory and maximum speed might have been new to Japan, but the practice of moving powerfully through water with one's body was centuries old, dating to feudal times when samurai used swimming as a means of defending clan territory. They had a warfare stroke for swimming in full armor, a way of treading water with just their legs so that they could point bows and arrows at enemy targets, and a vertical jump that allowed them to extricate themselves from whirlpools or tangles of seaweed or to catapult onto a boat. They had specific strokes for lakes, oceans, and rivers, each technique adapted to challenging and specific conditions. The swimming martial arts, called *Nihon eiho,* gave rise to bustling schools and innovative teachers. By the time of the 1924 Games, with the samurai era long over, Tokyo and Osaka coaches had turned their attention to the pursuit of speed.

The Japanese were the truest sea people, they believed, heirs to a rich and honorable tradition. For the two men on stage that night in Hollywood, that 1924 race might have been just a game — albeit a high-stakes one — measured in microseconds, millionaires' handshakes, and bronze, silver, and gold trophies. For Takaishi the consequences went far beyond that, and the possibility of failure overwhelmed him. All these years later, it's not hard to remember. In his mind's eye, Paris was like the succulent in his garden whose rare flowering was impossible not to wish for.

Three men, three skin colors, one race: In the most beautiful city stadium ever built, with the fastest swimming strokes ever seen, they had ushered in the modern Olympic age.

ONE

PARIS
1924

"This stirring feature was held in the finest swimming stadium ever built, and every seat was taken long before the opening gun sounded."
—Grantland Rice,
New York Herald Tribune

ON SUNDAY, JULY 20, 1924, twelve thousand spectators — the men in bowler hats, the women twirling parasols — leaned forward in their seats at the sold-out, swelteringly hot Piscine des Tourelles outdoor stadium in Paris, waiting on the starter's gun. Douglas Fairbanks Jr., Mary Pickford, and the famous sprinter Charley Paddock, just dethroned as the world's fastest man, sat in lower boxes. The august French director of the Olympiad, Count Justinien Clary, was unmissable with his wizard length white beard. The Games' founder, the diminutive Baron Pierre de Coubertin, was there too, delighted by the arena's positive energy. Outbursts from Italian fascists and spectator riots had tainted the previous weeks, but this moment was golden, like a Fresnel lens, bending many points of light into a singular beam so strong and luminous it could cut through the darkness of a stormy sea.

All had turned out despite an ongoing heat wave that scorched the city with 100-degree temperatures. On tap was the long awaited 100-meter swimming showdown between Chicago's brash world record holder, Johnny Weissmuller, and Hawaii's stoic Duke Kahanamoku, the two-time defending Olympic sprint champ.

Competing against each other for the first time ever at the Olympics, the two stood side by side on the edge of the pool deck, the lanes separated by ropes supported with floating cork. Crouched for the start, their arms stretched behind them like airplane wings, each man was strikingly handsome, their muscles outlined in wool singlets. Coming out of an era when leisure-seeking beachgoers wore full-body swimsuits, Kahanamoku and Weissmuller now looked the way young men ached to look: physical, free, and desirable. Boilers installed only weeks earlier heated the water to a race-optimum seventy degrees.

Weissmuller, barely turned twenty, had strutted confidently to the pool, welcoming the cheers of the crowd. Kahanamoku, the elder statesman at thirty-four, was notably more reserved.

Though the two men were public comrades on the same American team, the Games were still in their infancy, with athletes more aligned with hometown sporting clubs than the stars-and-stripes-branded national organization. Weissmuller was the face of Chicago's Illinois Athletic Club (IAC). The city's mayor, William "Big Bill" Thompson, had cofounded the club a couple of decades earlier, spearheading construction of a twelve-story building on South Michigan Avenue with a twenty-yard pool in the basement. A mammoth Olympic-themed frieze stretched across the building's facade, Zeus commanding the center and his mortal descendants sprinting, jumping, and throwing to his left and right.

Kahanamoku was the face of territorial Hawaii, which had raised the funds for all three of his Olympic appearances. He and his Waikiki beach friends had become locally famous years earlier, when they started their own grassroots club, an answer to the restrictive, white-only clubs in Honolulu. They called it Hui Nalu, or "Club of the Waves," and in calligraphic script penned its mission statement on a scrap of paper. Hui Nalu was like nothing anyone had seen in amateur sports: a world-renowned championship swim team whose members were largely brown skinned and native born.

Hawaiian-bred champions like Duke were seen as the natural product of a semicivilized ocean environment. By contrast, Weissmuller was thought of as a modern human engineering marvel, the product of the best coaches, the best pool, and the most advanced techniques.

America had become the dominant swim nation in the 1920s, especially in the crowd-favorite sprint events. Once-supreme swim strokes from England and Australia had been usurped by the American crawl, and the rest of the world was now playing catch-up. But all the stakeholders were there in 1924: the British, Aussies, and Swedes, all with the tall and rangy body type believed to be ideal for slashing through water at record speeds.

———

JAZZ AGE 1920S WAS THE PERFECT TIME for the emergence of a sport that produced larger-than-life creatures who embodied innovation, physical perfection, and, above all, speed. These were fast times, with everything changing at a breakneck pace. As a

1920s British news clip about the era announced, "Everything is going up, from the stock market to aerial stunts."

Superhuman endurance feats were good, superhuman speed was better. Bullet-shaped race cars overtook steam-fired motorbikes which had overtaken bicycles raced on banked wooden tracks. Ballroom dancing gave way to the Black Bottom and Charleston. Prohibition had no answer for smugglers and speakeasies. Young, discharged servicemen fled the World War I battlefields, seeking something new and exciting.

The impossible was possible, from climbing through the clouds to the world's highest peak to plunging into the world's deepest and most remote gorge. Lost civilizations — the magical Shangri-la, the Amazon's Lost City of Z — seemed in reach and were pursued. Oceangoing luxury liners were crossing seas at unheard-of speeds. Daredevil aviators set mouths agape, like seventeen-year-old Elinor Smith, who flew under all four bridges spanning New York's East River. Showstopping sportswomen proliferated, some earning as much as $15,000 a day to risk life and limb. A nineteen-year-old Nebraskan walked on the wings of a biplane without a safety harness; a sixteen-year-old from Long Island, atop her horse Red Lips, dove from a sixty-foot-high platform at an amusement pier in Atlantic City; a twenty-year-old Arizonan named Viola, newly arrived in Los Angeles with a trendy platinum bob, stood triumphant on the chestnut brown shoulders of a Hawaiian surfer off Laguna Beach, a look of euphoria beaming forth as they rode to shore.

An infatuation with the fit, unclothed human body spread across prudish home shores. Strongmen, virile and bare chested, flexed on the covers of glossy physical culture magazines at newsstands. Bathing beauties emerged in boardwalk contests. Camera lenses widened then zoomed in.

Swimmers became icons, first in sports pages then in Hollywood films, brave saviors to drowning starlets, or handsome foils to a league of funny men from Charlie Chaplin to Harold Lloyd.

The sport modernized, moving from cold lakes to heated pools and from dirty rivers to gleaming stadiums. Multiday races were held in towns from Peoria to Spokane. Fast times became faster. Previous records were no longer challenged every four years but every month; great rivalries emerged internationally but also between the East Coast and West Coast and Hawaii and the mainland. Scientists were called in, paid coaches arrived, money changed hands. The best swimmers, once part-time vaudeville performers diving for live fish or holding their breath and playing dead underwater, were now full-time racers obsessed with a singular, barrier-breaking goal: to swim 100 meters in less than a minute. These athletes could now swim faster than most Americans could run. Especially notable: Women, once considered too physically weak and delicate for competition, were allowed to join Olympic teams.

Pools begat pools at a staggering pace. No longer only at elite city men's clubs or soul-saving YMCAs, they appeared everywhere. In 1924 in the U.S., there were thousands of new pools, some as large as ball fields. Once called "tanks" — cramped and almost square, with life preservers mounted every few feet — pools were now long, rectangular stretches of water with taut lane dividers and black stripes painted on the bottom, straight and true as milled planks.

The pool mania wasn't limited to America. Hundreds appeared in France, a war-ravaged country where there had been few pools. Tokyo, leveled by a 1923 earthquake that took more than 100,000 lives, was rebuilt with countless pools dotting the landscape.

Swimming was pragmatic, a laudable life sport endorsed by civic leaders and family doctors. It was increasingly democratic, available to more people than ever before. The shameful exception was people of color, who were barely allowed at pools and beaches but were battling to get in. You didn't need to walk on an airplane wing or drive a race car to feel the thrill of letting loose. Swimming was fast and frenetic — the fluttering, breathless equivalent of a flapper dance.

THE MOST INTRIGUING COUNTRY to be transformed by the Roaring Twenties was Japan. Propelled by its young, Europe-smitten princes, Hirohito and Chichibu, no culture was changing faster. On downtown boulevards in Tokyo, it wasn't unusual to see young women strolling, some in full-length kimonos, others in colorful, gauzy blouses and flapper skirts. Tokyo and Osaka had become cosmopolitan centers to rival New York and Berlin, with luxury department stores, teeming dance halls, and cafés. Filmmaking thrived, the marquees popping with avant-garde titles such as *A Page of Madness* or Hollywood-style samurai dramas.

Young, boundary breaking women worked during the day and did what they wanted at night. Lithographs showed female athletes in Western-style swimsuits and bobbed cuts with kiss curls, poised atop high diving boards or in solo racing dories, bare arms strong and straining against oars. The liberated modern girls, *mogas,* appalled their elders: They smoked, drank, even divorced.

Within the Olympic scene in Paris, the unlikely emissary of Japanese modernism was Katsuo Takaishi, a nineteen-year-old unknown from an Osaka neighborhood along the banks of Yodogawa River. He impressed in the preliminaries, especially with his fast, powerful start. For the 100-meter final, he was in lane three, next to Duke and two lanes away from Sam Kahanamoku, whom Takaishi virtually tied in the semifinal heat. His small stature was incongruous with others' on the pool deck. His feet looked childlike compared to Duke's paddlelike size thirteens.

Takaishi had never competed, nor previously traveled, any-where outside his native Japan. He was coached by an Osaka junior high school PE teacher, Den Sugimoto, who had, along with his students, studied American swimming textbooks to adapt samurai-era strokes. When his students, including Takaishi, shock-ingly defeated the elite traditionalists from Tokyo universities a few years earlier, they were derided as "Monsters from the West."

At poolside, the slight Sugimoto was part of an assortment of largely anonymous coaches. The exception was William "Big Bill" Bachrach, or Bach, the American team coach who had discovered Weissmuller. Once characterized by his 350-pound girth and a money belt full of gold coins, he was now much slimmer and had toned down his personality to befit the dignity of the Olympics. The outcome of this race would make him a legend, and a wealthy one. He had reluctantly swapped the ratty bathrobe he liked to wear at the IAC for a tailored suit. Just before leaving for Paris, he had appeared at a club luncheon in Chicago, entertaining his lads by showing up in his familiar robe, which he opened to expose, as he put it, "what was no longer there." After the laughter died down, he added, "I can see my toes for the first time in years."

The Olympic record for the 100-meter was 1:01.4, set by Duke in 1920. This race would be faster if each racer started brightly, turned cleanly, and desperately drove each other to the final touch. For the first time in history, the judges would use Swiss-made pocket chronometers accurate to one-hundredth of a second. But Bachrach, Sugimoto, and David Kahanamoku, Duke and Sam's brother, had their own timepieces raised and ready. The brown, yellow, and white bodies were a rare and intoxicating sight. The stakes were self-evident. Motion picture cameramen flicked their switches, and Radio Paris began its broadcast to a waiting nation. Winning the race, the swimmers knew, meant everything.

TWO
QUEENS BREAK
1898 – 1912

"On land the South Sea Islander is an indolent, shiftless being, the height of whose ambitions appears to be to see how long he can lie undisturbed."
—Jim Nasium, *The Philadelphia Inquirer,* in an early profile of Duke Kahanamoku

A DAZZLING FULL MOON illuminated Honolulu Harbor in the early morning hours of August 13, 1898, as the steamship *Gaelic* arrived from San Francisco. The nervous uncertainty onshore was palpable, so much so that a small boat was sent out to the vessel to hastily check on the condition of the returning Hawaiian monarch, Queen Liliʻuokalani. She was said to be dying, a rumor that trailed her train car east to west across the United States and subsequently across the Pacific. The recent influx of red fish in the harbor, a traditional harbinger of bad luck, spiked fears higher.

The queen was fine, the scout boat confirmed, but still there was death in the air. As native Hawaiians had known for weeks, Lili'uokalani had been unsuccessful in persuading American lawmakers to reverse the overthrow of her independent nation. Instead, the U.S. government, led by the new administration of William McKinley, had sided with the group of powerful white capitalists — the so-called Committee of Safety — who had staged a coup five years earlier, removing Lili'uokalani from power and later placing her under house arrest for five months. On this trip, the queen had spent many months in the U.S. Capitol, filing so many appeals, she recalled, that "I have written enough for the wastebaskets of Washington."

As Lili'uokalani disembarked the *Gaelic,* the scene was mournful. Grief-stricken followers trailed her royal carriage along the oleander-scented Waikiki waterfront to Washington Place, her official residence. In the coming daylight hours, the low weeping and agonized chants would be replaced by a *ho'ok-upu,* a traditional ceremony dating back centuries in which subjects paid homage to a ruler safely returned from a long voyage. Throughout the day people descended on foot and horseback to the queen's residence, bringing modest bundles for tribute, until hundreds of her subjects filled the lawn and garden — a garden "to dream in," as one newspaper correspondent in attendance wrote. There were packages of taro roots, she continued, with their beautiful leaves attached; tropical fruits and rare upcountry flowers; dried fish wrapped in ti leaves; and live fowl. "Before entering the house [where they would approach prostrate with hands extended to the queen] each native deposited the gift on the lawn," wrote the correspondent, "and soon the chickens and live things made a fainting, fluttering pile . . . passed hand to hand and finally disappeared in the kitchen."

The royal band showed up playing the most famous songs that the queen, herself a talented published composer, had written. Two years earlier, freed from house arrest, she had translated into English her Hawaiian-language love song "Aloha 'Oe," ("Farewell to Thee"), knowing it would come to be thought of as an anthem of pride, even resistance. As the band played and hula dancers slowly swept side to side in ancient rhythms, the sound of weeping rolled through the queen's open doors, gentle but powerful, like the unceasing Waikiki surf.

Two weeks later the deal was done, and the American flag was raised over 'Iolani Palace. The queen, refusing exile in order to "show my people how to meet this," didn't attend the ceremonies but chose instead to stay at her residence, wrapped in a cloak depicting the Hawaiian flag. She was a woman in private life now, she said, but "my heart is my country, my flag, my people. My heart is Hawaii."

Queen Lili'uokalani remained in Honolulu as promised. She lived at Washington Place, but as time went by she increasingly favored her charming Waikiki Beach cottage fronting one of the surf breaks. Open on two sides, featuring a living room filled with Hawaiian artifacts, the home was called Ke'alohilani, "royal brightness." She called her retreat "my pretty seaside cottage," a place where she found leavening joy. The queen composed music, translated favorite Hawaiian works, entertained close friends. "I danced among the rooms," she wrote. "It was my own."

When she sat on her wraparound front porch, word would circulate, and the most talented young surfers lined up offshore at a favorite break named for her. They were there to perform for their queen. One of them, a teen named Duke Paoa Kahanamoku, was well-known to Lili'uokalani and everyone else in the city. He was a prodigy.

As she looked out to the waves, she saw Duke on a long-board he made himself — his early creations from redwood planks eventually graduating to a traditional *olo* board sixteen feet long and weighing more than a hundred pounds. "*He Kaʻeʻaʻeʻa pulu ʻole no ka heʻe nalu,*" she often said, acknowledging a clean, dry ride. What the queen saw, in his power and grace, surely reminded her of the royal ancestors who once were the only ones still practicing the ancient sport. Closely tied to Hawaiian religious traditions, surfing was known as "the sport of kings." Liliʻuokalani herself was a surfer.

Heading back for another ride, Duke began long hoe, the windmill stroke, in calm fashion, easily powering through the incoming surf. Beyond the break, as he had done a thousand times before, he stopped, waiting for the right wave. When it came, the sprint began: His head low, he dug in with deep, overhand, pulling strokes — a burst of energy to match the wave which had the capacity to build in strength and form for thousands of uninterrupted miles. The gymnastic display was described in a 1911 magazine story in which the astonished writer saw an approaching "mountain of water" then "a vigorous and deft paddling with all the strength and skill that can be put into trained arms, and great effort is made."

Week after week, Duke performed for an audience of one on the break that still evokes her memory, Queens. Years later, when asked about his effortless swim stroke, Duke would say he didn't know where it had come from, it just was. But it traced back to those early days spent on a surfboard, giving *leʻaleʻa* (pleasure) to the queen.

White thieves had stolen her kingdom. But in the joy, power, and youthful independence of Duke's wave riding, which linked past to present, Liliʻuokalani felt undeniable hope. The

American flag now flew high above 'Iolani Palace, but the surf was theirs alone.

———

BY THE TIME HE WAS EIGHTEEN, Duke was already viewed as a special talent, though he didn't see it himself. He was the first-born child of Duke Kahanamoku and Julia Paoa, both of whom had families with close associations to Hawaiian nobility. Duke Kahanamoku Sr. was born August 2, 1869, coinciding with a state visit from Prince Alfred, the Duke of Edinburgh. As it happened, the prince had expressed "a desire to see Hawaiians collected together," leading to a traditional feast hosted by Princess Bernice Pauahi Bishop. (Her husband, the American Charles Reed Bishop, founded Hawaii's first major bank.) Since Alfred was interested in native customs and a late-afternoon downpour had curtailed the outside entertainment, the princess led her guest to the Kahanamoku household, where her close friend had just given birth, an event that coincided almost to the day with the Royal Navy HMS *Galatea*'s arrival in Honolulu Harbor. The name Duke was given to the baby boy to please the prince and honor his visit. Years later, referencing his father's diary, Sam Kahanamoku insisted that his parents, so caught up in the Anglomania that gripped Oahu, changed the family surname to Edinburgh, going back to Kahanamoku only around the time Duke Jr. was born in 1890. When Duke was three years old the family moved to the Kalia neighborhood along the Waikiki beachfront, which was part of a large tract of land given to Julia's father during the monarchy and home to numerous relatives, including a growing band of cousins around Duke's age.

Duke Sr., a clerk and later a police officer, was not a

competitive swimmer, but Kalia was the province of some of the best native swimmers in Oahu, the best of whom was Kimokeo, the revered Hawaiian Islands sprint champion in the late 1890s and early 1900s. Described as a knot of muscles with an overhand, leaping style, Kimokeo was mostly relegated to native-only races. But in 1897 and 1898, in a boost to local pride, he beat a white Californian in a series of 100-yard showdowns on Regatta Day.

During Duke's youth Kalia was renamed Fort DeRussy after the U.S. military acquired seventy-plus acres of shoreline property and filled in historic fishponds and taro fields to create battlements. Kalia natives received minimal compensation for their land and quickly saw the traditional look and feel of the neighborhood vanish, replaced by a bustling military outpost and soldier R&R haven. Resentment grew between young Hawaiian men and the haole visitors who cut through their yards and caused disturbances after a night of drinking. Isaiah Walker, an author and Hawaiian historian, recalled that his great-grandmother was given only $2,000 for her four and a half acres of beachside Kalia property after the military condemned it as uninhabitable. At considerable expense, she failed in the courts to reverse the decision. The mood in changed Kalia in the early 1900s was tense. The resentment was largely subsurface, but it was there. The Kahanamokus were right in the middle of it. "His community was basically taken by the military," said Walker. "Those are tensions that shape you."

Still Duke Sr. and Julia chose to stay in Kalia and raise their children in the freedom of the ocean. Stories abounded of Julia giving young Duke, then his numerous siblings, full license to explore the water around them, almost as if the sea could be trusted in a way the newly contested land could not.

Duke and his younger brother David played in the cool

freshwater of the ʻĀpuakēhau stream, which flowed down from the verdant Mānoa and Pālolo valleys, entering the bay near the Moana Hotel. Duke's earliest memories of the ocean came from pushing a cracker box board out into the surf. "You can take a small board and go a long way," he said years later. "I used to swim out, turn around, and come back through the surf." His first time swimming in deep water came on a canoe trip with his father and uncles. After getting seasick in the pitching surf, he was instructed to dive overboard, the cooling water being a well-known remedy for nausea.

Duke was fourteen when he entered Honolulu's Kamehameha School for Boys, part of a heralded school system started by the Bernice Pauahi estate to educate native-born children. The curriculum was rapidly changing. The schools had recently — at the orders of the white provincial government led by Sanford Dole — begun to emphasize forced assimilation edicts, similar to what Native Americans endured on the mainland. "Kill the Indian in him, save the man," was the philosophy. Traditional cultural practices were eliminated at the Kamehameha schools and the Hawaiian language was forbidden inside and outside school walls. The boys wore military-style uniforms and were directed into the manual trades. According to biographer David Davis, Duke was taught hand- and machine-sewing skills to become a tailor and handwriting skills that made him "a voluminous letter writer throughout his life." In his last year at Kamehameha in 1909 (he would have a brief stay at a public school before dropping out), Duke played basketball and football, ran track, and starred on the championship soccer team. As a tall, broad-shouldered teen he became known among his peers for his water talents, though many white islanders believed native swimmers were not suited to sprinting and were good only at distance because, according to the Honolulu *Evening Bulletin*, "they were always in the water." By 1909 he was a fixture in Honolulu Harbor, and that same year was recruited, along with another native Hawaiian swimmer, for a hotly contested relay race between two white rowing clubs, Healani and Myrtle.

The race was held before a huge crowd "gay with that flutter of feminine clothing, everyone leaning perilously over the water at wharf's edge," reported the *Hawaiian Gazette*. Each leg was about fifty yards. Kahanamoku, the untested Healani anchor, was identified in the previous week's *Hawaiian Star* as a "wonder in the water . . . a Waikiki surfboard expert called Duke." He started his leg twenty yards behind the other anchor, George Center. There appeared to be no chance for Kahanamoku, but his gameness "appeared so strongly . . . the spectators yelled themselves hoarse."

He had closed the gap to one stroke with three yards to go when he inadvertently struck Center's leg in a wild finish, losing at the final touch. Still, Kahanamoku came away from the experience knowing, as he would say, "there was something in me to be a great swimmer." The papers reported that he needed work swimming straight but was plainly much faster than the older Center. At the time the most acclaimed canoe and swim racer in Honolulu, Center saw in Kahanamoku a talent well beyond his own.

After Duke's debut, the Myrtle and Healani clubs didn't stage another match the following year as expected, despite the 1909 event being described by the *Gazette* as having "thrills enough to make up for sixteen horse races and twenty-four baseball games." At the end of 1910, the *Honolulu Advertiser* reported that nothing had happened in the last year and a half and the sport of swimming had "died out." The white clubs could readily see that the native-born superstar was poised to supplant them.

Kahanamoku had turned his full attention to the new club he had conceived two years before with fellow surfing friends Kenneth Winter and William "Knute" Cottrell. Their club resulted from Cottrell overhearing a remark from a member of the all-white Outrigger Canoe Club which "disgusted us quite a bit." Like the other clubs in Honolulu, they created an insignia and even later composed a fight song; but unlike the white clubs, they added a mission statement that made them decidedly different. Their organization wouldn't be based on social connections or skin color but pure athletic merit. It would offer a home to native Hawaiian athletes long kept out of the popular, club-based competitive paddling and swimming events in Waikiki. Home base was the ocean in front of them, an expansive, ever-changing playground, from the dynamic Queens break to the still water at Bishop Slip. There was never any clubhouse. They used the Moana Hotel basement bathroom as their changing room. They hung out beneath the hotel's broad-leafed hau tree, where Kahanamoku and many early members — the so-called Waikiki beach boys — gave tourists surfing and canoe lessons.

Fees were $1.00 annually. The members were appealingly self-deprecatory, initially calling themselves VLS (Very Lazy Surfers) or the "poor man's club," before settling on Hui Nalu (Club of the Waves). They wore simple white or black tank tops with a round "HN" logo. Their founding sentiment was brotherhood, the title of their mission document being "Fellowship — (the 'why' of the Hui Nalu)." Kahanamoku and the two other founding members knew they were doing something different and made sure to photograph it, posing casually in the sand in front of an outrigger canoe and beneath the hau tree, then formally in slacks, button-downs, bow ties, and straw boaters.

They were idealistic nobodies, but led by Kahanamoku the Hui Nalu soon grew to be the strongest team of swimmers ever assembled, dominating the national scene for the next six years. All the top swimmers in Honolulu joined, including, uniquely, several female athletes. From the beginning the club was integrated and color blind. Duke's light-skinned hapa-haole founders looked nothing like him. Both born in Honolulu, they were the sons of white, mainland-born fathers. Cottrell's mother was Hawaiian, Winter's was Chinese.

When Kahanamoku was interviewed in 1911 after the swimming event that would change his life, the reporter said he wanted only to talk about Hui Nalu. "He pledges body and soul to it," he wrote, with plans to assemble the first Hawaiian team to compete on the mainland. The membership rolls had swelled from three to twenty-seven. "He speaks of Hui Nalu in like manner as a priestess to her cult."

Kahanamoku's vision and enthusiasm were surely informed by experiences that came from living in a place once his own but now someone else's. He never in his life publicly claimed the mantle of resistance and self-determination, but as a young man he didn't have to. Hui Nalu spoke for itself.

At the same time Hui Nalu was gaining notoriety, a powerful patron of sorts emerged: William Rawlins, a Honolulu-born white attorney. He had been a swimmer at Yale University, participating with other Hawaiians on a 1901 team that won the first ever national collegiate championship. As a longtime Healani member, he had seen Kahanamoku perform in the 1909 relay race and later asked if he could informally time him over 100 yards. He encouraged Kahanamoku to recruit more members for Hui Nalu and to practice more regularly. In 1911 Rawlins helped organize the first Hawaii chapter of the national Amateur Athletic Union (AAU), the governing body of amateur sports based in New York. He also announced a nonsegregated, open swimming event in Honolulu Harbor, featuring race distances from fifty yards to half a mile. Hui Nalu would make its team debut against Healani, a club that barred Duke from membership. At the time no national record was recognized without a club affiliation. Rawlins, the son of a sugar plantation owner, never claimed to discover Kahanamoku or coach him, but he was indispensable to both Duke and the Hui Nalu team, a necessary bridge between two worlds — theirs and his.

Rawlins knew Kahanamoku could set world records and went to much expense to ensure his times would hold up under national scrutiny. The thrice-measured straightaway course was set up off Alakea Slip, the start point being a wooden plank and the finish line a taut overhead rope. Three timekeepers and four judges were employed. The invited public, primed for a sporting spectacle after days of teasing newspaper previews, came in massive numbers, lining the commercial wharf where a naval battleship, a towering German coal barge, and a San Francisco–bound passenger steamship provided backdrop. Members of the Royal Hawaiian Band played. Canoes along the wharf were filled with sailors in dress whites while above them, beneath the shelter of long warehouse roofs, the Waikiki citizenry peered down. The conditions were ideal, reported the *Honolulu Advertiser*, with cooling trade breezes for the fans and water as calm as a "mill pond" for the racers.

In the feature 100-yard sprint, Kahanamoku and his fellow dark-skinned Hui Nalu teammate Dan Keaweamahi anticipated seven Myrtle and Healani opponents but only three showed up. When the starter's gun fired, Kahanamoku broke away instantly, extending his lead over the four other men until there appeared to be no one following him at all. All three timekeepers clocked identical finishing times: 55.4 seconds.

At the time only five swimmers in the world had finished the 100 in under a minute. The open-water American record, held jointly by the New York Athletic Club's Charles Daniels and John Scott Leary of The Olympic Club in San Francisco, was one minute, a full 4.6 seconds slower. In the 50-yard and

220-yard sprints, Kahanamoku also crushed existing world records — in the former, beating the runner-up George Center by thirty yards. The only person seemingly unaffected by his world records was Duke himself. When an *Advertiser* reporter arranged a time to meet him for his big interview, he found him shoeless and asleep under a palm tree. "Such graceful indifference to clamoring reputation in the making would have broken a half dozen fluttering and liege hearts on any beach in any state," he wrote. "It would have been taken as a sign of easy superiority. The takers would be wrong."

Hui Nalu soundly defeated Healani and Myrtle club swimmers, capturing all of the seven races, most of them easily, including the relay. The Outrigger club, rumored to fear the embarrassment of losing to the newcomers, never showed up. A day later, an anonymous Outrigger member wrote an editorial for the *Advertiser*, saying Kahanamoku shouldn't collect his team's trophy, because "he is one of those Hawaiian boys who make their living by taking tourists out for canoe surfing in the Waikiki breakers." Such work, the man argued, made Kahanamoku a professional "so far as the Outrigger organization is concerned." Another anonymous writer mentioned the $30 prize Hui Nalu collected for winning the canoe race and claimed it disqualified them as amateurs.

Outrigger retracted the accusations the next day, but it marked the beginning of a campaign that would plague Kahanamoku for the next fifteen years. After almost every major victory, rumors that he was professional, not an amateur, would swirl, and the AAU investigations would soon follow. Healani and Myrtle continued to try to shut out Kahanamoku and Hui Nalu, refusing them the use of their six-oared practice canoe and ensuring that the feature race on Regatta Day in September would be a two-club match, not three.

In Kalia and other native neighborhoods, Duke's rewriting of the American record book sparked joy and retellings of past mythic water feats from royal forebears. On the mainland, however, the reaction to the wire stories was doubt and disbelief. AAU officials said the times were an impossibility; that elite records might fall by a fraction of a second but not whole seconds, and certainly not four seconds plus. The islanders might try timing with stopwatches, the AAU reportedly suggested, not clocks.

The paternalistic assumption that trustworthy records needed to be set on the mainland, not a backward place in the middle of the Pacific, understandably struck a nerve. "We are some sporting nation," said an article in the Sunday *Advertiser*, "but it must be admitted that that part of 'we' which hangs around the corners of Tecumseh, Maine, and 45th Street, New York, are sometimes inclined to turn a collection of supercilious noses skyward over any American record or world's amateur record of any sort being by a 'South Seas Islander' who they might actually think at this moment is blowing the ashes under a pot destined for parboiling a missionary."

Six months later the AAU's record keeper, Otto Wahle, finally replied to Rawlins's request to certify Kahanamoku's time. Wahle was an émigré who medaled for the Austrian swim team in 1900 and moved to New York a year later, soon becoming a coach at the New York Athletic Club. He had little interest in dignifying the Hawaiians but had been nudged into action by a peer of sorts, the Hawaii-born physician Luther Gulick, director of phys ed of the YMCA who created the Y's triangular mind-body-spirit logo.

In his letter, Wahle told Rawlins that Kahanamoku's 100-yard record couldn't be approved. He argued that many little things could have affected the time, like drifting of the starting platform, faulty timing devices, or currents that gave the swimmers a push.

Also, they had seen this before. In 1905 Dan Renear, a police officer and champion swimmer living in Hawaii, had similarly shocked the East with a one-minute flat time in the 100, setting a new world record. Renear's subsequent performances on the mainland were nowhere near that fast. In fact, Renear finished dead last in his debut contest, a regional race in Philadelphia.

For all these reasons, Wahle wrote, Kahanamoku, "an unknown," would only be recognized after swimming in regulation tanks, against known swimmers doing the most technically advanced strokes taught by master coaches like Wahle himself. If he wanted his times to be considered official, Kahanamoku should travel to Pittsburgh and Chicago for the 1912 Summer Olympic trials.

Islanders had already anticipated the "come prove it" message, and by the end of the year, a fundraising effort had begun. Donors were listed in the newspapers, and benefit events such as baseball games, bicycle races, and dances filled the winter months. Early notable donations were from a remote leper settlement and the dense congregation of pure-blood Hawaiians living in Hana on Maui. "If all the gifts were as large in proportion to the means of the givers, the fund would have been oversubscribed weeks ago," said the fundraising chair.

On February 7, 1912, Duke and several Hui Nalu comrades, bedecked in leis, left Honolulu Harbor aboard a steamer. The group was comprised of fellow Olympic hopeful Vincent Genoves; Lew Henderson, their team manager; and Edward "Dude" (pronounced "dudie") Miller, a trusted trainer. Miller organized the beach boys' thriving tourist services and had traveled to the mainland previously as a bandleader. The Hui Nalu, including Duke, called him, "The Commodore."

Several hundred well-wishers saw them off at Matson Wharf with a quintet singing "Aloha 'Oe," the national anthem composed by Queen Lili'uokalani. "And it was off and away," reported the *Hawaii Gazette*, "with the speedy water artists on whom the territory is banking to bring her much fame and advertisement."

A few days earlier the *Honolulu Advertiser,* without comment, had reprinted a cartoon from a mainland paper captioned, "Hawaii has two athletes to send to Stockholm." A pair of dark-skinned, barefoot men were pictured with agitated faces, running full gallop, one swinging a machete, the other, a crude club. They wore grass skirts, giant rings in their ear lobes and, in case anyone was confused, carried surfboards.

THE HUI NALU TEAM had hurriedly left Hawaii short of their fundraising goal and short on time. The national championship races, held on back-to-back weekends, had been flipped, the first ones now in Pittsburgh, not Chicago. Getting to Pittsburgh meant their arrival in San Francisco was followed by a same-day departure for Chicago. While waiting for their train connection from Chicago to Pittsburgh, Henderson photographed the young island stars in their dress suits, playing in the snow, Kahanamoku crouched in front of a knee-high "first snowman." They pulled into Pittsburgh on February 20. The Olympic middle-distance qualifying races at the Pittsburgh Athletic Association Natatorium were in just two days.

George Freeth, a Hawaiian champion surfer and diver living and performing in Southern California, wrote a friend: "I see by the papers that Duke and Vince are on their way to Pittsburgh for the [Olympic] tryouts. There is only one chance for them to get beaten, and that's in a small tank. A tank 100 feet long in that part of the country is a pretty long tank. It is a shame that they could not come down here [Redondo] for a month to get used to tank work. We have three tanks here."

On the evening of the twenty-second, the pool's balcony and several closed windows were covered in American flags. A simple chandelier hung high above the deck. What little seating was available was oversold, the patrons seeming all to be cigar smokers. Grimy, odorous clouds collected along the ceiling, descending lower as the evening progressed.

The twenty-five-yard tank (twenty-five feet shorter than the length mentioned in Freeth's letter) had lifesaving rings attached to rails every ten yards. Having only ever swum in open water, an overeager Kahanamoku couldn't help himself in his first 220-yard event. Arms firing rapidly, his feet fluttering like whirring propellers, he went out too fast, dramatically cramped midway and, in front of hundreds of gasping onlookers, sank to the bottom of the pool. For the first and last time in his life, the semiconscious Kahanamoku needed to be saved from drowning.

Dozens of papers printed articles with headlines like one in the *San Francisco Chronicle*: "Duke Kahanamoku Collapses in Race." The embarrassment was profound. When the news reached Hawaii, there was disbelief, then fatalistic sighs. "For twenty-four hours," a Hawaii columnist later wrote, "[Kahanamoku] was the joke of the country — a championship aspirant almost drowning in a tank."

Two nights later, Kahanamoku won the fifty- and 100-yard sprints, the latter in an eye-catching 57.45 seconds. Two days after that, he and his team traveled to the University of Pennsylvania, where George Kistler, Dan Renear's former coach, had invited them to train for the Chicago qualifying events. Kahanamoku broke a tank record for 100 feet, one length of the pool, and easily defeated the local phenom, John Shryock, the 100-yard collegiate champion. His blistering 57.15 time for 100 yards was even more remarkable since he did it without any of the tank swimming tutorials he supposedly needed. The headline in a Philadelphia newspaper read, "Foreign Swimmer Competes at Penn."

On March 13, at the venerable Chicago Athletic Association (CAA) Kahanamoku won his third straight race, securing his berth on the Olympic team. In Pittsburgh, CAA swimmer Perry McGillivray had buried the drowning Duke. Two weeks later, Kahanamoku soundly defeated him, making McGillivray the second pick for the Olympic 100-yard race. Gaining in confidence, Kahanamoku acknowledged his rivals in Chicago were fast, but they were "nothing but tank swimmers."

The "foreign" misnomer in the Philly paper was common — few thought of Hawaii as part of the United States. But the slight was comparatively innocent. In Chicago, the *Tribune* referred to Kahanamoku repeatedly, in apparent jest, as "Count Kahanamoku." In San Francisco he was a "dusky lad and giant native" and the "submarine spook." A Los Angeles newspaper announced, "Hawaiian fish man in L.A." In Detroit, he was described as one of two "dark-skinned" athletes (the other was Howard Drew, the Black sprinter) slated to join the U.S. team. Another paper simply called him "the guy with the funny name." In Philadelphia, Kahanamoku agreed to be photographed in a loincloth, as if primitive clothing were his wardrobe staple. Most reporters found Duke's quietness and awkwardness in answering their strange questions as evidence of intellectual deficiency. Only in the shark-infested waters of his native islands did a boy like Kahanamoku realize for the first time, observed the *Philadelphia Inquirer*'s Jim Nasium, "what his hands and feet are hitched onto his dark brown body for."

After the Olympic trials, Kahanamoku returned to Pennsylvania, where he lived with Lew Henderson's family while training at the University of Pennsylvania with Kistler. A former world champion swimmer in England, Kistler immigrated to the U.S. in 1891, working in a coal mine before becoming a local swim instructor. In 1897 Penn hired him to oversee the campus pool and build an undergraduate swim team. That same year, he organized Penn's first meet and, the following year, he coached the team to the intercollegiate national crown in front of 14,000 spectators at Boston's cavernous Mechanics Hall.

Kahanamoku raced against Kistler's swimmers, handicapping himself by launching well after the others to see if he could catch them at the touch. He worked on his start, practicing a long, shallow dive and quick getaway; he performed turn after turn, honing a push-off he had never needed do in open-water races at home.

Kistler called him the most talented athlete he had ever seen. The AAU's Wahle had mocked Kistler six years earlier for presuming to get Dan Renear into race-ready shape to defend his world record. With Kahanamoku's selection for the U.S. team, Wahle had to accept he was wrong about Hawaii swimmers, wrong to doubt the time Kahanamoku had set in Honolulu Harbor, and wrong about Kistler, who would be considered one of America's best coaches and the father of collegiate swimming. Kahanamoku wrote to his dad that he loved training with Kistler and hoped to train with him again after returning from the Olympics.

Though Kahanamoku had been selected for the U.S. team, Genoves had not. They had been viewed as close to equals among Hawaii friends who watched them practice every day, launching off the Moana Hotel pier. In late March, after the Chicago meet, Genoves returned home, accompanied by Henderson and Dude Miller, who the Hawaiian papers called his "chief cheerer-upper." Genoves hadn't performed well, never seeming to recover from his debut outing in Pittsburgh, where he finished last. On the second night there, he didn't even race in the 500-yard event, a distance perfectly suited to him which he was favored to win. He starred in the hometown events during Honolulu Harbor's second annual meet in early June, winning the 440- and 880-yard events and the mile. But he decided not to join the Hui Nalu team that would travel to the mainland beginning in 1913 under Duke's leadership. He stayed home.

The stark difference in Kahanamoku and Genoves's outcomes on the mainland, and their reaction to adversity, put into relief the quietly fierce determination Duke possessed in an alien, often hostile landscape. A year earlier, the *Honolulu Advertiser* wrote: "They say that some land shells are found only within a few feet radius and are not found outside that particular circle. Duke Kahanamoku exists on the Waikiki beach only."

And yet he didn't. You couldn't tell what he was thinking, but he seemed to know his silence was a power, not a handicap. His personal resilience had been tested in Pittsburgh.

Native Hawaiians lured to the mainland experienced disorientating confusion and culture shock. That Kahanamoku was willing to persist was clear. Perhaps having grown up in a place where the indigenous people were treated as second-class citizens made him uniquely capable of compartmentalizing and working around the edges.

In Kahanamoku's last race before departing for the Stockholm Games, he set a new American record for 220 yards at New Jersey's Verona Lake, a splendid course lined with flagpoles flying the stars and stripes. In a middle-distance race he wasn't favored to win, he clipped .6 off Charles Daniels's mark. The competition, featuring the best American swimmers, was to determine the four-man relay team for Stockholm. Unexpectedly,

Kahanamoku won a slot and would now be competing in two events at the Games.

By the time he got on the SS *Finland* bound for Stockholm — which tracked a longer, southerly course in the wake of the *Titanic* disaster two months earlier — there was a satisfying sense he had done exactly what he'd hoped to do.

On June 14, 1912, the American Olympic team left the Red Star Pier on the North (now Hudson) River before thousands of madly waving spectators and a band playing "The Star-Spangled Banner." Before leaving New York, Kahanamoku and his teammates were presented with a dress uniform: a trim-fitting blue blazer with patch pockets and the national team shield on the sleeve, white flannel trousers, white shoes, and white cap with the insignia on the visor. The ensemble was completed by a silk hatband for the cap, an American flag, and a streamer with the words, "Bring Home the Bacon."

Each morning at 10:30 a.m. and again at 2:30 p.m., the 164 athletes worked out on deck while passengers and a phalanx of newspapermen, including *The New York Herald*'s James S. Mitchel, looked on. Mitchel, a massive Irishman and the unofficial dean of the correspondents on board, had competed at the inaugural modern Games in Athens in 1896 and was acclaimed as the greatest "weight thrower" of his day. His pet description of the Olympics as "the world's greatest sport carnival" was apt.

The deck had a ribbon of cork track, wide enough for two runners and deemed more or less sufficient but for the intermittent ocean swells that threatened tumbles and knee dislocations. A postage-sized canvas swimming tank, with room for one, was suspended from railings and filled with chilly seawater. The swimmers were fitted with harnesses, a taut overhead rope fixing them in a near stationary position as they stroked to nowhere. Wahle, sternly guarded the tank from bystanders, but when he eventually walked away, other athletes would avail themselves of a pleasing, post-workout dip.

Javelin throwers stayed active, tying yards of shipboard line to the ends of their spears then launching them off the starboard side, claiming direct hits with whales and porpoises. Discus throwers, having gotten the ship carpenters to bore holes through their metal disks, threaded them with ropes and launched those overboard, too. Heavy shot puts and medicine balls flew and thudded in landings; fencers' sabers clanged in the dining saloon; and marvelously attired marksmen raised dueling pistols, shooting into the thick ocean air from the stern, where a revolver gallery had been erected. Less ominously, cardigan-clad tennis players whacked balls against a backstop with a line drawn across it at net height. The nine-man bicycle team pedaled stationary bikes, assured that they were securely lashed to the vessel.

To a sports-mad twenty-one-year-old Kahanamoku, it was nirvana. He snapped photos with a new 3A Graflex camera he purchased in the city, and played hapa-haole music on his ukulele, swaying his fluid hips to hula during evening talent shows.

You can sense the ease he felt from a photo taken on the SS *Finland*'s deck. Teammate Jim Thorpe, in a tweed cap and light three-piece suit, is stationed at one end of a long bench and Kahanamoku is at the opposite end, three or four others sandwiched between them. Thorpe is grinning mischievously, and Duke, in a dark, hooded sweatsuit and loose-fitting beret, looks like he is happy just to be there, in on the laugh.

THREE
THE OLYMPIC AGE
1896 – 1912

"What a wonderful thing, the crawl stroke."
—Author Jack London in the last
weeks of his life, reflecting on his
visits to Waikiki in the early 1900s

ON MAY 28, 1912, before the American team made its way east for its departure for Sweden, a benefit show kicked off on the other coast to defray travel expenses for California's athletes. Headlining the event was an "Olympic Minstrel" performance, starring the "last word in black-faced funny work," Wesley Ruggles. Then twenty, he would later become a successful Hollywood actor alongside silent movie star Charlie Chaplin. Ruggles took the stage at the Los Angeles Auditorium along with several other "tambo" performers. Wearing white gloves and hiked-up dark trousers, their lips whitened to look as fat as peaches, they slayed the crowd, playing music like "That Baboon Lady Dance." The Olympic athletes themselves took part, performing physical stunts. The night was deemed so successful, the organizers promised an encore performance of "burnt cork and tambos" in the coming days.

The Los Angeles fundraiser — similar ones were popular throughout America at the time — was a reminder to Kahanamoku, Thorpe, and the three other dark-skinned athletes on the U.S. team how they were viewed at home. They knew that while they were expected to be showcase products of the American experiment — Island Natives, Indigenous Americans, and Black athletes now "civilized" and proudly wearing the United States team colors — they also were laughed at for their strange origins and economically poor upbringings.

In 1912, Olympic sports in the U.S. orbited around exclusive clubs and elite Ivy League sports teams, neither of which included the five nonwhite athletes. (The first U.S. Olympic roster in Athens, organized by the Boston Athletic Association, consisted entirely of Ivy League athletes with the exception of one.) The ennobling power of amateurism, the bedrock of the modern Olympic Games, was part of a cosmos not their own. Each man was made to sign a document for each event he participated in, promising never to accept prizes or money in competition, never compete against a professional, never coach athletics for compensation, or be "sold, pawned, hired out, or exhibited" for income.

Thorpe, twenty-five, was from the Sac and Fox Nation; twenty-four-year-old Lewis Tewanima, the 1911 New York City Marathon winner, was Hopi; and nineteen-year-old Andrew Sockalexis, a runner-up in the 1912 Boston Marathon, was Penobscot. Drew, twenty-one, was a Black sprinter from Springfield, Massachusetts, who had fled the Jim Crow South with his parents and had dropped out of school for a time to work. Kahanamoku rounded out the group.

The year 1912 was to be a breakthrough moment for all five — Kahanamoku, Drew, and Thorpe, a pentathlete and decathlete, were all gold-medal favorites — but it could also be a disaster, as previous Olympics had been for nonwhite athletes before them. George Poage was a Black hurdler who won two bronze medals in St. Louis in 1904, but many Black American athletes were bitterly disappointed he didn't join them in boycotting the Games because of racially segregated seating and facilities. The five men were aware that their athleticism was prized but not their heritage. Being grateful for where they were going but also proud of where they came from was a knot they didn't know how to untie.

The visionaries of the U.S. Olympic movement saw the men not only going abroad to win medals but also to illustrate how they and their people had been won over to American ideals. Tewanima would later tell the story of how administrators at the assimilationist boarding school Carlisle Indian Industrial in Pennsylvania had forced him to hand over his Hopi earrings and cut his long hair. Considered wards of the federal government, too backward to be trusted with rights and responsibilities, Indigenous Americans weren't even citizens. It would be another twelve years before they gained U.S. citizenship.

Drew, a sensation who easily won the 100-meter sprint in the trials, probably struggled most. As a teen he had refused to enter the prestigious Boston Athletic Association running races, citing their racist stance against admitting Black members. Later in his career, in San Francisco, he was forced to walk to a race (which he missed) when bus drivers refused to stop and soldiers harassed him, calling him "yellow" and telling him to "take a hike." The newspapers made fun of him, saying he couldn't "find his way to the fair."

Because none of the five could independently afford travel to cities where qualifying events were held (in contrast to the college boys and professional men who overwhelmingly made up the team, some of whom had expenses covered by the millionaire philanthropist Andrew Carnegie), they had to ask the

Olympic authorities for permission to fundraise. At the eleventh hour, the American Olympic Committee reneged on its offer to pay for some of Thorpe and Tewanima's travel expenses, saddling the Carlisle School with the bill. Drew almost didn't go to Stockholm because U.S. team authorities delayed his request to fundraise not for himself but to help support his wife and two infant children in his absence.

Thorpe, already famous for leading Carlisle to the top tier of collegiate football, expected to be an attraction at the Stockholm Games. But back home in North Carolina, he existed in a precarious place. Some praised his performance in regional baseball leagues while others demeaned him as lazy and undependable, ridiculing his heritage and the tepee where, as one columnist wrote, he probably lived. It was hard to imagine a white, Ivy League teammate being photographed, as Thorpe was before the 1912 Games, wearing only a jockstrap.

Sometimes their diminishment was more nuanced, such as when sportswriters declared the men were born with their athletic gifts. They were naturals who rarely even practiced. Reporters marveled at Thorpe and falsely claimed he didn't move a muscle during the steamer passage to the Games.

They had to be ready for the insults, they knew. When Great Britain's heavyweight wrestler Louis Bruce became the country's first Black Olympian in 1908, he was given the nickname "Darkey Bruce," and his real first name was lost to sports historians for generations. Canada's Black sprinter John "Army" Howard was welcomed to the Stockholm Games, but before boarding the ship to Europe he had to stay at a separate hotel from his white teammates.

Despite the obstacles to overcome, the concessions to make, and the possibility their Olympic opportunity — or they themselves — would unravel, they were there, in the arena, amidst the biggest and best gathering of athletes in the world. It over-rode everything else. The pride was palpable.

———

THE FOUNDER OF THE MODERN GAMES, Baron Pierre de Coubertin, gave mixed signals about the disruption caused by the American athletes of color. Some saw it as a welcome sign that he didn't publicly protest; others saw a French noble very comfortable with an overwhelmingly aristocratic field. Yet for Coubertin, his priority was not democratizing his invention but seeing that it survived. In 1912, it didn't look good.

The modern Olympics, which began in 1896, had not gone well in each of its four previous editions. The inaugural Games, held in Greece, had few non-Greek athletes, and the following Paris Games, in 1900, had gotten so lost in the excitement over the World's Fair, also in Paris, many didn't even realize the Olympics were taking place.

Social reformers saw marathon distances as inhumane as injuries mounted, many unknowingly caused by drugs such as opium and strychnine, which were legal and liberally employed. In 1912 the future World War II American general and hero George S. Patton said he received a near-lethal amount of "hop," or pure opium, from the U.S. team trainer prior to the 4,000-meter cross-country modern pentathlon run, causing him to collapse at the finish line in front of the Swedish royal box. Other contests, like tug-of-war and rugby, regularly sparked brawls, often exacerbated by long-simmering ethnic grudges.

Unlike track and field, swimming wasn't a part of the ancient Olympics, but Coubertin knew that Grecian history abounded with stories of heroic military sea crossings, and evidence pointed to ancient Greeks using a variety of swim strokes.

Plato was popularly credited with believing that a man who didn't know how to swim was an uneducated man.

The first three Olympic swimming contests were abject failures, however, held in open water or filthy canals. In 1896, the gold-medal winner, the Hungarian Alfred Hajos, who learned to swim after seeing his father drown in the Danube River, said he was less worried about winning than surviving the fifty-degree Bay of Zea. Officials had rowed the quivering athletes out to sea, directed them to swim through heavy waves back to shore (hollowed-out pumpkins marked the course), and fired the starter's gun. The sole American launched with the others screamed "Jesus!" and immediately returned to the float. The 1900 Paris Olympics featured, for the first and last time, "obstacle swimming," in which the unlucky participants had to shimmy up a pole then alternately climb over and swim under a row of boats in the contaminated Seine River on the way to the finish line.

But the unforgivably worst Olympics, at least in Coubertin's eyes, was the American one, which occurred in St. Louis in 1904. The problem was James E. Sullivan, a sports-magazine publisher turned amateur athletics organizer based, like Wahle, at the New York Athletic Club. Sullivan was broad-shouldered and tall; Coubertin was neither. A peace-loving poet by nature, Coubertin would come to despise the bombastic, win-at-all-costs promoter.

Sullivan's "America First" obstinacy as director of the St. Louis Games insisted that all events be measured in yards, not meters, the European standard used in all Games before and since. The largely less-than-elite Games (top athletes from Europe refused to travel to the U.S.) might have been a drowsy footnote to Olympic history, but Sullivan also staged a parallel Anthropology Days competition, recruiting indigenous men from the concurrent World's Fair who had been brought from the Philippines, Japan, the Congo, Patagonia, and elsewhere to serve as "living exhibits" for the fairgoers' entertainment. In one popular display, representatives from a Filipino ethnic tribe, the Igorots, who occasionally ate dog meat in ceremonies, would be made to slaughter and consume dog each morning.

Sullivan tested his "primitive" recruits in Olympic disciplines they had never seen, never heard of, nor were particularly interested in. It wasn't a minstrel-like spectacle engineered for laughs but a serious eugenics experiment. Sullivan and a leading ethnologist and anthropologist named William McGee were intent on disproving the belief that the "average savage," on account of living in the wild, was physically stronger, faster, and more agile than the white man. "Barbarians Meet in Athletic Games," announced a headline in the *St. Louis Post-Dispatch*.

Over two days, Sullivan conducted his experiment before several hundred unimpressed spectators. The Indigenous Patagonian strongmen underwhelmed, as did the javelin throwers and sprinters (the winner politely waited for the others before crossing the finishing line). The Ainu shot-putters from northern Japan couldn't be convinced to try to better their scores with a second throw.

Coubertin called Anthropology Days, now tangled up in the public's mind with his regal Games, "an outrageous charade." Sullivan, for his part, concluded, "The whole meeting proves conclusively that the savage has been a very much overrated man from an athletic point of view." His colleague McGee, a former head of the U.S. government's Bureau of American Ethnology, affiliated with the Smithsonian Institution, believed the Games established in "qualitative measure the inferiority of primitive peoples, in faculty faulty if not intellectual grasp."

Sullivan's Games also managed to sully the Olympics' most revered event, the marathon. To test the "purposeful dehydration theory," he directed course crews to set up only one water station, at the twelve-mile mark. Competitors collapsed in ninety-degree heat along the trailless, hilly, dust-choked course, which a World's Fair official called the "most difficult a human being was ever asked to run over." Eighteen of the race's thirty-two starters dropped out. The winner, Thomas Hicks, needed doses of strychnine sulfate, egg whites, and brandy to keep upright the final miles, then collapsed after finishing, requiring an hour of postrace emergency medical attention before he could get back on his feet.

The St. Louis Games did nothing to diminish Sullivan's role in American athletics; instead, he rose even higher and was the unquestioned chief of the powerful U.S. delegation steaming across the Atlantic to invade Europe. The same "savage" and "living in the wild" athletes he had sought to discredit in 1904 he had welcomed to the 1912 team. His eugenics mission was temporarily put aside. The bottom line was winning American gold.

THE AGE OF THE GAMES welcoming all colors and classes was still far away — one observer in 1912 described the U.S. team as a "mongrel mix" — but in one sport, the clash between white and nonwhite athletes was surprisingly prevalent. It had to do with the new speed stroke in swimming and who was responsible for it.

When Captain James Cook sailed into the Waimea waters off Kauai in the late 1700s, he saw natives swimming with their traditional double overhand stroke. Indigenous people in the Americas and other continents did much the same. The late nineteenth century English short-distance swimming champ John Trudgen said he had learned his namesake hybrid stroke, for a time considered the fastest stroke in the world, by watching a native swimmer in South America. His arms fired rapidly overhand but his legs used a wedge-like kick, a holdover from the much more popular breaststroke.

In the lead-up to Stockholm, the Aussies had made their case for honing the stroke to near perfection. For more than a decade the noted instructor Frederick "Professor" Cavill said he and his sons had studied Pacific Island swimmers on travels abroad. In 1898 a Solomon Islands swimmer, Alick Wickham, arrived in Sydney, affording even closer analysis.

Wickham, the mixed-race son of a European ship captain and a native Polynesian, was a sensation at Sydney's Bronte Baths. He was blindingly fast over short distances and bold beyond comprehension. In 1918 he dived off a 205-foot cliff in Melbourne in front of 70,000 spectators.

When Richard Cavill, the youngest of Professor's sons, went to England, he completed the family mission and finally perfected the Wickham-like speed version — a double overhead stroke with an up-and-down thrashing kick. Cavill became the first person to break the minute barrier for 100 yards, finishing in 58.5 seconds in a 1902 handicap race. In the meantime, his older brothers found their way to the West Coast of the United States, where they were evangelicals for the new stroke, spreading the gospel through clubs and exhibitions.

The Cavills, relentless promoters as well as swimmers, described their master stroke in a way that would stick. They said, or at least were credited with saying, it was like "crawling through the water." When American Charles Daniels, at the London Games in 1908, used the crawl to set a 100-meter world record and add to an Olympic medal count begun at the 1904 Games, it further convinced the world the Cavills had cracked the sprint code.

The old sidestroke and the jerky Trudgen stroke were pushed aside. The distaste that genteel English audiences expressed when they saw Ojibwa athletes from Lake Superior slamming the water with overhead arms and kicking legs at an exhibition decades earlier was pushed aside as well. A transformation in competitive speed swimming was taking place, thanks to one obsessed family.

The white swimming world's growing interest in the crawl, and subsequent claims to own it (depending on who won records each year it went by the American crawl, the Australian crawl, or even the British crawl), went largely uncontested. But the ascendance of Duke Kahanamoku was a reminder of the crawl's indigenous origins, a tether to the ancient past and to Wickham, the "bloke with the stroke." Long before English swimmers were blowing up trying to sprint as fast and far as they could on a single held breath, Hawaiians were flicking their heads side to side to inhale on every stroke. It was startling to think about. It was as if the Wright Brothers had come to learn an ancient North America people had built a glider and sailed it across the sky.

Many experts reflexively maintained that any Pacific Islander crawl was crude, needing a modernizing, educated hand. The Aussies theorized that Kahanamoku's stroke was a slightly modified Australian crawl, probably passed down to him by Aussies visiting the islands. They would prove as much after seeing him in Stockholm. Nobody acknowledged that Kahanamoku's stroke was ancient, refined over thousands of years, and performed by ancestors and Polynesian royalty to a degree that he said probably surpassed his own efforts.

Years later Kahanamoku and his brothers, in a series of interviews with broadcaster Lowell Thomas Jr., emphasized that the "revolutionary" Hawaiian crawl was the product of native forebears, though perhaps tweaked by their father, Duke Sr. "My father told [Duke] it's best to keep your legs moving exactly like a clock," recalled Sam Kahanamoku. "The Australia kick was the left leg with the right arm. My brother doesn't use that, he uses a continual straight rhythm exactly like a propeller.

That is not the American crawl or the Australian crawl, it's the Hawaiian crawl."

————————

LEW HENDERSON, THE HUI NALU team manager, had proven an unexpectedly poor correspondent. The local newspaper editors, and hence the citizenry of the five Hawaiian Islands, spent weeks wondering what the boys were doing on their way to the Stockholm Games and why Henderson, a draughtsman who had designed the well-regarded poster for the Honolulu Floral Parade, wasn't filling them in. The Hui Nalu, known for bestowing colorful team nicknames ranging from Steamboat to Toots, gave Henderson a new one. Silent Lew, they called him.

The news was coming secondhand, via New York writers traveling with the team or by drab wire-service copy. Henderson's Western Union telegrams were almost artful in their penny-pinching brevity, with little more than a notice of arrivals or departures. At Yale, only days after the tumultuous events at the Pittsburgh trials, Henderson wrote: "Duke and the boys arrive New Haven ten fifty."

Henderson left the team altogether in March to return home with Genoves and Dude Miller. The news updates stopped completely. Kahanamoku was now traveling alone, and he was already famous for keeping his thoughts to himself. He was unlikely to be heard from again, despite everyone in Hawaii feeling party to his adventure.

The Honolulu reporters, out of desperation, began descending on the Kahanamoku Waikiki home, hoping they had heard something. As it turned out, Duke had been writing to his dad almost daily since his arrival in San Francisco in February. Duke Sr. had been to the mainland himself at roughly the same age, when he traveled as part of a small singing troupe to New York and the 1893 World's Fair in Chicago. At a cyclorama exhibit showing images of the Kīlauea crater, he and seven native companions sang like the "call of the lovebirds," reported the Hawaiian language paper *Ka Nupepa Kuokoa*. Native hula girls danced. Duke Sr. was thrilled that his eldest son was walking in his footsteps.

He agreed to share his son's letters, many of them printed in their entirety. A surprisingly full portrait emerged of a young man expressing himself in a breathless, excited way that few outside family and friends would recognize.

He flashed through sightseeing trips like he'd never get back to the mainland again: to Times Square, the bloody stockyards of Chicago, the Carnegie-built jewel of a natatorium at Yale. He went to popular song and dance shows at theaters in Chicago and New York and to a restaurant on Broadway for a poi supper, thanks to some Hawaiians he happened to meet. In the letters to his dad, he enthused more about the side excursions than the record-setting pool performances. He wondered about going to college at the University of Pennsylvania, where Kistler encouraged him to enroll. "This is a great trip, dad," he wrote.

There was nothing much in the letters about the 100-meter race to come, or the German and Australian sprinters who most experts favored to beat him, or the grumbling among some other nations that a Hawaiian shouldn't be eligible to represent the U.S. Only in one letter to his mother did he admit he felt nervous.

On June 21, the U.S. delegation arriving in Antwerp for the connection to Stockholm included athletes, a hundred or so fans, and sixteen-year-old Harry Naughton, a Toledo boy who hid in a lifeboat as a stowaway. Because he was considered a good omen, he would become the team mascot. Kahanamoku was unbothered by the nine days at sea, cheerily starting a telegram to Henderson with, "Dear old Pal," and ending it, "Best regards to the Hui Nalu. Aloha Nui to you. DUKE."

King Gustaf V, a wiry sporting monarch who played competitive tennis into his seventies, often under the alias Mr. G, opened the Games on July 6, encouraging a friendly contest between rival nations. The Team Amerika stadium entrance in the warm, clear sunshine was impressively large and expertly choreographed. "The Americans have been well received . . . including Thorpe and [Louis] Tewanima, the Indians, who are suspected of carrying tomahawks and scalping knives, and Drew, the fast little darkey sprinter," wrote a New York *Evening World* correspondent.

A sea of U.S. athletes, passing before the royal box in rows of four, seemed to stretch forever, all of them dressed smartly in blue blazers, white slacks, and straw boaters respectfully doffed to their chests. Japan, by contrast, had only two athletes in its first Games, dressed in white T-shirts and shorts, one of whom carried the flag. In the Games' first controversy, they were criticized for neglecting to lower it before the king. The host nation Swedes, in a sight that clearly pleased Gustaf, marched in last, their numbers staggeringly large and diverse. The dozens of female competitors shocked James Sullivan, who had refused to include women on the U.S. roster. The AAU ruled out all participation, then amended the prohibition, banning women from "any event in which they would not wear long skirts." Female swimmers and divers were barred. Sullivan would pass away before American women finally had their coming out in 1920, when they not only swam, and won in numbers, but did so in clingy performance suits.

In the run-up to the Games, Stockholm grandly advertised itself as the "Venice of the North" — perhaps a bit of hyperbole, but the Swedes had prepared better than any previous Olympic host and had, without question, superb facilities. The first ever Olympic pool was a 100- by 20-meter area of the protected

Djurgårdsbrunnsviken Bay in central Stockholm. This "improvised bath" was framed by land on one side and a steamship pier on the other, enclosed by a line of cleverly arranged pontoons. A writer from London's *Daily Telegraph* described the water as "smooth, shimmering like satin." Tall grandstands for 3,000 rose from the shoreline, beyond which were thickly forested highlands. The royal box was centrally placed, just a few rows above the deck. The newspapermen had their own box seats and a specially built telegraph and telephone pavilion (complete with white Doric columns) outside the stadium, from which they could file their stories. Colorful bunting draped the stadium at water level and a dozen flags from participating countries flapped from lines strung above the pool.

The swimmers, shadowed by officials striding the deck as they raced, wore numbered linen bath caps in different colors so spectators and judges could easily identify them.

On July 6, Kahanamoku, in a red and white cap, had set a blistering world record time in his first qualifying heat, despite water that was dark and impossible to see in and despite having to march in the opening ceremonies earlier in the day. The 100-meter favorite, Germany's Kurt Bretting, was five seconds slower. In describing Kahanamoku's astonishing 1:02.6 time, an observer remarked: "The performance of the phenomenal Kanaka [sic] quite came up to expectations. He employs a special type of crawl, with the motor-power derived from the ankles alone, and not from the hip or knee joints."

Kahanamoku looked like a shoo-in for the gold when he and the other American contenders missed the semifinal heat in a schedule mix-up. The German Federation protested any exemption being made, but the international swimming jury agreed to let the Americans try to qualify in a special trial. They had to beat the time of the third-place finisher in the semifinal heat from which they were absent. Two of the three Americans did, including Kahanamoku, earning a berth in the finals.

The stadium was packed, and Kahanamoku was the obvious fan favorite, greeted with his own chant. "Hawaii! Hawaii! Hawaii!" it went, "U-S-A . . . America . . . Duke!" The royal box contained King Gustaf; his wife, Queen Victoria; and the crown prince and princess. (The day before, King Gustaf had surprised Kahanamoku at his practice, asking him for a preview exhibition.) At the west end of the pool, where the finalists collected for the start, members and guests of the Stockholm Rowing Club leaned off a second-story deck of the boathouse.

In a scintillating performance, Kahanamoku pulled away from the field in the first fifty meters, then allowed them to close the gap in the last fifty when he turned to look at where they were. A motion picture crew caught the final meters. In the middle lanes, Bretting and Aussie Cecil Healy kicked furiously, their backsplashes causing water to spray everywhere. Kahanamoku's arms moved rapidly but there was no seeming effort with his leg kicks, and minimal splash. His speed was explosive but seemed almost invisibly generated. His legs ticked a steady beat in the dark harbor water and, because of the hint of magic and evidence of something different, no one would soon forget it.

After his touch, Kahanamoku sprang from the water with a beaming smile he couldn't hold back. He looked genuinely shocked, like he didn't know what to do. He was still dripping wet, his wool singlet clinging to his body, when a cameraman futilely tried to wave him to attention as handshakes came at him from a crowd of men in suits and derby hats. One of them was Colonel Robert M. Thompson, the most prominent backer of the $100,000 American Olympic effort, "a millionaire," in Duke's awestruck words to his dad. On the passage over, Thompson had requested Kahanamoku sing "Aloha 'Oe" and dance the hula.

Kahanamoku matched the world freestyle record of 1:02.4. It was a new Olympic record as well, bettering Charles Daniels's old mark by more than three seconds. The U.S. swimmers won a total of four medals, Kahanamoku awarded half of them. (In addition to winning gold for the 100-meters, he led the relay team to silver.) Days afterward, he again swam before the king of Sweden, who had taken a special interest in the "dark-skinned Honolulu man-fish." In exhibition appearances after the Games in Hamburg and London, he raced before more royalty, including Emperor Wilhelm II, host of the next Olympics in Germany. Henri Berger, bandmaster of the Royal Hawaiian Band and a friend of Queen Lili'uokalani, was in Europe at the time and came to the exhibition. He greeted Duke in mock German: "Vell done, mine poy, zis iss der vay be do dings mit Honolulu."

In an ode to Duke, the Hawaiian language newspaper *Ka Hoku o Hawaii* recounted the meeting with King Gustaf. "Gathered there . . . was the King, Queen, and the Heads of State of other Nations, when the winner was announced along with his time. The skies were filled with cheers. Voices ringing out in the skies were like the roar of thunder. At this time, the hand of the King was seen waving to the Duke of Hawaii."

Like fellow gold medalist Jim Thorpe, Kahanamoku was a hugely popular figure at the Games, fawned over for his strength and skill. Both men were well-liked by their fellow competitors. They managed to glide past the gapers, laughing off the crushing disappointment some fans expressed at seeing Indians and Islanders with neither a headdress nor a nose ring.

For the next weeks and months, the capitals of competitive swimming would be buzzing with analytic investigations into the newest, best stroke: the Kahanamoku crawl. The secret was thought to be how many fluttering kicks he took with each stroke.

"He will willingly exhibit his stroke and kick in the water to anyone who is interested," reported one coach. "Up and down he will swim with his long-reaching crawl stroke, flat on the water with an easy roll to one side and easier one to the other. When asked how he kicked . . . he was quite at a loss to explain and said he did not know, but just kept going naturally."

Some English officials bemoaned the fact that their team fell to a well-funded U.S. onslaught, including one of the team's "black men," Duke Kahanamoku, "born and bred among a people who live in the surf." The Australasia team, which would have won gold in the 100-meters if the Americans had been disqualified, begrudged the U.S. its victory. "America did not draw the color line," a Sydney columnist protested. "Duke is a colored boy. America wanted him and shut her eyes to that fact." Later, the Aussies said they had evidence from an Atlantic City resort that Kahanamoku was a paid professional, which should disqualify him from the gold medal. Their second-place finisher, Cecil Healy, should be awarded it instead.

It was all for naught. Like a thunderbolt hurled across the gentlemanly Olympic world, Kahanamoku established Hawaii as the new hotbed of swimming. At twenty-one, he could be expected to only get better and set more records. It was hard to imagine who might offer him a contest at the next Olympics in Berlin. But just as the world's top Olympic swimmers watched Kahanamoku, he was also assessing them. His impression was clear: He knew the Hui Nalu swimmers back home were as good as any he had yet seen. Hawaii's dominance would continue not just through him but through his teammates waiting to be known. Perhaps as a sign of his brimming confidence, he did a swan dive off the stern of the ocean liner *New York* when it stalled in choppy waters on its way across the Atlantic to the United States.

When Kahanamoku finally returned home, after eight months away, his Hui Nalu teammates and thousands of others met his arriving ship. Public donations had been collected, and a gift was announced: an $1,800 beach house next to his family's on Ala Moana Road. Supporters had already put the deed to the home in a trust. It was a tribute in keeping with ancient Polynesian tradition, no different than the queen's last *ho'okupu*.

"It's a fine thing to have your friends express their aloha for you in this way," Kahanamoku wrote in a published statement about the gift. The day would quickly come when the AAU would have an issue with the house.

Sanford Dole, who had led the American overthrow decades earlier and as the president of the republic enacted the "English-only" legislation banning the Hawaiian language in schools, was one of the "distinguished men" to attend Kahanamoku's welcome-home luau. Dole, his flowing white beard parted in an upside-down vee, commended the champion's modesty and the example he set by showing what clean living will do for athletes of "all bloods."

The year concluded with the announcement that James Sullivan had accepted the job of sports director for the Panama-Pacific International Exposition, the massive World's Fair to be held in San Francisco in 1915. The athletics, promised Sullivan, would be bigger and better than anything at the Olympics.

Kahanamoku excitedly made note of the event. Hui Nalu was going. Hawaii would get to tell its story to the world. The only question was what these sports competitions would truly look like. Whether a replay of the disastrous Anthropology Days or a legitimate test of athleticism, the next big global sporting event would be left entirely to Sullivan's wide-ranging and devilish imagination.

FOUR

HOTBEDS
1905 – 1913

"Gut Heil"
>—German phrase for "good health,"
>etched in large block letters on the
>front gable of the Turnverein Vorwaerts
>("Forward Turners") Hall in Chicago

JOHNNY WEISSMULLER'S ANCESTORS were ethnic-Austrian émigrés who came to the Banat region of Hungary hoping for a
fresh start. For a time, they carved out threadbare livings on free,
war-decimated lands bordering the Danube River. When their
cereal harvests — wheat, oat, barley, and more — collapsed in
the late 1800s, his family collected in the German-speaking enclave around Freidorf, or "free village." As a commune, it was
originally exempt from taxes. But the Weissmuller clan and their
neighbors were increasingly isolated and oppressed. Births in
Freidorf were recorded in Hungarian, a language most people in
the area didn't speak. German-language schools were forbidden.

The exodus of Banaters to the U.S. would approach peak numbers in 1900 as bank failures roiled the countryside. Peasant farmers had their loans called in and their lands taken. In 1882 alone, 15,000 farms were liquidated. Some 150,000 desperately impoverished emigrants, many of them agricultural laborers with no fields to tend, left Hungary between 1900 and 1914.

At the turn of the century, Peter Weissmuller was a man whose prospects were especially forlorn. He was a recent widower whose wife had died from heart disease. He was also childless, as his first-born son, Johann, and a set of twins died in infancy. His day work was being replaced by cheaper machines. In June 1903 he remarried, and eighteen months later he and his new wife, Elizabeth, and their infant son, also named Johann, boarded a ship for America, intending to join a relative in Pennsylvania. They had $23.50 in their pockets.

As the mother of a seven-month-old and another baby on the way, Lizzie, twenty-four, knew the myriad dangers that awaited them. One danger was particularly anxiety-producing to a young family in steerage on a rough twelve-day passage across a turbulent ocean: drowning.

It wasn't an abstract fear but a very real one, rooted in a horrific episode that occurred in New York and was recounted from immigrant to immigrant, the news eventually reaching small hamlets the world over, especially German ones.

On June 15, 1904, the *General Slocum,* a 263-foot-long, side-wheel excursion steamboat, was cruising up the East River when a fire started in the bow. The crew jumped overboard and the pilot, unaccountably, headed for North Brother Island, half a mile away, steaming into the teeth of a wind that stoked the blaze. The passengers rushed to the stern to escape the advancing flames. The screaming, the black acrid smoke, and the hundreds of panic-stricken passengers leaping into the water to their death was a spectacle witnessed by thousands of New Yorkers assembled on the riverbanks. The fire quickly consumed the ship, which sank two hours later. Bodies washed ashore for days at North Brother Island and other points around Hell Gate. The majority of the 1,400 on board were women and children from St. Mark's German Lutheran Church on the Lower East Side. They had been headed to an annual picnic on Long Island Sound to celebrate the end of Sunday School for the year.

A rescue-boat worker described hundreds of grotesquely charred bodies on the collapsed upper deck or floating in the river. A survivor who attempted to help others said the cork-filled life preservers were rotten and useless. An Astoria man who rowed out in the powerful currents at Hell Gate said he personally saw fifty children drown.

Pastor George Haas at St. Mark's estimated 800 had perished, including his own wife and child. Five hundred of them were children, who either burned to death or drowned. Funerals were held nonstop for weeks in the churches of Kleindeutschland, Little Germany. The death count would rise to 1,021, making this one of the worst maritime disasters in U.S. history. A marble obelisk, erected near the church two years later by the Sympathy Society of German Ladies was etched with the words: "They are Earth's purest children, young and fair."

The national response to the disaster was immediate. Educators put new emphasis on "waterproofing" children; in Chicago, waterless "swimming" classes were held in the public schools. "After the pupil has learned the art of swimming his or her mother will be much less likely to see his or her name next year in the column of *The Tribune* which is devoted to summer drownings," declared the Chicago board of education's director of physical education.

Donations and letters of remembrance were still being collected six months after the tragedy when the Weissmuller family sailed into New York Harbor for the processing stopover at Ellis Island.

After a short stay in Pennsylvania, where Peter worked in the coal mines, the Weissmullers settled in Chicago in 1906, living in a Cleveland Avenue flat on the Nord Seite, the thriving northside neighborhood of German immigrants. Peter worked at a local brewery and Elizabeth waitressed at a popular German social club, Turner Hall. Such clubs had migrated from Germany, where they had originated to inspire robust fitness among youth who would be called on to withstand the Napoleonic army. Like the Lower East Side churches of New York, the Turner Halls of Chicago sponsored civic outings for mothers and young children at the new crop of city parks and, more urgently, at Lake Michigan beaches, where reformers had begun to invite poor youngsters for an introduction to water safety. Instead of forbidding access, as the beat cops strained to do, Chicago officials, like those in dozens of other cities in the wake of the *Slocum* tragedy, had begun to try to familiarize small children with the body of water they lived next to.

In 1912, the same year Duke Kahanamoku was crossing the Atlantic for Europe, the Chicago waters thrummed with activity. Municipal pools, spreading throughout the city, sponsored a popular learn-to-swim program for girls that led to a claim that Chicago, with residents making 644,979 pool visits each summer, was the cleanest city in America. The number of summer drownings reported in the *Chicago Tribune* had dropped from a record 156 in July 1906 to the point where the column was discontinued.

. In Lincoln Park, where a roped-off bathing pool had been created at the edge of Lake Michigan, thousands of poor children, having been taught how to swim, were said to be, according to the *Tribune,* "happy with a happiness that is almost pathetic." Johann, seven, now known as Johnny, and his little brother, Peter, were among them. "So, with much laughing and splashing of water these children of the poor take their fill of pleasure, as happy as if there were no dark tenements, no foul alleys, no scant clothing, and no scantier meals. For the time they are the happiest on Earth."

At the North Side and Central YMCAs, the instructors taught novices three strokes: the traditional English breaststroke, the Trudgen, and the one that had quickly became the craze, the American crawl. The YMCA, home to year-round swimming for Chicagoans unable to afford private clubs and teams, became the Weissmuller boys' second home. According to family lore, the eleven-year-old Johnny lied about his age to get around the Y's twelve and older minimum age entry requirement.

THE CIGAR-CHOMPING MAN WHO would soon serve as the boys' coach, manager, and surrogate father had just left his job as swimming instructor at Chicago's Central YMCA. William Bachrach had a new vision. At thirty-two years old, and living with his widowed mother, Leonora, it became clear to him what he really wanted to do.

He had fallen into an era when swimming and a pioneer class of racers was beginning to command the Chicago sports scene. Journalist H. Jamison Handy, in the early morning hours after a shift at the *Tribune,* taught himself to exhale underwater as he crawled, dramatically setting new marks in the early 1900s. Breaststroker Michael "Turk" McDermott was a national champion at multiple distances. Sprinters Ken Huszagh, Perry McGillvray, and Harry Hebner were all U.S. Olympians living in Chicago. Hebner's innovation, a backstroke sprint using crawl-like principles, looked so different it was originally banned before being allowed at the Olympics and adopted by elite swimmers.

Chicago's fear of swimming was real, but so was the wonder at seeing it done well. Bachrach initially saw his purpose as teaching Chicagoans to swim, even going so far as to publicly challenge a rival swim instructor to determine which stroke was easiest for beginners. But he soon saw the potential in speed and began to dream about creating a record-breaking team of his own. A born salesman, he envisioned the marketing potential. He could sell his peerless, Adonis-like mermen to the newspapers, to fans, to businessmen, and to politicians who loved glad-handing at popular sporting events. When he took a coaching job at the Illinois Athletic Club on South Michigan Avenue, which featured a lavishly tiled swimming tank and Turkish and Russian baths, it was to do just that. He could feel his fortunes radically changing.

A decade earlier, Bachrach had been in Cuba, serving in a war already over. American imperialism had found its stride: Hawaii had been colonized, along with the Philippines, Puerto Rico, and Guam. Cuba would be next. Bachrach, the ne'er-do-well brother of high-profile Chicago defense lawyers and son to an immigrant German Jew, volunteered on May 16, 1898, leaving Springfield, Illinois, a week later for Jacksonville, Florida, where he spent months in sweltering training conditions as a private in Company One of the Second Illinois Infantry. The Spanish-American hostilities ceased in August, but Bachrach and his company continued on, sailing to Cuba to join an occupying force that October. It was a tumultuous year for a group of young men lured by the promise of grand adventure but who instead slowly rotted away in the tropics, going for months without shoes, underwear, or pay. Before he was mustered out in the spring of 1899, Bachrach and his company got a reputation for troublemaking and insubordination. Their mutinous band was put under house arrest when they refused to sail to Cuba aboard a filthy animal transport. After they arrived, their despised superior officer fell ill and needed to be sent home. The men joyfully sang, "I Don't Care if You Never Come Back."

For Bachrach's trouble, he got to drill for months without seeing a moment of action (absent the card games at Camp Cuba Libre). When he returned to Chicago, he fashioned himself a battle-steeled warrior, swimming in a couple of races, including his one and only championship race, an AAU 100-yard regional in the Milwaukee River in 1899. He finished fourth in a five-man field from which one entrant dropped out. It would be a signature punchline in his many wisecracking interviews to come. He took his first job at a tank on the South Side in Washington Park, where he stayed for almost five years, developing a young Michael McDermott.

In 1910 he took charge of the Central YMCA program, preparing McDermott for a broadening slate of races. Their notoriety, coupled with his brothers' downtown connections (Benjamin Bachrach helped Clarence Darrow defend Nathan Leopold and Richard Loeb in the "crime of the century" in 1924), earned Bachrach a new job two years later at the troubled but ambitious IAC.

When the handsome, twelve-story building overlooking the lake opened in 1906, it was touted to fill a "notch in the skyline and promote sports in the Middle West . . . which in ten years will result in Chicago becoming the real athletic center of the United States."

Now the club was in upheaval. At the start of 1912, it fired its corrupt board officers. The swimming team had lost to the Milwaukee Athletic Club in the last meet of the year. At the club gala, the elevator operator, a newly engaged twenty-five-year-old, had been crushed when the car tumbled down the shaft, the horror magnified when club members carried the mangled body through the main banquet room. Things couldn't get much worse.

Bachrach restored the IAC to its former glory and by 1922 would be the most famous Olympic swim coach in the world, managing the career of one of the city's first athletic superstars, Johnny Weissmuller. The concept they devised to captivate the 1920s swimming world wasn't based on aboriginal swimming technique but a recently invented modern wonder, the motorized hydroplane. A speeding swimmer, Bachrach claimed, could create the conditions to hydroplane, too. In Weissmuller, he said, man and machine became one.

The young, disgruntled Private Bachrach would have been hard-pressed to imagine the titan he would become. At the height of his dominance, he weighed twice his service weight, drawing more comparisons to a German butcher than to a standard bearer of physical culture. He smoked cigars day and night, flashed a mouth of gold teeth, and routinely wore only a loosely drawn bathrobe around his posh club. "What a pair of overalls is to the bricklayer, the cassock to the clergyman, tights to a chorus girl — that's what Bachrach's robe is to him," wrote his favorite newspaperman, Clarence A. Bush. He had friends in the highest places in Chicago and the lowest, too.

Bachrach's timing, so wrong in 1898, was perfect fourteen years later. With his arrival at the IAC, the stage was set.

———

IN ADDITION TO BACHRACH AND WEISSMULLER, the YMCA welcomed yet another striver who would play a role in putting Chicago on the world sports map. Elwood Brown was at the evangelical heart of the YMCA. Born in Cherokee, Iowa, the son of a Baptist minister, he spent his teen years in Oregon with his missionary parents before returning to the Midwest, where he was a star basketball player on the Wheaton College team. His first job was at the Central Y, where he likely crossed paths with Bachrach at local swim competitions. In 1906 Brown migrated west to direct sports at the Salt Lake City YMCA, one of hundreds of Ys sprouting up across the West.

Four years later, in January 1910, his life changed dramatically when he accepted a job in Manila at the first YMCA in Asia. For Brown, there was one primary reason to venture where nobody like him had been before: There were an estimated 550 million souls to save in China Sea countries.

Following a common assimilation blueprint, Brown, twenty-seven, attempted to convert as many of those half-billion people as possible, in this case by organizing a vast Olympic sports program. Modern sports had been unknown in the Philippines prior to American occupation. Swimming was one of the few activities they knew, though the idea of racing against a timepiece for random-seeming distances was unknown.

Brown began with hundreds of bored and slightly vengeful clerks forced to relocate to the mountain town of Baguio, where their American employers fled to escape the oppressive summertime heat in the city. Brown introduced a workout regimen and happily reported that the mild acts of Filipino sabotage, such as clogging toilets and disabling telephones, decreased. Sports, as his early days in Chicago had shown, were often surprisingly effective to combat vices. Brown then got permission to teach Western sports in the public schools and to sponsor an amateur winter sports carnival for everyone in Manila, American soldiers included. "The American soldier was more inclined to take a swift kick at the Filipino than anything else, but athletics brought them together," Brown would later write. "On more than one occasion, a speedy Filipino runner would beat a white man."

Brown believed that, in the same spirit, it might be possible to bring together national teams from Japan, the Philippines, and China in an Olympic-style competition of Western sports. Less than two decades earlier, Japan and China had fought the First Sino-Japanese War, resulting in a combined 50,000 casualties in nine months of fierce battle. The mutual animosity had not lessened. Few held out hope Brown would be successful.

An added reason for doubt was that Brown had an impressive hard-lined philosophical foe in Japan's Kanō Jigorō, the founder of modern judo and head of the Tokyo Higher Normal School. He opposed the Christianity cloaked in team pursuits such as basketball and volleyball and was dedicated to Bushido, the "warrior way," a moral code of conduct through which an individual paid tribute to the emperor. Jigorō was pretty sure that Japan, a rising world power, didn't need Western sports, much less a civilizing Christian transformation.

Jigorō was well schooled in the classic martial forms of swimming and had even developed a popular stroke of his own. He had recently been appointed the lone Asian member of the International Olympic Committee (IOC) under the direction of Pierre de Coubertin. When he headed to Stockholm in 1912, he didn't support Brown or the Asian games he desperately wished to launch.

And yet Brown was tireless, moved by the godly mission before him and the concept of muscular Christianity that merged physical strength with moral virtues. In the nineteenth century novel *Tom Brown's School Days,* which guided Elwood Brown and gung-ho evangelicals like him, the protagonist cares for and helps develop a weaker schoolmate, each drawing spiritual and physical sustenance in the process. For Brown, each Asian participant in one of his YMCA sports could experience something similar.

He carved out the agreement in less than a year, calling his event, to be hosted in Manila in February 1913, the Far Eastern

Games. In participating countries, the event was simply called the Olympics.

Brown wasn't without insight, but it was hard to know if it was meant as irony or pride when he described the inaugural Games as a "strange spectacle" with "three types of oriental peoples competing in purely American contests and using the English language."

———

PRIOR TO BROWN'S GAMES, THERE HAD BEEN one memorable Olympic-style event, held in Japan. On August 13, 1898, in the busy cosmopolitan port of Yokohama, an unusual swimming race took place, pitting, for the first time, top Japanese swimmers against foreign competitors. The foreigners belonged to the prestigious ex-pat Yokohama Amateur Rowing Club. A bristling tension surrounded the event. Three decades earlier, American naval commodore Matthew C. Perry had arrived with his fleet of what the Japanese would call "black ships," forcing the ratification of pro-Western treaties that opened the door to the previously isolated country. Westerners established a foothold in business and society circles — Yokohama was the most British city in the Far East — a fact that was provocatively illustrated by the rich, white, waterfront sporting clubs. Yokohama Amateur Rowing Club was one of the best in the city, with some 300 strong, well-heeled British, Aussie, and American members.

Anglo colonialism and arrogance were never far from the surface. A year earlier, club members at a regatta in Mukojima, east of Tokyo, took in a local swim meet. The Suifu-ryu Ota-ha swimming school, one of the twelve classical swim schools in Japan, organized the meet, and most of the competitors used popular strokes such as the *konukite* and *hitoenoshi* developed generations earlier for overcoming fast currents.

The body postures struck the rowing club members as odd and backward. Their loud commentary drew local notice, then a public challenge: a series of competitive races to be held the following year in front of the Grand Hotel at modern distances — 100 yards, 440 yards, and 880 yards.

By 4:00 p.m. on the appointed day, English boats and sampans filled with spectators clustered Tokyo Bay, and the nearby yacht club overflowed. Rickshaws raced past tea traders and silk merchants along Bund Street to get passengers to the waterfront in time.

The race officials — judge, starter, and timekeeper — were all English. Regardless, brothers Mototomo and Motoki Mizoguchi, from Tokyo's Ota-ha club, dispatched their foreign rivals in two of the three races, the 100-yard sprint and the quarter mile. In the former race Mototomo edged his foreign rival by a foot with a time of 1:20, but in the longer 440 it was no contest; Motoki won handily. The Japanese didn't use the en vogue overarm Trudgen stroke used for record-setting in the West but the traditional strokes of their samurai forebears. The English-language *Japan Weekly Mail* reported the club's losses months later but stressed that "the second string of our opponents finished last in all three races."

The events in Yokohama went unnoticed in England but not in Japan, where the victories had a huge effect on competitive swimming. As with the first modern Olympics two years earlier, successful individual performance could be extrapolated to say something about the culture and nation from which the athletes hailed. It was pointed out that competitive swimming events had taken place in Japan for centuries before the Yokohama event. The first European race, in England, wasn't until 1837.

Japanese historians dated their country's swimming tradition to Emperor Jimmu's founding of the nation in the seventh century

BCE and competitive racing to the first century BCE. An imperial edict in the 1600s mandated that swimming be taught in schools. Always a battle technique, swimming was eventually folded into the samurai catalog of eighteen essential martial arts. Illustrations from the more peaceful Edo period (1600–1867) show beginners with rope harnesses and kickboards, or beach scenes with young families splashing, diving, and moving through water, or adolescents engaged in horseplay below wooden piers. Elite practitioners in the Kobori-ryu swim school were named "master of waves," the very best awarded the Bosui scroll, which translated meant, "to have forgotten that one is in water."

By contrast, Western nations had, for the better part of 500 years, studiously avoided the water, fearful of fatal diseases that bred there.

Every swimmer and coach in Japan would come to know the story of the Yokohama meet, including a recent university graduate named Den Sugimoto, who was hired in 1911 to teach physical education in Osaka at the Ibaraki Middle School, his alma mater.

Sugimoto, twenty-five, had no coaching experience in swimming. He had no pool. And though Osaka Prefecture had advised comprehensive ocean training in schools as early as 1912, the trips to the ocean that other schools took were judged to be too expensive. The school was spartan, frugality a philosophical mainstay.

Sugimoto had loved to swim as a boy, often staying in the water for five or six hours, and he wanted a Western-style pool for Ibaraki. The idea was more than novel — the Japanese had yet to build such a pool. Even with the free labor of his students, he had no budget for building supplies and had to start with a rudimentary pond. He scrounged logs and planks for the periphery and carted in gravel for the bottom. After dark he filled the pool with clandestinely diverted river water that was supposed to irrigate rice crops.

Moss bloomed on the pond's surface. Bottom soil churned up by swimmers' feet darkened the water, making it impossible to see. Locals washed their clothes in the pond, farmers dumped clumps of manure. And yet on Friday, June 26, 1914, the first day of classes, there was wild excitement. A notice said only that students should bring loincloths and towels to school. There were a lot of white bodies, remembered one student, but in the summer sun, a few would turn black.

Sugimoto had given the honor of teaching to a traditional expert. He began lessons in the shade, with Zen exercises. When commanded to enter the water, students responded, "Yes, sir!" A red-capped assistant — as with judo, swimming levels were color-coded — taught them strokes from the Kankai-ryu school, which Pacific Coast clans had developed for long ocean swims. Kankai-ryu was far older than Tokyo's popular Suifu-ryu Ota-ha school, which headlined the Yokohama races.

Exactly when Sugimoto started coaching himself isn't clear, but when he did, it wasn't to teach what he called classical "one-handed" methods from the old schools. It was to introduce a stroke no one had dared to try in Japan: the modern American crawl. He decided he wanted to develop swimmers to compete in the Olympics.

Over the years, Sugimoto and his students, including the wispy Katsuo Takaishi, would build a true Western-style pool reinforced with concrete, adding a boiler to warm the cold river water. They studied old American swimming manuals to understand what the rest of the world was doing, blending East and West styles to come up with something entirely new.

They would finally arrive at the Paris Games having adapted modernity to ancient traditions rather than the other way around. They came despite a magnitude 7.9 earthquake months before — the Great Kantō Earthquake — which destroyed the capital of Tokyo and Yokohama to the south.

Yokohama was instantly buried by an avalanche of seawater and thousands of collapsed buildings, then engulfed by raging, wind-whipped fire. In Tokyo and Yokohama there were as many as 150,000 dead, making the earthquake one of worst natural disasters in history.

The three-story Grand Hotel and the Yokohama Amateur Rowing Club had come tumbling down, killing everyone unlucky enough to be inside for noontime dining. One rescuer recalled seeing "a human skull, and spinal column, and thighs without a body" in the rubble at the Grand's main entrance. The whereabouts of thousands of residents were unknown, including the Mizoguchi brothers and many of their foreign rivals.

The mass burials and agonized grieving was followed by a great moral debate about whether Japan was being punished for its embrace of Western mores and lifestyle, an indictment that included the fancy yacht clubs, the decadent nightclubs, and even a seductive European-based construct the imperial government had recently fallen in love with — the Olympic Games.

————————

JUST AS THE YMCA IN CHICAGO groomed Weissmuller and friends, the Ibaraki pool became an incubator, promising something different. The focus shifted from competency to speed. Almost as unlikely as a pool being built by poor barefoot students in Osaka was a young boy perfectly suited to thrive in it.

Katsuo Takaishi was that boy. Self-taught and self-possessed, he grew up on an estuary of the Yodo River and, like Sugimoto, loved swimming more than anything else. "I don't remember when I learned to swim," he recalled, "but by the time I entered elementary school I must've been pretty good." He swam in all seasons; Sugimoto fondly recalled his student training well into November "when the leaves of the poplar turned yellow and scattered on the surface of the pool."

In a way that nobody could see coming, unique talent was blossoming in Osaka and Chicago — where opportunity suddenly presented itself and where knowledge was landing in the exact right hands. While Hawaii shared the limelight with its indomitable champion, the future had already emerged in the form of two relentless coaches and two barely adolescent boys who would follow them anywhere.

Duke Kahanamoku had a target on his back.

FIVE

TROUBLE
1913 – 1915

"You a brown boy, get little bit dark skin, stay away."

—Legendary Waikiki beach
boy Harry Robello on
wooing female tourists

KAHANAMOKU WAS A GLOBALLY revered superstar, a person of color celebrated abroad and feted from coast to coast. He walked through a blizzard of confetti on Broadway when the victorious U.S. team was welcomed home; it was the second-ever ticker-tape parade in New York City. In California he was presented with a gold watch engraved with his initials.

At home, he was the same Duke, sworn to Hui Nalu and settling back into his Waikiki beach-boy routine — giving surfboard and canoe rides by day, playing music by moonlight.

In October 1913, it became shockingly clear how different, and incompatible, his old life was with his new one.

Kahanamoku found his name in headlines around the world, but this time, it wasn't for his Olympic achievements. He was identified as corespondent in a divorce suit involving an English society woman who was white.

The woman, Rhoda Wilson, and her husband, Noël Deerr, had been married for barely a year. They met when Wilson had literally fallen into Deerr's lap when a wooden grandstand collapsed at the London coronation of King George. Deerr, a biologist, was part owner of a sugar plantation and had to rush back to Hawaii in the middle of their courtship. He eventually met up with Wilson at New York City Hall, where they were married. They bought a Cadillac touring car and had it shipped to Honolulu.

Their romance was celebrated in newspapers worldwide. The *San Francisco Chronicle* tabulated the distances covered by the couple in their quest to be with each other: 21,000 miles of ocean voyages and cross-country train rides. Not much was made of the pale Deerr's appearance, but Wilson, just nineteen, was beautiful, her radiant face and aquiline nose portrayed above the fold of the Sunday paper. "She is worth a couple trips around the world," Deerr said.

The alleged affair with Kahanamoku, when it was reported, did not strain credulity. Torrid beach romances came and went. It was understood that, in the balm of sun and warm water, the normal restrictions of class and color could be suspended if done in the right way. Native women beckoned in mainland travel posters. Young athletic men dived for coins flung from deck rails of arriving ships. Feelings stirred in white tourists who stepped off a Matson's Line boat and bowed their heads for a white lei, knowing they were thousands of miles from home. Secrets abounded; yearnings were discreetly indulged. "Can you imagine what it was like for me, going to a Catholic school on the mainland, to have a man take me surfing?" a beach boy remembered a nineteen-year-old female companion telling him. "To sit on top of me, on the back of my legs, skin to skin. In the water."

The dangerous proximity of men and women bathing together in minimalist outfits had led the mainland to segregate the sexes — in Chicago's Lincoln Park, a fence was erected on the beach, in San Francisco, men and women used separate tanks — but Honolulu wasn't like that.

Kahanamoku and Wilson were frequently seen together at Waikiki, where their relationship began with surfing lessons only weeks after his triumphant return from the Games. Months later, in early May, she registered at the Hotel Aubrey in the windward village of Hauula, where Kahanamoku appeared in the guest book. The hotel and its picturesque setting astride a beach ringed with mountains was a favorite honeymoon destination, recently featured in a scandal in which a native island worker eloped with a young society woman who evaded her disapproving mother and the detective she hired. George Aubrey, the proprietor, ran tasteful ads in the Honolulu papers offering chicken dinners with "trimmin's" served by well-trained Japanese maids.

Wilson had been gently warned by her teatime companions in Waikiki that her lack of discretion had people talking. Duke's Hui Nalu friends were similarly concerned. Sure enough, the October 11 *Maui News* reported that Wilson had been seen at the Hotel Aubrey with Kahanamoku: "It is said that on one occasion the swimmer and the fair Englishwoman journeyed to Hauula, where she became a guest at the hotel there and he a caller. She stopped for a week and the days were spent in walks up the gulches, both of them garbed in [nothing but] bathing suits.

The affair had ruined their marriage, Deerr lamented in his court complaint, saying that his spouse of only a year refused to sleep with him. "Deerr says she has not been wife to him since November last year and, as a baby is alleged to be expected by

Mrs. Deerr, the husband asks himself a question or two," the *Maui News* reported. "The complexion may settle the question."

The *Maui News* article broke just as Kahanamoku was preparing to leave for San Francisco's Sutro Baths, where he and his Hui Nalu teammates had successfully raced just a few months earlier. In a send-off the night before their departure, Prince Kūhiō, an avid sportsman and the lone member of the former royal family elected as a territorial representative to U.S. Congress, had presented Duke, the team's captain, with a cane once belonging to Hawaii's King Kalākaua.

When the team left Honolulu aboard the *Wilhelmina,* the mood was somber. Unlike the raucous Hui Nalu send-off in July, where 5,000 people swarmed the dock, there was no hoopla at the pier and no lei-bearing girls wishing the men well. Kahanamoku looked visibly upset and said he was not guilty of the charges and would clear his name when he returned. His intermediaries said he might make blockbuster disclosures which would involve the names of several prominent civilians and service officers who were "just as attentive to the beautiful Englishwoman as he was." It was an extraordinarily explosive message, both for the people involved and the Hawaii Promotion Committee, which saw its artfully created aloha image vulnerable to crusaders looking for any reason to blast the vice-ridden islands.

Then the story vanished, or least Kahanamoku's role in it. Names were not named. A divorce settlement was made, and Wilson returned to England. Deerr would leave too, gaining the proper distance and perspective needed for the other passion in his life, the scrupulously researched masterwork *The History of Sugar.*

Some of the same broad storylines — a young society woman entangled with a prominent, possibly promiscuous native athlete — would have a less sanguine ending two decades later, when Joseph Kahahawai, a local boxer whom Duke knew, was murdered vigilante style. Falsely accused of raping a white socialite named Thalia Massie, his body was found in the trunk of Massie's mother's car, setting in motion an explosive, nationally obsessed-over case that threatened the finely brokered peace between classes and races. Four were convicted, including Massie and her mother, but *The New York Times* suggested beach-boy culture had a hand in the tragedy. A New York tabloid published a cartoon of a white woman in a black evening gown being strangled by a club-wielding, half-naked native with his grinning cohorts closing in. The guilty trial verdict and immediate gubernatorial sentencing commutation from ten years to one hour outraged all sides. Martial law was narrowly avoided.

Kahanamoku later described his post-Olympics self as "dumb," referring to his errors of judgment but perhaps also to his inability to comprehend how his status had irrevocably changed. He understood the sacrifice in being Hawaii's export to the world. He had played the part and was loved by even those who had reason not to love him. Rivals became friends, stern foreign coaches softened. His singing voice was serene and free, breaking ice, smoothing the tensions within a room.

Settling back home, he expected his duty as national ambassador to fall away like petals from a fiery hibiscus bloom. But in the trade-off for a fame he never courted, he lost a precious and valuable commodity his native-born Hui Nalu teammates still possessed: anonymity. By 1913, his private life would be precariously balanced between what he was and what he had to be. His white adversaries on the mainland could afford to put their sole focus on filling the record books James Sullivan churned out for the American Sports Publishing Company. In a time when he was in his prime and might have joyfully explored the outermost boundary of how fast a man could swim, Duke Kahanamoku was simply trying to stay afloat.

———————

SAN FRANCISCO'S SUTRO BATHS was a massive complex of pools in a glass and steel structure on the Pacific Shore at Point Lobos. The millionaire Adolph Sutro had built this water playground in 1896 as a gift to the city. It featured six saltwater pools and one freshwater pool, all kept at different temperatures. During high tide, water from the Pacific would flow into the pools at a rate of 1.7 million gallons an hour. There were seven slides, a springboard, and thirty overhead rings for swinging into the water. Twenty thousand bath suits and 40,000 towels were available to rent. Promotional events ran the gamut from the Leander Sisters performing their "Cupid and Psyche" dance to dwarf boxing matches to swim races which required participants to eat a bagful of donuts beforehand. There was stadium seating for 7,000, but crowds often were estimated at twice that. Ticket holders entered through a stately Greek portal lined with Sutro's collection of natural history artifacts then descended to the pool's promenade level via a witheringly steep 100-foot grand staircase. Storm-whipped ocean breakers routinely broke through a protecting sea wall and shattered glass panes.

An Edison Motion Pictures crew came in 1897 to illustrate the "people's palace," showing happy bedlam as teeming masses of bathers in dark one-piece rental suits splashed, roughhoused, and flopped on top of one another.

Safe exercise and hygiene for poor people were Sutro's aspirational goals, but woeful accidents were commonplace, like the one that befell Al Hobern the same weekend Kahanamoku would be racing. The twenty-five-year-old civilian attempted a "soldier's dive" but neglected to brake himself by spreading his arms underwater and instead severely lacerated his scalp on the pool's concrete bottom and needed emergency rescue.

Kahanamoku and the Hui Nalu team had been at Sutro only three months earlier, when he set multiple records and won nearly every event in front of 6,000 spectators. To train during the passage, Duke had a tank rigged on the forward deck. On the same trip, at San Francisco's Olympic Club, he set three world records, prompting the club's swimming director, the Aussie Syd Cavill, to say, "I have seen all the best of them, but I have never seen anyone who even compares with him."

At Sutro Baths on October 24, 1913 — as part of a festival to celebrate the 400th anniversary of the Spanish "discovery" of the Pacific — Kahanamoku was even better, winning all four of his individual events, from fifty yards to 880. With Hui Nalu badly trailing in the concluding relay race, Kahanamoku opened up the throttle, and the team won by a gaping seventy-five yards. It was a performance "never seen before or since in any part of the world," said *The San Francisco Call.*

Kahanamoku's versatility and stamina at Sutro — he won five events in a single day —seemed to reveal a level of single-minded motivation not seen in him before. The "dusky-skinned Hawaiian's one-night stand" was, according to the *Call,* a sports milestone.

Sutro Baths was the site of successive Hui Nalu triumphs in July and October 1913, but when the men returned in 1914 and again in 1915, they would face a uniquely ambitious opponent: William Bachrach's IAC team.

For the first time, the best of Hawaii and the West Coast would collide with the champions of the Middle West. "It is not often we get an opportunity this far west to measure 'crawls' with the far east, and this is a chance that should not be overlooked," the Sutro Baths posters touted in 1914.

There was something off-putting just the same, something that smacked of go-getting professionalism. A barnstorming amateur team from a region not their own, made up of inland tank specialists guided by an immigrant German from corrupt Chicago, had gotten an invitation to Sutro, promising a big turnout at the gate.

Everyone knew the tawdry story of Bachrach's predecessor at the IAC. Dick Cavill, of the ubiquitous Cavill family, had been hired in 1910 to build a swimming dynasty. In part he had succeeded, starting a water polo program which would go on to furnish national championships. But after nine months, he was abruptly dismissed. Cavill lasted another few months at the "Millionaire's Row" Pittsburgh Athletic Association before he was told to pack up for Australia, fired for flagrant indiscretions with female pupils. While less attractive ladies took care of his instructional duties, Cavill invited select students to shed their voluminous swim bloomers for what one reporter described as "lace and silk" creations. He and well-positioned male colleagues could then appreciate the women's "underwater gyrations."

Bachrach more than cleaned up the program, he resurrected it, boosting its reputation right away with a series of deft and witty instructional articles published in the IAC's monthly magazine, *Tri-Color*. In explaining why most swimmers tired after fifty yards, he wrote, "The reason is simple. As soon as they rise from the plunge they go through the water like grace through a camp meeting for the dozen strokes or so, and soon tire out." Swim memberships increased, and Bachrach entertained everywhere he went. When a rumor circulated that he might not know how to swim (since nobody had ever seen him in the pool), a mock club investigation took place. Was he hesitant to swim because he didn't want his hair to get wet? "Yes," he said, "I do not want to lose that Titian hue."

At the same time he restored the club's image, Bachrach dramatically rebuilt the IAC team, recruiting the best racers in the city to thrash the Chicago Athletic Association, their Michigan Avenue rivals. He lured the "breaststroke king" Turk McDermott away from the CAA and recruited backstroke gold-medalist Harry Hebner, the tireless pioneer H. Jamison Handy, and another versatile Olympian, Perry McGillivray. Arthur Raithel, a product of Crane Tech, a trade school on the immigrant-dense near west side, had quickly emerged, setting fifty- and 100-meter times that Bachrach promised would challenge Kahanamoku's.

The three-day meet at Sutro Baths, held over the July 4 weekend, was billed as the greatest swimming event ever to take place on the West Coast. Twenty-five cents for general admission, $1.00 for the choice seats. For days the returning Hawaiian team had been the toast of the city. Reporters descended on their hotel, the Stewart, for novel esoterica. The swimmers trained on "devil fish" — sun-cured octopus that their mentor William Rawlins brought over from Honolulu in a large jar, securely cushioned in a suitcase. "Duke smiles like a schoolboy when he munches devil fish," wrote one reporter.

The meet kicked off on Friday night with a half-mile and fifty-yard sprint qualifier, both of which Kahanamoku lost, the former to the youngster Raithel. Bachrach had wisely lowered expectations for his team, citing travel-sore legs and balky ankles. With his team exclusively used to freshwater and small, twenty-five-yard tanks, he added, the seventy-five-yard saltwater Sutro Baths course favored the open-water swimmers from Hawaii. In reality he was laying a trap. If they were defeated, as he suggested they probably would be, it would be because of elements beyond their control, not conditioning or talent. If they won, it was because they were good enough to overcome any adversity.

The coach drew wide and lively reactions at the meet. He was a character you might expect to see next to prizefighters or horse trainers, not amateur swimmers congregated on a pool deck. "To the casual observer, Bachrach would appear more at home in a spacious comfortable Morris chair, sipping the cooling extract from a stein or drawing frequent puffs from a 'jimmy' pipe than he would in the water," wrote a bemused correspondent from Washington. "He is a large, florid man, weighing 240 pounds, with short cropped red hair and a skimpy red moustache. He is of Teutonic origin and speaks with the slight accent of the Vaterland."

Things started brightly for Hui Nalu on the second day, when Kahanamoku nipped Raithel and McGillivray in the 100-yard and 220-yard events, respectively. In front of thousands of fans yelling themselves hoarse, Kahanamoku made a cleaner turn than McGillivray at the halfway mark to gain his slight edge.

But the races unfolded far differently on Sunday afternoon. The IAC unexpectedly won the 50-yard sprint (Raithel beat Kahanamoku) and employed a tactic in the 440 in which one swimmer went out at an impossibly fast pace to trick the other favorites into exhausting themselves trying to follow. Afterward, Hebner, the "rabbit," didn't deny the strategy, saying yes, he was trying to "kill off" their rivals. Local officials dimly viewed Bachrach's team tactics. The spirit of a race was supposed to be every man swimming for himself.

In front of a sold-out audience, the IAC easily won the concluding event, the 300-yard relay, symbolic of the best sprint team. The anchorman Kahanamoku finished his seventy-five-yard leg several seconds behind. The IAC time was eight seconds faster than the Hui Nalu team mark set the previous year. Over three days, Kahanamoku was the only Hui Nalu member to win a race.

The weekend was a devastating blow to Hui Nalu, which ultimately finished a distant third in the team competition behind the IAC and its island rival Healani. It's unclear why there wasn't a unified Hawaiian team as there had been in previous years, but what was clear was the dominance of the Chicago tank swimmers.

The win wasn't a fluke. The IAC hadn't lost a national competition since Bachrach took charge. The club's water polo team was equally unbeatable, with McGillivray inventing the "lob shot," and Handy requiring, as the club magazine boasted, a "brutal guard, plus a lax referee to smother him."

The 1914 team that put the IAC on the map didn't have a spectacular headliner like Duke, but the squad had enormous depth and range of experience. With Bachrach's encouragement, they viewed the Hawaiians as rivals and saw themselves as smarter and more hardworking. Handy described the diminutive all-arounder McGillivray as a "student of the swimming game," while Kahanamoku was a "giant" who had "every natural advantage endowed by nature." Bachrach was more circumspect in his comments when it came to Kahanamoku, holding out hope he might lure him to race for the IAC and be the crowd-drawing, moneymaking headliner they were missing.

The IAC team would take a victory tour of the West Coast, swimming in lucrative exhibitions from L.A. to Spokane. Bachrach had found novices, one paper said, and "now their names are famous throughout the sporting world."

Bachrach's theories about swimming technique were skeptically regarded in the East, but he had a knack for getting the best out of his swimmers. Both Handy and Hebner, his team veterans, loved him. Under previous coaches, Hebner wrote, "the team seemed to stand still and gained very little fame locally and nationally . . . but now they had a Miracle Man in swimming that can be compared with the wonders of the world."

The Hui Nalu team headed home immediately, a blowout welcome in Honolulu abruptly canceled by club organizers. Kahanamoku wasn't with the others. He was informed by cable that his job with the Honolulu water department had been terminated. He opted to remain in California, staying with a

Hawaii friend, George Freeth, and swimming under the colors of the Los Angeles Athletic Club, where Freeth was an instructor.

The following summer, the film actor and director Hobart Bosworth cast Kahanamoku as a sailor who comes to the protagonist's rescue and in the process performs, according to the script, "some swimming tricks." Before the national release of *Beachcomber*, Kahanamoku learned that the AAU was intensifying its crackdown of amateurs who went professional. The recent rulings, coming in the wake of James Sullivan revoking Jim Thorpe's 1912 Olympic medals on the grounds that he played semipro baseball, determined, among other things, that Kahanamoku couldn't accept the gift of the house given to him by the people of Hawaii.

Some in the international sporting community had reacted to the Thorpe scandal with glee. The AAU, it claimed, had struck a devil's bargain, choosing to win at all costs by using working-class athletes rather than members of the privileged classes for whom the Games were largely intended. Some critics, like the disgraced Cavill, said the American swimmers had escaped the scrutiny paid to their higher-profile track-and-field brethren. Kahanamoku was a professional just as sure as he was. "He's no fool," insisted Cavill.

From the winter of 1913, when Thorpe was compelled to confess, through 1915, the AAU considered charges of professionalism against hundreds of amateur athletes, some, like Kahanamoku, on multiple occasions. It created new bylaws and restrictions, among them a rule preventing athletes from performing their chosen sport in movies. Kahanamoku could maintain his eligibility so long as he didn't swim on screen.

For the first but not last time, Kahanamoku had nowhere to turn. A promising film career had to be cut short. *Beachcomber* was pulled, appearing in only a few theaters. He had no job to return to and for a time seemed destined to stay in L.A. Then, in late November 1914, in a surprise to all, he boarded an island steamer and went home.

He said he wanted to reunite with Hui Nalu to race against the IAC at Sullivan's self-styled Olympiad at the World's Fair, to be held in San Francisco the following year. Kahanamoku had not forgotten his vow, made after the 1912 Games, to assemble a championship team for the event. The territory of Hawaii, expected to be a major exhibitor, had always been a priority to Pan-Pacific organizers, who strived to combine cultural spectacle with the latest scientific advancements in American society. Eugenics factored largely. According to the fair program, a visitor could catch a swimming race, a hula dance, and a lecture on forced sterility of "imbeciles," all while enjoying a breezy Golden Gate afternoon.

Bachrach had successfully protested the exposition's decision to hold the swimming events in open water next to the San Francisco Yacht Club. At his insistence, the races would take place in tanks. A dominant, all-white swim team raised in man-made pools and taking on a Hawaiian team nurtured in wild surf was a dream contest for spectators and scientists alike. It was almost as if Anthropology Days was blessing them all over again.

———

JAMES E. SULLIVAN was long dead before the first starter's gun was fired at his World's Fair wonder games. He had died the preceding September on the surgeon's table at Mount Sinai Hospital during a botched operation on his intestines. His funeral procession in Manhattan was attended by thousands as a horse-drawn casket made its way from his home near Columbia University up Broadway to St. Aloysius Catholic Church. He was remembered as an early champion of the Pastime Athletic Club and "somewhat of a distance runner."

In one major sense, the Games were better in his absence. Women athletes were allowed to compete, a reversal from Sullivan's categorical declaration that "right here rests the salvation or the ruins of athletics in this country. Women have little or no place in athletics."

But his golden lineup of athletes never really materialized. Records didn't "fall like leaves in autumn." The first modern pentathlon in America came and went. The "world's greatest track," a straightaway instead of an oval, wasn't so great. The total number of entrants did not exceed the Olympic Games, another unfulfilled promise. Competitions or exhibitions of "every known sport that was practiced throughout the civilized and savage world" did not happen. In the end, William F. Humphrey, the president of San Francisco's Olympic Club, who replaced Sullivan, had to make a recruiting trip to New York and Chicago weeks before the fair opened, scrambling to assemble a respectable field.

When Kahanamoku's eight-man team arrived in San Francisco, they found nine powerful IAC swimmers waiting for them. They also found miles of waterfront transformed. It was only a decade since the city was destroyed by the 1906 earthquake. In an area where nothing stood there was now a perfect grid of structures, their red-tiled roofs and alabaster walls gleaming against the endless blue of the Pacific. Before the grand opening in February, millions of visitors had already toured the grounds.

At the western fringe of the expo lay the dusty athletic fields, auto racetrack, and aviation runways; at the eastern end were the popular, lowbrow amusements of the Joy Zone. In between were man-made lagoons, festival halls, international pavilions, and palaces of industry and the arts, exhibiting everything from a transcontinental phone call to new breeds of corn. Occupying the skyline was the Tower of Jewels, a 400-foot-tall Italianate structure covered in cut glass. At another corner, somewhat curiously, was a brand-new, Mediterranean villa–like YWCA.

It wouldn't take much for a visitor — with planes buzzing overhead and automatized machines milking cows — to be dazzled by the promise of the future. But there was also reason to be vigilant about the present. Lectures at the Palace of Education warned of the dangers of soaring immigrant birthrates and Caucasian race suicide and stressed the need of systematic sterilization of defective humans. A sizable exhibit was given over to the Race Betterment Foundation, John Harvey Kellogg's organization that promoted "race hygiene" as a method of improving bloodlines. One talk, typical of the exhibit's offerings, was titled "Mongolian Types of Idiocy."

Nearby, in an area of the Joy Zone off Van Ness Avenue, was an enormous plaster head of a stereotypical Black tribal savage. The "African Dip" beckoned, an attraction well-known around the country in which a Black person sat above a dunk tank, targeted by ball throwers who were white. One exhibition hall offered a clever variation, giving guests an opportunity to throw at an assortment of racial types. If you beaned, say, the Oriental, and successfully knocked off his hat, you won a cigar.

Kahanamoku was a dependable presence at the stately Hawaiian Pavilion off Baker Street, where he sometimes performed (as did the Hui Nalu's Dude Miller), lending his celebrity to hula and hot music acts like steel guitarist Joseph Kekuku and the Royal Hawaiian Quartet. The attractive building, surrounded by tall trees, boasted the longest lines at the fair, the biggest draw being mammoth aquariums stocked with indigenous tropical fish. There was a steady die-off of them from disease, but reinforcements kept arriving on steamships traveling from the islands. Frieze panels, in the words of exposition literature, depicted "old legends on which the imagination of the islanders have fed for centuries," while moving pictures and lantern slides showed island treasures, from the world's greatest active volcano, Kīlauea, to the world's greatest extinct one, Haleakalā, "House of the Sun." On a central arch, several sculpted surf-riders slid down the tops of breaking waves.

Attentive fairgoers would have learned a lot about Hawaii and its modern history: about King Kamehameha and his unification of the Hawaiian Islands in 1795; about the arrival of Protestant missionaries from Boston upon Kamehameha's death in 1819; about how the evangelicals kept coming, with their opportunistic sons and grandsons becoming massive landowners and wealthy agricultural kings; about the import of Portuguese, Japanese, and Korean laborers that shifted population trends; and about the last ruling monarchs —Kamehameha III, the "good-hearted king"; Kalākaua, the "Merrie Monarch"; and Queen Lili'uokalani, the last of the line. Above all, fairgoers would learn about the cultural richness Hawaii tried to bring forward into the new, largely disinterested century.

In June, to commemorate Kamehameha Day, outrigger canoes had cruised the lagoon, blazing with electric lights, outside the Fine Arts Palace. A faux Queen Lili'uokalani and her court simulated a "night in Hawaii" with 2,000 Hawaiians, white and native, in attendance. Prior to the celebration, Hawaii's governor, Lucius Pinkham, gave a speech that emphasized the islands' raison d'être as military insurance for the mainland: ". . . she exists for the protection of your Pacific Coast, your cities, your commerce, and the mighty material and the political progress of the United States of America."

The Hawaiian exhibition exceeded the promotions committee's wildest expectations. Visitors to the fair increased by fifty percent, leading to a decade-long mania for ukulele and native compositions, soon to be adapted by popular Tin Pan Alley musicians and Irving Berlin. *Ka Nupepa Kuokoa,* one of many Hawaiian-language papers that covered the exposition, reported "the ukulele is in great demand from all over America," forcing Jonah Kumalae, O'ahu's foremost ukulele maker, to produce and ship 500 a month. Mark Twain's writing about Hawaii swept travelers westward: "No alien land in all the world has any deep, strong charm for me but that one . . . its balmy airs are always blowing, its summer sea flashing in the sun; the pulsing of its surf-beat is in my ear."

Kahanamoku walked the avenues of San Francisco with an unmistakable pride and confidence. His participation in the World's Fair was, in a sense, the culmination of all he wanted and all that was wanted from him. As the official report published by the Panama-Pacific committee explained, "The relations between San Francisco and the 'islands' have always been close. To them we are always the 'Mainland,' to us they are always 'the islands,' as though there was no other." Heading into competition, he led a supremely talented team, unified by their manager, William Rawlins. Unlike the disparate group that Bachrach's club had trounced the year before, all eight Hawaiian swimmers would compete under the flag of a team created specifically for the exposition, the Honolulu Athletic Association.

After the Friday opening races, in which Kahanamoku won the 50- and 220-yard races, the two teams, Chicago and Hawaii, were close in the team standings. Hawaii was favored in the featured events on Saturday night, the 100 and the four-man relay.

What transpired was unprecedented in a major championship event. It started with Kahanamoku's victory in the 100 which, despite a handshake acknowledgment from the runner-up Raithel and thousands of cheering poolside fans, was unaccountably judged a dead heat. The decisive voice was William Humphrey, Sullivan's replacement as director of the exposition's sporting program. Despite Rawlins's official protest, Kahanamoku again lined up for a race he had already won. And he won again, this time setting a new world record.

The last event, the relay, would determine the team champion. Starting yards behind the IAC's headline anchor sprinter, Kahanamoku caught McGillivray in the final few yards, touching the wall a foot ahead. The stomping, sweating crowd made the glass-enclosed stadium fog up and feel like a terrarium. The jubilant Hawaiians dressed quickly to get to dinner and celebrations. It was well after midnight. But huddled off the deck, the judges vigorously debated. A couple of minutes turned to five, ten, twenty. Finally came the announcement of a dead heat and a new race, to take place in ten minutes.

Rawlins again protested. This time, exhausted and upset, none of the Hawaiians, least of all Kahanamoku, had anything left to give. Bachrach's team easily won the rerun and with it the Panama Pacific International Exposition title. Kahanamoku was publicly mute. But his team was certain the race had been stolen. "It was a case of anything to beat Hawaii," said assistant manager Harvey Chilton. "It was a barefaced holdup."

The Hawaiian swimmers felt that they and their island heritage had been disrespected. Rawlins said it was very possible his all-Hawaii teams would not return to San Francisco and Sutro Baths. As it turned out, they didn't. This would be the last major national race to be held before world war put the Olympic Games, and the intensifying Chicago-Hawaii rivalry, in storage for the next half decade.

At the close of 1915, Duke Kahanamoku was the unrivaled king of sprint swimming. He was at his peak and would wonder, years later, what he might have accomplished had he emphasized breaking records the way others like Weissmuller did. He mused that fifty-one seconds flat for 100 yards (about a second faster than Johnny's world record time) was possible in his prime, but it wasn't what interested him. Victory was enough.

Back at home, he was popular with visitors to the islands, all of whom wanted to meet him at the wharf and the beach. When the YMCA opened its brand-new pool, the finest on the island, he helped to mark the occasion by participating in "fifteen to one," a vaudevillian act in which fifteen native swimmers repeatedly dived into the pool to catch one mullet fish.

On December 5 an event would unfold which, like Kahanamoku's entanglement with Rhoda Wilson, was both uncharacteristic and completely understandable. White seamen traveling on the SS *Great Northern* steamship were drinking at Waikiki Beach's Seaside Hotel bar when they ordered an older Polynesian patron to leave because they didn't wish to drink "side by side with a nigger." When he refused, they beat him viciously. News of the incident quickly spread.

The *Great Northern* was a high-profile undertaking in Honolulu, the model for a new fleet of fast ships preparing to attempt a speed record for a transpacific crossing. At the gala to welcome the ship officers a day earlier, city officials had selected "twenty-five pretty and pleasing girls to distribute leis."

Within minutes, a dozen native men had assembled at the Moana Hotel. Primarily, according to a local paper, "well-known members of the Hui Nalu, including Duke Kahanamoku." The Hui Nalu men jumped the *Great Northern* sailors, settling the physical score and causing injuries that sent some of the sailors to Queens Hospital.

If this incident revealed the "real" Duke, a complex and conflicted character fed up by racial injustice he and others suffered, nobody — including Kahanamoku — could rightly say. But with the Berlin Games canceled and American involvement in the Great War looming, his Olympic swimming career seemed likely over.

SIX

NORD SEITE
1917 – 1920

"Two years ago, it was a distinction to be known as German American. Today one almost mentions it under his breath."
—Archbishop of Chicago George Mundelein, in a
    1916 speech referring to anti–German American
    sentiments on the eve of the U.S. entering
    World War I

"Chicago has grown but it hasn't changed. As soon as a colored person moves in, the whites move out."
—Myra Alexander, a lifelong Black resident of
    Chicago, describing the city's pervasive racism
    in a 1980 interview with Studs Terkel

NORD SEITE CHICAGO WAS IN TURMOIL. With the densest collection of German Americans in the city (and Chicago having the largest population of German Americans in the country), it was targeted for persecution from the moment the United States formally entered World War I on April 6, 1917.

German-language courses in Chicago public schools were pulled from the curriculum, despite German being the most popular foreign language in America. German-named goods, German-named dog breeds, and German-named streets were all renamed. The neighborhoods of Berlin, Hamburg, Lubeck, Coblentz, Rhine, and Frankfurt disappeared from Chicago maps. The Germania Club became the Lincoln Club. Turnverein Vorwaerts became Turner Hall. Families changed their German surnames.

Lutheran churches, the heart of Chicago's German American community, made urgent appeals to parishioners to buy liberty bonds to prove their patriotism. The CAA on South Michigan Avenue fired its German-born employees. The Schoenhofen family, well-known brewers, had their property seized for alleged collusion with the Germans.

An entire culture, once flourishing and admired, was suppressed, sent into fearful forced hiding.

For a young boy identified as German, a first-generation immigrant, the hostility extended from the lakeshore at Diversey Avenue to neighborhood playgrounds like Stanton Park, where Johnny Weissmuller was often found. Fights were common. In an authorized biography in 1964, Weissmuller remembered confessing to starting a brawl to a priest at his neighborhood parochial school, Saint Michael's. "I was a punk kid," he said. But gangs provided some protection against other gangs roaming out of their enclaves to find sons of brewers and truck farmers (another nickname for the neighborhood was the Cabbage Patch) who, like their parents, were now called "Huns."

At the height of Chicago's anti-German hysteria in 1918, Johnny Weissmuller's father, Peter, went out the door of the family's home and never returned. In subsequent years, as Weissmuller grew into his Olympic fame, the family said Peter had died. In one of his last interviews, at seventy-one, Johnny told a reporter that he "lost" his father at fourteen. That was true, if not completely accurate. Peter Weissmuller — brewer, gambler, and, for a brief, unexplained time, deportee — was very much alive, as everybody knew, living blocks away on the North Side, where he would marry another woman and raise another family. He died in 1938.

Weissmuller and his younger brother, Pete, were left to navigate the city on their own. Like it was for a lot of poor kids in Chicago, school offered neither encouragement nor interest. The boys took odd jobs, including errand running for the bookies their father was fond of.

Johnny and Pete were exactly the type of lost boys social reformers thought about when they built city parks and opened the first public beach at Lincoln Park. The decade's watchwords were hygiene and exercise, and behind the campaign was the YMCA, whose clubs were seemingly everywhere. At the North Side Y they could swim. There was no free instruction, but Johnny was free to work out the fast strokes he had seen others do.

By fourteen Weissmuller was already known for his swimming ability. He had been steered to Lane Tech, an all-male high school swimming powerhouse.

Throughout the city, swimming clubs began to regroup as troops started to return home in 1919. By this time, Bill Bachrach wasn't viewed as the top man any longer. That was Harry Hazlehurst, a swimming coach who had made his name at the Hamilton Club. He became more well-known when he left in 1917 to head the training program at the Great Lakes Naval Training Station north of the city, where he prepared 500 "jackies" each day, many of them new enlistees who didn't know how to swim. Sewage-fouled Lake Michigan was believed to be a disease source — in just a couple of months, the 1918 flu pandemic killed 8,500 and sickened 40,000 in the city — so Hazlehurst trained his sailors in thirteen large tanks.

Some of the city's leading competitive swimmers, including Bachrach's team mainstay McGillivray, followed him to Great Lakes. He boasted his gobs were trained by a "half-dozen of the greatest speed swimmers in America." One of the tanks was built for competitive trials, and he had his coaches swim in regular exhibitions meant to build corps morale as well as to set records.

For Bachrach, his reign appeared to be over.

After the war, Hazlehurst accepted a post at the CAA with the idea that he would create a swim team to match the club's track team, which for decades had been acknowledged as the best in the city.

The exact date when he first saw Weissmuller swim isn't known. But it was surely the suffocatingly hot summer of 1919, when an explosion of racist mob violence put a halt to all normal activity in the city. The violence was not directed at the German populace, which was cautiously emerging from the shadows, but Black migrants, the city's fastest growing demographic. The episode was sparked by a question everyone in Chicago thought they knew the answer to: Who could swim where?

On Saturday, July 26, the city was excitedly preparing for one of its signature summertime events, the two-mile Chicago River marathon swim. Tens of thousands would line the banks and bridges and seemingly the one person missing was the event's irrepressible founder, sponsor, and cheerleader, Mayor Bill Thompson. He had started the river marathon in 1908 to promote his new club, the IAC, hoping to siphon-off interest in a running marathon sponsored by another club. Thompson, who had been derided as "Kaiser Bill" for his wartime defense of German Americans, was on a characteristic boondoggle trip roping steer in Cheyenne, Wyoming, leaving his deputies aboard the USS *Commodore* to start his race. In eleven years, the IAC had won all but two of the races, its last loss in 1910. When the starter's gun went off at 2:00 p.m., thirty-seven swimmers leapt into the harbor at Randolph Street, bound northward for the famously cruddy water of the Chicago River and the local fame that Thompson's silver-plate victory cup would provide.

Out on the river, Bachrach occupied a seat in a rowboat that paced his swimmer, Buddy Wallen, a former Hazlehurst pupil he'd recently poached from the Hamilton Club. McGillivray, a four-time winner, was at the oars. He had returned to the IAC.

Amidst his crew's urging, Wallen expanded an early lead and won using the old Trudgen crawl stroke. At the Wells Street finish line, he was yanked from the water by happy teammates. It was the conclusion of a perfect summer's day, affirmation that all was back to normal, world war and racial violence finally in the rearview mirror.

But Sunday told a different story. On Sunday, hell returned.

————————

IT NEVER DID COOL DOWN. Just after midnight on July 27, it was still eighty degrees, and by midafternoon it was an oppressive ninety-five. Everyone in Chicago was looking for relief at the Lake Michigan waterfront. The segregated South Side beach at 29th Street, a few blocks east of the Black Belt, was packed.

Eugene Williams, seventeen, was clinging to a railroad tie drifting offshore when a white adult shouted at him, believing he had crossed the invisible line separating white lake water from Black. Incensed, the man hurled stones, striking Williams in the head, his friends said, and knocking him off the tie into fifteen feet of water. A subsequent commission report couldn't confirm a head wound to Williams but said the constant assault of stones and a white swimmer coming toward him likely caused him to lose his grip and drown.

Black beachgoers summoned a Chicago policeman, identifying the stone thrower, but the white officer refused to arrest him. Frustrations erupted into fights, then gunfire.

The tragedy of Williams's senseless death, and another fatality hours later, were only the beginning of almost two weeks of rampaging violence which fanned across the city and laid bare its virulent racist streak.

Tuesday was the worst day of violence, despite the deployment of 3,000 state militia troops. The day before, the *Tribune* had published an illustration depicting Black and white swimmers with high, clenched fists, standing in Lake Michigan on opposite sides of a long dividing rope. A white, muscular figure had one arm threateningly raised and the other pointing to the rope. "The color line has reached the north," the caption read.

"Hunting the Hun" was replaced by hunting Blacks. Many assailants were young thugs sent out by white gang leaders who used the riots to punish Black migrants moving closer to their neighborhoods. "There were instances of thousands of white men attacking Negro homes, pulling the men out and beating them," the *Tribune* reported. The white rioters fired guns into dozens of Black homes; some 2,000 raided Black residences on one block of South Hermitage Avenue alone. The noted Black newspaper editor William Linton was with some 500 Black youths gathered in front of Walgreen's at 35th and State when nervous police officers opened fire, killing five and wounding twenty. Some of their rifles were tipped with bayonets. Henry Baker, one of twenty slain that Tuesday, was kneeling in front of his window on East 37th Street, reading his evening prayers, when he was shot in the eye.

The gangs, armed with revolvers, knives, torches, metal rods, and baseball bats, cast a widening net, roaming well beyond the initial battle zone on the South Side, moving downtown and further north. On the West Side, a white mob reportedly pulled a Black man off his bicycle, beat, kicked, and stabbed him, shot him sixteen times, then poured gasoline on his dead body and set it afire.

At the ornate Sherman House and Palmer House hotels, white mobs stormed in to kidnap Black employees. The violence became so widespread that the *Tribune* hired an airplane since it was impossible to report from the ground.

The Nord Seite briefly erupted in fighting, too. It was the last neighborhood to see violence before the battles finally stopped later in the week. At the time Weissmuller was working as a bellboy and elevator operator at the Plaza Hotel near Lincoln Park. The kitchen at the North Side Turner Hall, where Lizzie Weissmuller worked, prepared more than 700 sandwiches and "pails and pails of hot coffee" for the Chicago Avenue station where policemen and refugees from the fighting were crowded.

The several hundred arrested were primarily Chicago youth who were booked and ultimately released. Most were Black but there were significant white arrests, too. The investigative commission believed the city's ragtag athletic clubs, such as Ragen's Colts and the Hamburgers, were responsible for many of the attacks. The riot's stone-throwing instigator was identified as George Stauber, a twenty-four-year-old Bavarian immigrant living a few blocks from the beach. "Red Summer," as the riot would be known, ended with 38 dead, 537 injured, and 1,000 Black families made homeless. If you hated a person because of their skin color and had come through the riots in one piece, it was likely you now hated them more.

It was virtually impossible to be a white teen living in

Chicago in late July 1919 and not to be a part of the trouble or know those who were. Johnny Weissmuller, once a target as a German-born kid and now finding himself part of an angry majority that sought to crush Black newcomers, responded by heading to the water. On August 10, just days after the troops went home and peace was restored, the untrained but talented fifteen-year-old entered his first major swimming race.

Held at the Lincoln Park Lagoon, the races were part of a water carnival that had been jeopardized by the riots but remarkably went on as planned. The carnival, sponsored by the CAA, featured swimming, rowing, and wildly popular novelty events like wooden-tub races and a jousting match called "canoe tilting" in which combatants mercilessly raked their rivals with oars to try to knock them into the water.

Thousands lined the lagoon, some in Packards and Fords, most of them keenly eyeing another novelty — a series of women's races starring the visiting Aussie Fanny Durack, holder of multiple women's swim records.

Tucked into the undercard on Saturday was a competition of junior swimmers racing for their neighborhood parks. Weissmuller was a revelation, winning the 50- and 150-yard freestyle as well as the 50-yard backstroke, and leading his Stanton Park team to victory.

Two weeks later, at the outdoor Sherman Park Natatorium, again racing for Stanton Park in junior-division races, he won the fifty- and 100-yard sprints in record times for the city, twenty-eight seconds and 1:04, respectively.

Sometime that fall he began training at the beautiful CAA pool. Late in the year, however, he abruptly left the CAA and Hazlehurst's calm tutelage. Bill Bachrach was ascendant again, having finally obtained a star headliner: Norman Ross, a swimmer Bachrach had coveted since 1914 when Ross was with the

Olympic Club in San Francisco. After the war, he relocated to Chicago, signed with the IAC in March 1919, and began setting records nationally and internationally. At the Inter-Allied Games in Paris, Ross won a five-mile marathon on the Seine before 300,000 spectators, the largest crowd in history to attend a swimming contest. Any swimming prospect, Weissmuller included, would have dreamed of being on a team alongside Ross.

When Pierre de Coubertin announced the Olympics would resume in 1920 and that the swimming trials would take place at the Lincoln Park Lagoon, Bachrach was at full boil.

———

AS DOUBTFUL AS IT SEEMED IN 1915 for Duke Kahanamoku to return to the top ranks of competitive swimming, he had been lured back two years later when Hawaii arranged a meet featuring him and his heir apparent, the stockily built Spokane boy, Norman Ross. The centerpiece of the Winter Carnival at Naval Slip was an evening showdown under the lights: the young man taking on the older man in the 100- and 220-meter finals. The shorter race was thought a toss-up but in the 220, Ross was the clear favorite.

Kahanamoku's father, Duke Sr., had died a month earlier from a heart attack, so the races held understandable weight and emotional pull. Before the largest audience ever to attend a Honolulu swimming event, Kahanamoku won what the papers called the "greatest race in history," a come-from-behind victory in the 220-meter. In the 100-meter sprint he set a new world record.

The reaction of home fans, some of whom suspected he was past his prime, felt extraordinary to Duke. Years later, when he sketched out the sporting moments that meant the most to him, this was at the top. "The most exciting swimming meet we've ever had in Honolulu," he wrote. A sportswriter at the *Honolulu*

Star-Bulletin breathlessly described the end of the race: "Something inside burst, and hats, cushions, and any movable thing was thrown in the water . . . . The crowd cheered. The crowd yelled. They do that always when a man makes a game fight." Another paper declared that Kahanamoku was "better than his past best." He owned the beach at Waikiki, and most of the rest of Honolulu. Even Duke was shocked. "220 yards was Norman's race," he would write. "The odds were five to one in his favor. I swam in that race as the third man."

A writer for the Hawaiian language *Ke Aloha Aina* newspaper described Ross supporters as being *kukule lakou e like me ka moa i pulu i ka wai* — dejected like a chicken drenched in water — adding, "Long live Hawaii because of [Duke]."

Earlier that summer, friends observed, Kahanamoku was as settled and comfortable as he had ever been. He was often seen in the company of Eleanor Snodgrass, a young white music student visiting from the Bay Area. Their relationship was exuberantly chronicled in her private scrapbook, which nobody would see until it appeared at an auction house 100 years later. The pair tandem surfed and pressed closely to one another on the beach. In several snapshots they are being goofy in the front seat of a car sculpted out of sand. Duke inscribed her favorite book of poetry and charmingly drew a picture of Diamond Head and the bay.

Snodgrass, the daughter of a bank president and niece to two Southern state congressmen, told a mainland newspaper reporter that she had gone to Waikiki with her mother on a brief Knights Templar trip that they extended to the entire summer. Snodgrass said she had been made an honorary Hui Nalu member and described the thrill of the first time Kahanamoku dared her to go surf riding with him beyond the breakers. "I took his dare in a jiffy," she said. "I stood on Duke's shoulders . . . time and again I thought certainly I should be dashed off, but we rode safely to the shore. I simply could not get enough of it after that, and Duke took me on his shoulders trip after trip."

The relationship didn't draw the hot attention or sharp criticism of Kahanamoku's earlier affair with Rhoda Wilson Deerr. A mixed-race couple was still frowned upon — even in Waikiki — but the proper guardrails of the time were in place. Snodgrass's mother was with them in the evening, Duke's beach-boy pals were there during the day. Perhaps it was as simple and innocent as two young people sharing a bed of sand and a surfboard. What is clear from her scrapbook is that Kahanamoku had found a person he deeply cared for who felt the same about him. His Winter Carnival victories might have flowed from this easy if elusive season of contentment.

Snodgrass would marry two years later, but she never disappeared from Kahanamoku's life. She lived in Waikiki and became a member of the Outrigger Canoe Club, which had invited some native Hawaiians to join, including Duke. In later years, she ended a personal note to him: "Remember I love you very much . . . 'wife #2' Eleanor."

By 1918, a new crop of controversies and troubles had arisen. Some questioned why Kahanamoku applied for temporary exemption from war service, which he received, and why he later delayed reporting for duty. "Duke Kahanamoku, a Hawaiian, recently established a tank record in Chicago," said one editorial in reference to a 1918 swimming exhibition. "The duke would hold a higher place in our estimation if he had established the tank record on the Marne. Many a lad who was considered 'onry' at home is proving a hero in chasing the *Boches* back to Berlin and adding to the glory of the flag."

That summer Kahanamoku had been on a U.S. and Canada tour to benefit the American Red Cross, during which he appeared in newspapers knitting scarves to be auctioned in the cities he passed through. He had applied to the war department for draft exemption because he was the sole provider for his family's dependents, but his status was changed during his tour and he was to report in Hawaii at the end of October. He missed the date because of an emergency seventeen-day hospitalization for Spanish influenza in Washington, D.C. His return was further delayed because his business manager had left him in the U.S. without any money. Kahanamoku was on a ship bound for Hawaii, where he planned to report for Air Corps duty, when the armistice was announced on November 11, 1918.

Friends vouched for him and his story but still, he heard the whispers.

NO SOONER HAD BACHRACH SIGNED ROSS to the IAC than he issued a challenge to Kahanamoku. Honolulu boosters, cajoled by Bill Rawlins, agreed for the first time to host and cover expenses for the visiting swimmers and coach. But when Bachrach, Ross, and other IAC swimmers arrived in the fall of 1919, Kahanamoku was struggling to recover from his life-threatening bout with the flu and uncertain about his race condition. He couldn't be persuaded to compete against Ross in the much anticipated rematch.

As a result, the IAC was triumphant, dominating the Hawaiians and in doing so again becoming the hottest swim team in the country. One of the more memorable photos from the trip showed Bachrach in a black bathing singlet, his bare legs spread in Waikiki sand, cigar in mouth, posed in front of Duke's sixteen-foot surfboard. Ever the opportunist, he still had hopes of recruiting Kahanamoku to his team. In a final interview before returning to Chicago, he said, "You don't realize the two things for which the Hawaiian Islands are famous for in the minds of most people in the United States are Duke Kahanamoku and the crater of Kilauea — with the crater second choice."

Kahanamoku had participated in various promotions for the races against the IAC, including hosting a dinner party, but it wasn't nearly enough in the view of the same writers who lionized him two years earlier.

One writer suggested Kahanamoku's true character was nothing like a champion's. He didn't buy Duke's explanation that he hadn't recovered from the flu to adequately train. An incensed Leonard Withington, sports editor of the *Pacific Commercial Advertiser* and head of the local chapter of the American Legion, called him a coward and a slacker, a criticism considered particularly scathing since "slacker" was a term applied to those who evaded the Great War. He was a Hawaiian unworthy of being of Hawaiian blood, Withington said.

This attack might have reminded Kahanamoku of a story Norman Ross had written for the *Star-Bulletin* during his first visit to Honolulu. "The life of a champion is a hard one," he observed. "As long as he is on top he is great . . . the minute he is defeated, or gives signs he is not the man of old, the same friends turn on him."

Kahanamoku responded to Withington's article by suing the parent newspaper, *The Honolulu Advertiser*, asking for $50,000 in damages. The complaint, issued by the law firm Brown, Cristy & Davis, cited that Kahanamoku was "brought into odium and contempt" and that he has been "humiliated and debased."

The *Advertiser* was owned by Lorrin Thurston, a white lawyer who helped spearhead the overthrow of the Hawaiian monarchy decades before. Thurston had succeeded in imprisoning Queen Liliʻuokalani and heavily influenced assimilation policies such as forbidding the teaching of the Hawaiian language in schools.

The lawsuit, coming from a man whose ancestors were intimately connected to the royal line, was, in one sense, a remarkable declaration of indigenous independence and a critique of the systemic injustice all native Hawaiians endured as colonized second-class citizens. Queen Liliʻuokalani's death was still recent. She had died on November 11, 1917, just weeks after Kahanamoku's victories over Ross in Honolulu Harbor.

But in another sense, the lawsuit represented yet one more battle Kahanamoku felt obliged to fight. The strain revealed itself in a simple but poignant way: He said he could not sleep.

THE FIRST SWIM TRIALS for the 1920 Olympics took place on the West Coast and were primarily for California and Hawaii swimmers. The second trials, at Lincoln Park, incorporated those winners with Midwestern and Eastern hopefuls. Starring twenty-three of the country's fastest swimmers, the Chicago meet could not have gone better for the IAC host team. On Saturday, with the 100-yard and one-mile races on tap, some 20,000 spectators ringed the lagoon, just north of the poor kids' beach on Fullerton Avenue and away from an old cemetery that reeked of standing water and shallowly buried corpses.

A novel PA system announced the swimmers at each turn. With several war veterans in contention, a patriotic feeling was evident. Former naval machinist Eugene Bolden, now swimming for the IAC, won the mile, edging out Hawaii's Ludy Langer by a yard. Kahanamoku easily beat Ross in the 100. But the wire-story lead was the 200-yard breaststroke. It was won by old Bachrach protege Turk McDermott. The next day, Ross won the 440 as expected, in record time.

When Otto Wahle announced the Olympic team the

following Thursday, every Hawaiian was on it. The *Hilo Daily Tribune* reported: "All Hawaiian swimmers on team. Square deal for natives, official promises." A photo accompanying the story showed the seven swimmers posed in a Hudson super-six speedster, parked on the beach with Diamond Head in the background. An identical photo had run a year earlier when Bachrach visited, only the coupe was filled with Chicago swimmers. Bachrach's knack for promotion seemed to have rubbed off.

According to George Center, who was managing the Hawaiian swimmers, it was a tale of two receptions on the mainland. At the West Coast trials, the Hawaiians felt welcomed. Huge, adoring crowds came to the qualifying races, many of them showing up from the growing community of Hawaiians living in California. A Hawaiian band played, and fans volunteered to rub down the swimmers. Even swimmers not named Duke Kahanamoku came to the fore. "When Pua Kealoha crossed the line he gave the judges his famous million-dollar smile," wrote Center in a letter published in the Honolulu papers. "It knocked them dead, and the crowd too. You should have seen the Navy men go mad to get him smiling. Kodaks burst out of the crowds. I was a judge and with all the Navy men and Kodak fiends trying to snap Pua, I was hanging onto the ragged edge of nothing trying to keep from being knocked into the pool." When the team boarded the *Overland Limited* train for Chicago, they were euphoric.

But Chicago was different, Center wrote, and went on to detail the "numerous incivilities" to which he and his team were subjected. The team's host, the CAA, was chilly to them and Center had the impression the Hawaiians' strong performance in California was upsetting the plans of the committee chosen to select the U.S. team. Wahle, the chair of the selection committee, told Center that Kahanamoku was "through" and would "never make the American team."

Shortly before the U.S. team left New York for the Antwerp Games, Duke gave a free-ranging interview to *The Evening World*. As if to ridicule Wahle, who saw himself as leading the vanguard of scientific training methods for optimal sprint performance, Duke said he did nothing to prepare for racing and never had. He did not diet ("I eat anything") and he did not train. "Training? Why, I never did go into real training for a race. My training consists of going out and swimming around."

Kahanamoku likely remembered Wahle's comments made after his 1912 Olympic victories: "Duke came to this country devoid of knowledge of even the rudimentary principles of speed swimming. He learned all he knows about the art of swimming right here in the East, and it was here he developed the kick, which many regard as the foundation of his success. He was 'made in America' by Americans."

In July 1920 Kahanamoku, this time accompanied by Hawaiian comrades, left for his second Olympic Games. Initially rejected by the AAU, Bill Bachrach was given a coveted spot on the U.S. team staff following a loud protest by influential members of the IAC.

Left behind was a certain enthusiastic attendee of the Lincoln Park trials. But Johnny Weissmuller had seen everything he needed to see, and knew where he intended to go.

SEVEN

MONSTERS FROM THE WEST
1920

*"Every time I want to wash my face there's no
water, and we're so crowded I can't move. Some
of the men sleep in the morgue — more fun."*
—Aileen Riggin, a fourteen-year-old
U.S. team diver in a shipboard letter
to her cousin, written en route to
the 1920 Summer Games

THE TALL, ANGULAR U.S. Olympic Committee president, Gus-
tavus Kirby, in a top hat and long-tailed coat, had finally arrived
to meet the athletes at team quarters in Antwerp the day before
the start of the Games on August 14. Kirby, a New York attorney whose ancestor was the patriot Betsy Ross, proceeded to
give a robust pep talk for the "further athletic glory of America." When he concluded, the hundreds of athletes who were
gathered in the courtyard of a Belgian schoolhouse withheld
the expected throaty huzzahs. Instead, they were stony silent.

They'd had enough and had banded together in opposition to Kirby, his fellow American eminences, and the autocratic organizations they represented, the AAU and the American Olympic Committee.

Their complaints centered around their treatment as America's premier athletes and, more specifically, the trip to Europe, which was a disaster from the start. The ship that greeted them in Hoboken, New Jersey, was not the promised speedy ocean liner but a rickety troops transport, the *Princess Matoika*, borrowed on the cheap at the last minute from the military. When it arrived for its athlete cargo, the repatriated remains of 1,800 American soldiers were being offloaded, row upon row of coffins surrounding the team on the docks.

The conditions on board were deplorable. The noxious smell of formaldehyde filled the hold where they slept on chain-suspended bunks that swayed with the pitching sea. Most of the male athletes slept on deck rather than the rodent-infested quarters. The large delegation of American officials, however, was housed in private staterooms.

The trip to Antwerp took two weeks, more than twice as long as expected. In what came to be known as the "Mutiny on the *Matoika*," the team had drafted a protest letter signed by all 200-plus athletes. It blamed the executive committee for "laxity and gross inefficiency," and argued that such poor living conditions could make it impossible for the team to, in the words of the late James Sullivan, "bring home the bacon."

"Sleeping either in an ill-smelling hold, overrun with rats, and without sufficient ventilation, or on hard decks in rain; eating food served improperly due to the overcrowded conditions of the galley; poor sanitary conditions for the majority of men . . ." the athletes' complaint began. In Antwerp, the old schoolhouse awaited them, where they anticipated food from cans. Dan Ahearn, a gold-medal favorite in jumping, took one look at the primitive accommodations and disappeared, checking into a city hotel.

In his speech, Kirby ignored the letter entirely. Another American official, angrily gauging the athletes' disrespect, said the team risked disgrace in the eyes of their country if they persisted with their complaints. Norman Ross, the athletes' spokesman, nonetheless firmly reissued their demands for "proper accommodations" for the rest of the trip and the assurance of better conditions for future U.S. Olympic teams. If they were not met, Ross said, they would not march in the next day's Parade of Nations.

"Athletes had been considered docile or dumb and were generally impressed by the display of high silk hats, white kid gloves, and fashionable canes," Charley Paddock, the famous American sprint star, would later recall. "The team of 1920 was different. They represented the new generation in American sports."

The athletes' signatures were scrawled in the margins of the first page of the protest letter. One of the most prominent, writ large and more centered to catch the reader's eye, was Duke Kahanamoku's. A copy of the letter was a prized keepsake which Kahanamoku donated decades later to the Hawaii state archives. Kirby acceded to the demands.

Thirty-seven teams marched into the Olympic stadium for the opening ceremonies. Doves flew and a new Olympic flag, featuring intertwined rings representing the five inhabited continents, was raised in a message of world unity. But war was still fresh in everyone's minds, especially in Belgium. American swimmers who toured nearby battlefields said they had found remnants of the carnage. Diver Aileen Riggin picked up a boot and found the remains of a human foot inside.

It was only twenty months after the armistice. The Germans, banned from participating in the Games, were still enemy combatants. Even German Americans were unwelcome in allied

Europe. When Wahle, who was actually Austrian, abruptly shipped out to New York, leaving his assistants Bill Bachrach and George Center in charge of the swim team, the stated reason was an emergency at home. Center believed the real problem was his nationality. The "Belgians and other allied peoples" held it against Wahle, said Center.

When the Games got underway, the swimming conditions were awful. "It was a ditch," said Riggin, who was part of the first-ever squad of female American swimmers at the Olympics. "I had never seen anything like it. We heard later that this had been the city moat." The waters were murky and, though it was late August, only fifty degrees. Swimmers emerged with arms and legs "half frozen," according to Riggin. The lone Hawaii female swimmer, Helen Moses, was kept out of competition for fear of permanent physical damage. "She was too young to be chanced in that icy pool," Center said.

Nevertheless, the American swim results in Antwerp were spectacular. No country could beat the U.S. sprinters, most of whom were Hawaiian. Duke was at his self-assured best, winning his second-straight Olympic gold in the 100-meter, followed by two Hawaiians who won silver and bronze. Warren Kealoha won the 100-meter backstroke. In the final event, Duke, Pua Kealoha [no relation to Warren], Ross, and McGillivray won the 800-meter relay, smashing the world record by sixteen seconds.

Back home in Honolulu, the Hawaiians received top headlines for carrying the U.S. team. After reminding its rival the *Pacific Commercial Advertiser* that it called Kahanamoku a slacker the previous year, the *Star-Bulletin* observed, "If all the people in Honolulu who are giving three cheers for Duke in private would get together and 'hip hip' in unison, Duke would almost be able to hear in Antwerp."

Following the Games, the swim team traveled to Paris for an

exhibition hyperbolically billed the "Revenge of Nautical Olympians." The French had not been a factor at the Olympics, and everyone knew it wasn't a country of elite swimmers. There were only an estimated twenty pools in all of France and less than five percent of the population could swim. Still, the Parisians came out, tens of thousands packing the banks of the Seine.

The Americans swept the diving events and swim races, both Ross and Kahanamoku suspected of easing their pace in order not to humiliate their adversaries. A reporter from *L'Auto* magazine interviewed Duke as he emerged from the water after his 100-meter swim, asking his thoughts on French wine and smoking; the aviator adventurer Bernard de Romanet, the world record holder for the longest flight; and Georges Pouilley, the 100-meter French champion he had easily dispatched. "Very good swimmer," Duke said. The exhibition would later be credited with sparking a French interest in competitive swimming.

The Americans' performances were sandwiched around team culinary adventures and tourist visits to the Louvre, the Champs-Élysées, the Folies Bergère. Kahanamoku was said to make a solo visit to the Olympia concert hall to see Honolulu musician William Kulii Kanui perform in a melodrama about two doomed Hawaiian lovers.

Duke, Ross, and teammate Ludy Langer then boarded a flight at Le Bourget Airport taking them from Paris to another exhibition in Exeter, England. The Farman F.60 Goliath, the first commercial plane to fly passengers, was typically reserved for wealthy patrons, not amateur athletes. Ross and Duke were different; they were sports celebrities, an emerging new breed. In a photo published in *Le Miroir des Sports,* Kahanamoku is at the open door of the gigantic biplane, flashing a broad smile in anticipation of the death-defying two-and-a-half-hour flight. Seated in wicker chairs, passengers flew at seventy-five miles per hour at an altitude of 5,000 feet. Ross boarded despite having survived two airplane crashes during the war and vowing never to fly again. The sensation of diving into clouds and zooming low and fast across land and sea was an unbeatable experience, he admitted, "but if you fly, sooner or later you are going to fall."

———————

FRANCE WOULD produce Duke's best Olympic memories. He was hugely popular everywhere in Europe, George Center would recall, particularly Paris. French admirers, many of them female, caused a commotion at his appearances and had to be cleared away by police when they surrounded his taxi. The French reverence for artists, entertainers, and athletes of all colors was well established. The Black American world champion bike racer Marshall "Major" Taylor, hectored by bigots in his own country, came to Paris in 1901 amidst admiring headlines he never saw at home.

When Olympic founder and retiring IOC president Pierre de Coubertin announced that Paris would be the site of the 1924 Games, Kahanamoku, now thirty, was not expected to try to make the team. But Paris was a reason to go.

Duke was enjoying a free-flowing independence he had never known. Gliding in and out of clouds, looking down on a ruined but rebuilding land, he had cause to feel his expanding privilege. Much of his experience in Europe in 1920 would go unchronicled. The hundreds of travel photos he took were lost, and he kept the best, most colorful stories, as he always did, to himself. But those closest to Duke knew his true nature. They would not be surprised by a story from Antwerp to surface decades later. He had dared teammate Hal Prieste to shimmy up a fifteen-foot pole and, with security distracted, swipe the

Olympic flag. Prieste would keep the flag in his suitcase for decades, revealing the episode only when he returned the flag at the 2000 Olympic Games in Australia.

When the Hawaiians finally returned in November, circling Army airplanes welcomed them, dropping leis on the decks of the *Matsonia* as it entered Honolulu Harbor. Warren Kealoha dropped quarters overboard for the youthful native divers. "No pennies for this occasion, only two-bit pieces," he shouted above celebratory whistles and band music. Kahanamoku deferred to George Center to lead the procession from the wharf down a lane of flowers and a crush of well-wishers to the Young Hotel. At the gangplank, a reporter had asked Duke if he had learned French. "Oui, oui, Marie," he said with a smile.

In Chicago, the IAC's reception was more modest, but Bill Bachrach was enjoying his newfound notoriety. He was singled out in the official American Olympic Committee report, suggesting he would be Otto Wahle's heir apparent. He didn't have a top sprinter, but Chicago was viewed as the center of swimming in the new decade. Bachrach had a way with his swimmers and, more importantly, he knew how to raise the U.S. team profile. His boosting, as he called it, would propel American swimming to new heights as the next Games approached.

In appreciation, Bachrach received a significant raise from the IAC, his annual salary going from $2,700 to $3,600, a forty percent increase that made him the highest-paid swimming coach in America.

George Center, whose work at the Games went unpaid, was barely mentioned in Wahle's report, despite the magnificent performance of the seven Hawaiian swimmers he trained, some of whom had never competed outside Honolulu. In Europe the Hawaiians had competed in twenty-six meets and won fifty-nine medals. Center believed swimming's future was in Hawaii, not

Chicago, and he challenged the AAU governorship of the sport, suggesting the board be more representative.

But the AAU quickly snuffed out the proposed reforms. Wahle hadn't forgotten Center's comments about the poor treatment of the Hawaiian swimmers in Chicago, nor had he put aside his bias against Kahanamoku. Center didn't know it yet, but his days as a national coach were over.

———

AS MUCH AS THE DREAMS of the Americans were realized in Europe, those of the Japanese were not. They had sent their best swimmers to Antwerp: Kenkichi Saito and Masayoshi Uchida. The two had dominated the Far Eastern Games in Tokyo in 1917, and the willowy Uchida defended his sprint victories in Manila two years later. Saito, a muscularly built twenty-five-year-old born on Sado Island, had attended Tokyo Higher Normal School, the center of sports and competitive swimming in Japan. Uchida, along with his brother, had started a swimming club on Lake Hamana, famous in Japan for nurturing generations of swimmers.

Hopes were high, especially for Saito, Japan's best all-around athlete. "Should he be able to strike another two seconds from his time he would reach the world record established by the famous Hawaiian champion, Duke Kahanamoku," reported the *Japan Times*. On the way to Belgium, Saito and Uchida visited Princeton University and the New York Athletic Club, where they were timed at 1:03 for the 100-meter.

But the moment they arrived in Antwerp, there were problems. They had no experience swimming in frigid water. Their small stature stood out, as did their swim stroke. The prevailing competition stroke for sprint distances, and the one they likely used in Antwerp, was the *Chimba-Nuki,* a sidestroke in which the swimmer alternates using the left and right arms.

They were defeated almost as soon as they started, ousted in the preliminaries. Saito dropped out of the 400-meter semifinal altogether. Seiichi Kishi, president of the Japanese Amateur Sports Association, said they were viewed as "laughingstocks," more for their ancient swimming strokes than for slow times. To make matters worse, they and the rest of the fifteen-person Japanese team had no way home. They ran out of money and were stranded in Belgium. The Mitsubishi and Mitsui corporations agreed to donate $15,000 to retrieve them in exchange for not having to sponsor the Olympic team again. The national embarrassment was profound. For the second consecutive Olympic Games, Japanese athletes had failed to win a single point.

The returning swimmers blamed the archaic sidestroke, imploring the adoption of modern techniques. One American trainer said it was shocking "how little the Japs really knew about athletes." Some critics saw a deeper problem. "The overwhelming defeat the Japanese team suffered at the Olympic Games at Antwerp last year is not the fault of the Japanese team alone," said an editorial in the Japanese-English paper *Nippu Jiji.* "It is the fault of the entire Japanese people who failed to realize the importance of physical training. And how long will Japan, one of the leading powers of the world, be satisfied with such condition? The physical inferiority of the Japanese is an unchallengeable fact."

WHILE JAPAN WAS FLOUNDERING in Antwerp, there was a glimmer of hope back home, in the form of fourteen-year-old Katsuo Takaishi and the revolutionary team he was part of. Their breakthrough came at a national college swimming meet at Heda, about ninety miles southwest of Tokyo. "I will never forget it," said Takaishi, some fifty years later at a reunion of Ibaraki teammates and coaches.

To a kid from a busy port city, the dramatic natural scenery around Heda was a revelation. Mount Fuji rose on the opposite shore, "majestically above the white waves of Suruga Bay," Takaishi wrote in an article about the rise of the Ibaraki swim program. Heda was a small seaside village on the eastern Izu Peninsula. Steamers and sailboats landed and departed throughout the day, cruising between the peninsula towns. The races were held in a bay with a white sand beach protected by pine trees, crystal-clear water, and a fifty-meter-long starting platform. Takaishi couldn't help but obsess over what he didn't have — this idyllic place where the heralded Tokyo Imperial University swim team, the country's first college program, got to practice and perform. "They had a dormitory in the pine grove next to the beach," he wrote. "I was envious."

Hosted by the university, the amateur swimming competition at Heda was Takaishi's first national event. Hundreds of athletes were expected, most from the elite university programs across the country.

The little-known junior program from Ibaraki Middle School was a curiosity. Their times were said to be impossibly fast. Ibaraki's fourteen- and fifteen-year-old swimmers were several years younger and many pounds lighter than the college men. They came from a campus of old wooden buildings, where the students dressed in uniforms from a bygone era: navy-blue sleeveless kimonos with navy-blue *hakama* trousers. In keeping with the school's spartan philosophy, they were required to be barefoot year-round.

The coach, Den Sugimoto, was barely known in Tokyo, though he probably should have been. He seemed to have the energy of a dozen men. In addition to the popular swimming program at Ibaraki, he enlisted almost every student in an out-door class of nighttime mountain hikes. Takaishi fondly recalled clandestine trips he took with him at midnight to "borrow" river water, commandeering a pipe away from the rice fields and into their pool. Nobody would be surprised when Sugimoto, also an avid musician, returned from the 1924 Games in Paris with in-struments he had purchased to start an Ibaraki jazz band. Much later, to mark his fiftieth birthday, he walked 513 kilometers from Kyoto to Tokyo. He was an unstoppable force.

Only a year after building the modest Ibaraki swimming pond in 1914, he began construction of a true Western-style pool on the school's former playground. At almost fifty meters long, the pool extended onto municipal land, an error that resulted in the principal's dismissal — but the project wasn't stopped. Instead, Sugimoto had shrewdly tied the pool to a series of public-works projects being done all over Japan that year as tribute to Emperor Taishō's coronation in 1915. One group of students were shovelers who excavated the soil, while others were "basket crews" who lugged it away. They labored steadfastly during gym class and over summer break, and the pool slowly took shape.

It was brutal work. In a photograph taken at the time, there are dozens of barefoot student workers in white overalls and dark sashes, burying shovels into muddy embankments. Others work hoes or are perched on rickety stair-steppers, backs bent as they strain to turn the waterwheels that diverted inflowing water. It's a slightly mad scene — a series of mudholes that give little indication of the end goal — but the work laid the foun-dation for a dazzling future. And they knew it.

By December 1915 they could, according to Sugimoto, "see in their own eyes" that the swimming pool was taking form.

"They were so energized they continued to work hard even in the morning when frost pillars were standing in the cold sky and in the evening when light snow was falling." The Imperial Government recognized their achievement with a medal engraved with the royal chrysanthemum crest and the word "Banzai." The medal hung from a red-and-white-striped ribbon said to come from the pavilion drapes used at the coronation ceremony.

Two years later Sugimoto attended the Far Eastern Games in Tokyo, where he was inspired to start his own competitive team. He hired a Japanese medal winner at the Games to teach his student swimmers at Ibaraki.

As late as summer 1919, Tomekichi Nakata taught his old one-handed stroke and sternly held to training myths he had been taught. He forbade post swim baths, believing they softened muscles. The middle schoolers, swimming in insufferably hot weather and in water often covered in algae, heeded their teacher, despite the nauseating odor that clung to their slime-streaked bodies after practice.

But that same summer, Sugimoto read the American Charles Daniels's book about the crawl stroke and how he used it to set world records and win Olympic gold at the London Games in 1908. Sugimoto constructed a five-year plan to build a champion in time for Paris 1924. At the start of the school year, he used Ibaraki's annual 10,000-meter run to select athletes who showed the best endurance potential.

He convinced a reluctant Nakata to teach the new crawl stroke and see how students did with it. Nakata didn't want to part with the past entirely, but when he did finally let them use the crawl for an entire 100-meter distance or longer, they saw startling fast times.

Sugimoto debuted five swimmers at Heda in 1920, all of them using the crawl stroke. In his diary the night before the event, he wrote that he loved the group and knew how the older university athletes from Tokyo taunted them. "The day had come for us to see how well we could do," wrote Sugimoto. "The blue tide surged over Heda Bay and we waited for the battle to begin. How are the hearts of the warriors?"

The east-west rivalry between the Kantō and Kansai regions, and their respective capitals, Tokyo and Osaka, was centuries old, each swimming enclave viewing the other with bias. To Osaka, Tokyo was conservative, flat, unchanging; to Tokyo, Osaka was loose, light, common. The alternating overhand stroke that Sugimoto's students unveiled at Heda probably couldn't have come from Kantō, the stronghold of samurai and their famous schools of swimming. It had to come from Osaka. The new breed of Ibaraki crawl swimmers, whether endurance or speed oriented, didn't breathe the old Japanese way, with heads out of the water. They breathed like Charles Daniels, Norman Ross, and Duke Kahanamoku, the fastest swimmers in the world. Kantō officials weren't happy: "A terrible guy has come out of Kansai," wrote one in reference to Sugimoto. "He's taken over."

Sugimoto's swimmers won three disciplines and the team points competition, drawing notice throughout Japan. "When I got home I went to the beach to watch the sunset," he recalled, but soon found himself screaming, "Hooray for Ibaraki! Hooray for Ibaraki!" The country had suffered calamity at the Olympics, but the feeling arising from Heda was optimism. Sugimoto was so convinced of his path after the victory at Heda, he immediately began teaching the crawl to first years.

Back at the school's pool, the Ibaraki team posed with the winner's flag, all but one of the five swimmers wearing the traditional *rokushaku fundoshi*, a white cotton thong. Katsuo Takaishi, standing with the flag positioned waist high, looks like a mere child. Sugimoto wears a pure white robe and is seated with his feet in the wild grass that frames the rectangular hole they had famously dug years before.

Some of the Tokyo swimmers had a name for the Ibaraki crawl swimmers: monsters from the West. Scholars saw the continued erosion of Japanese identity in the Western-influenced strokes, something much more consequential than the fleeting thrill of winning a race. The Classical Swimming Federation, supporting and advocating for the traditional martial techniques of *Nihon eiho*, was quick to oppose the Western adaptations. The twelve premodern schools, developed for encountering every conceivable situation in the water, were in one sense highly pragmatic. In another, the strokes were ritualistic and ceremonial, a timeless part of the nation's ancient fabric.

Takaishi wasn't the star of the Heda meet. He struggled in the 800-meter race in choppy waters, his small stature so overmatched in going against the current he had to switch strokes, abandoning the crawl for the classical one-armed sidestroke. Though he seemed to be embarrassed to have relied on the old ways (he never did it again) he knew he was fortunate to have centuries of rich swimming heritage at his disposal.

But if his physical immaturity betrayed him at Heda, Takaishi impressed the one person who counted most. In the decisive race, a relay to determine overall team winner, Takaishi was fading in his second leg when suddenly he found another gear, making up ground in what Sugimoto described as an "extraordinary feat." He passed the other swimmer to regain the Ibaraki lead which his two teammates maintained, giving the team the title.

Sugimoto already knew that Takaishi was his most analytic, hardworking talent. He didn't have the physique for stardom yet, but he had belief and grit. He understood there was a direct line between the shovel he held to build the Ibaraki pool and the unceasing effort it would take to compete in what Sugimoto described as "the battles." It wouldn't be long before he won far more races than he lost. In one of his first Ibaraki practices, Sugimoto couldn't help but notice Takaishi's obsession. It was April and the pool was half frozen. Takaishi was one of the few who stayed in, clearing ice out of his way as he swam.

Strong-willed and adventurous didn't sufficiently describe Takaishi. As a boy, he swam in the river near his home, often after dark and despite a policeman ordering him to go home. His daughter Yuriko loved his story about a neighbor catching and beating him for stealing a watermelon. She thought it sounded like something from *Tom Sawyer*. "He jumped into a river and ran away, like a naughty boy," she said. According to family lore, he once brought a stray dog home, and when his parents said he could not keep it, Takaishi and the dog ran away. Eventually, his parents coaxed them back.

Takaishi, young as he was, was sure of two things: The crawl was his path forward, and he was the person to perfect it in Japan. His crawl, though imitative of a Western style initially, was completely different because the principles of swimming passed on to him were different. How he rolled his torso, how he used his arms to push against the water's density, how he nimbly directed his hands, how his ankles flexed as easily as a shrimp curled its body — it was all informed by his country's centuries-old approach to swimming. His crawl had a grace and beauty that was distinctly Japanese. Yuriko, who lives in Osaka, still remembers his form as "beautiful."

Japanese purists did not understand yet, but the crawl was already their own. The secret for potential wasn't some textbook technique. The secret, as Sugimoto liked to say, was that they were the sons of warriors.

EIGHT

COMERS
1921

"Chicago, the home of America's watermen, has produced another swimmer of international promise, a boy of seventeen."
—*Kansas City Kansan* on
Johnny Weissmuller

IT WAS JANUARY 6, THE START of the 1921 indoor swimming season and a renewal of Chicago's best intercity rivalry: the IAC versus the CAA. Norman Ross, back from Europe, was looking to break the 100-yard individual medley record in the tiny IAC pool. Along with fellow Olympians Perry McGillivray and Harry Hebner, he also hoped to set a new national sprint relay mark.

For the undercard, Bill Bachrach touted two sixteen-year-old juniors he heralded as "comers," Oliver Horn and Johnny Weissmuller. Of the two, Bachrach believed Weissmuller, whom he had begun training two months earlier, to be the most promising.

Timing officials and starters in suits patrolled the narrow

pool deck. Dozens of athletes in club racing suits came and went through the archways leading to the locker rooms. A decent number of fans, strolling South Michigan Avenue on this unseasonably warm Chicago night, walked in off the street. People stood on the balcony to watch, removing their hats to fit beneath the low ceiling.

When the IAC pool opened to the public fifteen years earlier, it was a "revelation in aquatics," according to the club magazine. There was space for 2,500 spectators, and the black tile racing lines on the pool's bottom were an early innovation. When the cornerstone of the building was laid, Frank Lowden, an Illinois politician who would later become governor, declared, "The poor man with health and physique is far richer than the millionaire with dyspepsia."

He likely would not have imagined the captain of the club's athletics program to be a 350-pound man whose wide girth and perpetual cigar smoking began most every newspaper story about the IAC. Weissmuller would never forget the first day he swam for him. "Bachrach was dressed in a tattered bathrobe, chewing a cigar, and his hands were perched on his spacious hips," Weissmuller told a biographer. "He took a cool, unfriendly glance at me: 'So, you're the great swimmer I've been hearing about.'"

Bachrach, the antihero of the manic, clean-cut, Christian physical culture movement, surrounded himself with fit men and women who only accentuated his rogue status. The cramped basement pool, a far cry from Sutro Baths and even many Chicago-area tanks, provided immense pleasure for the coach, who knew that the newer club pools had no answer for his fast swimmers. It was like a bedraggled city tennis court that begat champion players.

Records were a growing fascination that filled the nation's

sports pages. In one typical day, the *New York Tribune* reported speed records for motorboats and race cars, and pitching control as represented by Babe Adams's eighteen walks in only thirty-six games. Numbers, numbers, numbers. Bachrach was the first coach to recognize the trend, leading his swimmers to make record attempts in pools of all types, at varying distances measured in both yards and meters. His timers were instructed to note 50- and 100-yard segments of longer races to claim additional marks. Spalding's annual sporting almanac groaned with small-type numbers.

The name of the game was setting records — no matter how meaningless — and nobody played the game better than Bachrach. The promise of a record being broken gave people a reason to watch and, more importantly, a reason to gamble. The nonstandard IAC pool was a case in point. The 160-yard-relay world record, which would be set this night, was not recognized anywhere else except in Chicago.

The evening would be judged a superb start to the IAC season but for one result. In the junior division Weissmuller lost to the CAA's Herbert Topp in the 100-yard sprint. It was like one of Bachrach wisecracks — the swimmer who finished second in a two-man race. Weissmuller was nervous and had three false starts. The veterans looking on were dubious. "I wasn't that impressed at first," recalled Ross about the first time he saw Weissmuller swim. He was comparatively slow in the 100 but Ross thought his work ethic might help: Weissmuller would gladly spend all day in the water and was already known for following an IAC practice with an even longer workout at the YMCA. His interest in swimming was single-minded, almost Hawaiian, thought Ross. Weissmuller was not like him or others who did their laps then got on with other things.

Weissmuller's teammate Oliver Horn was victorious in the

other junior event, the 100-yard backstroke. A week later in St. Louis Horn won a senior-division 50-yard race in 26.2 seconds.

Bachrach might have been disappointed by Weissmuller's performance, but he wasn't deterred. An illustration in the club magazine that accompanied a story about the meet showed a maelstrom of hands and feet behind a pin-sized head. The caption read: "Young Wieshmuler [sic], a most promising world champ, spoofed the audience, by letting his opponent win. But in the future, look out for him." In the article, Bachrach joked that the real culprit wasn't jumpy nerves but Johnny's hair. His long auburn locks were stuffed into a swim cap, which flew off midrace. The poor boy couldn't see, Bachrach said. The next day, the wavy beach-bum hair was gone, per the boss's orders.

Bachrach reminded himself of what he saw the first time Weissmuller swam for him. He had terrible form — actually no form — and no pacing. He exhausted himself in the opening twenty-five yards, but he was long and skinny and shot through the water like a stick. Bachrach glanced down at his timer. The stopwatch didn't lie. Project Johnny began the next day.

Bachrach put him through unrelenting boot-camp workouts in November and December in anticipation of his January debut. When he came to him, Bachrach said, Weissmuller was a rail-thin 130 pounds. When he began setting records less than a year later, he was a physically sculpted 170 pounds.

Bachrach focused on correcting Weissmuller's form. His arms were too straight and swept too wide; he sloppily crossed his hands above his head, not keeping them on a straight plane aligned with each shoulder. "My legs were used in a mongrel way," Weissmuller remembered years later. "I had no system about breathing, body position, or anything else."

For weeks Bachrach had Weissmuller work on his arm stroke exclusively. To better arch his back he swam with a rubber truck tire around his legs, using only his arms to move through the water. The goal of the arm stroke was "pull and push." The pull came first: With the elbow and shoulder higher than the hand, Weissmuller moved his outstretched fingers almost straight down in the water. Then, at breast level, he "pushed" the water outward and back. The push ended at the hip, where he paused for a fraction of a second before the next reach and "catch." It got to the point that he forgot about his legs as they simply dragged behind.

The characteristic Weissmuller profile emerged when he added a rapid flutter kick: torso high, planing above the water rather than churning through it, his head almost comically clear of the water line and swiveling side to side like a fan following a quick tennis rally. Weissmuller remembered endlessly kicking himself across the pool while holding a rubber water-polo ball. He resembled a water-show porpoise.

The crawl precepts weren't new; not even the training tools of tires and balls were new. Some saw an obvious script: Weissmuller used Kahanamoku's kick, Ross's start, the tank turn of Harry Hebner, and the breathing of Jamison Handy, the Chicagoan who was the first to inhale through the nose and exhale through the mouth. Bachrach's unique gift to Weissmuller was the way he emphasized the importance and artistry of relaxing within the stroke. Relaxing at the same time as swimming at maximum speed was the key. Bachrach began some workouts by asking Johnny what he was thinking about. Weissmuller dutifully told him he was thinking about keeping his head up, or his shoulders flat, or how and when to bend his elbows.

How about relaxing, Bachrach would ask, aren't you thinking about that?

Weissmuller's angst-filled January performance proved only one thing to Bachrach: He needed more time. Weissmuller might be ready physically but not mentally. He needed more practice, more shoring up of confidence so that his nerves didn't betray his physical gifts. Bachrach made the unconventional decision to keep him out of all competition until the summer season.

As Weissmuller trained, Bachrach kept the competitive IAC swimmers busy into spring. On April 7 and 8 the IAC hosted a much anticipated water polo match against Syd Cavill's Olympic Club team. Cavill would want to forget the weekend — his swimmers lost amidst dubious refereeing and a pool that was so cramped it felt like a closet. In fact, Cavill resigned shortly after returning to San Francisco. But there was one thing he would remember about the trip: seeing Bachrach's latest find swim a 100-yard sprint during practice. Cavill, in many minds the man who introduced the crawl to America, clocked a boy named Johnny "Wiesmuller" (sic) at 54.8 seconds. As if to remind Weissmuller that he was not forgotten, the club magazine published his photograph that same month in an IAC racing suit, his closely cropped hair neatly parted in the middle.

In May and June, the whispers about a sprint phenom gained volume. A story in the *Kansas City Kansan* began: "Chicago, the home of America's watermen, has produced another swimmer of international promise, a boy of seventeen." Bachrach dubbed Weissmuller "a second Norman Ross," and said the boy had recently swum 100 yards in 53.6 seconds. The *Kansan* described Weissmuller as possessing every trait for a champion — tall and rangy, with long, supple muscles and excellent stroke form. "[He moved] through the water swiftly . . . with clean powerful strokes."

Even with the outdoor summer season upon them, Bachrach didn't rush Weissmuller onto a slate of events. It was anyone's guess as to why not. Bachrach didn't explain. It wasn't like him to hold back any of his athletes. He left money on the table at venues he could have filled with spectators eager to see a boy wonder.

Finally in Duluth, Minnesota, on August 7, Weissmuller appeared on the start list for his first senior event. The races were supposed to be held in front of the grandstand at Duluth Boat Club, but because of rough water the swimmers were moved to a protected area behind the stands. A Western Telegraph station had been set up not for the swimming races but for a rowing regatta in Buffalo, where Duluth Boat Club's men's eight was competing for the national title.

In the 100-yard race Weissmuller finished in 55.2, beating Herbert Topp. His 50-yard result — 23.2 seconds — was a dead heat that the officials debated before giving the edge to Weissmuller.

To Bachrach's chagrin, all the local hoopla was reserved for the happy news in Buffalo, related via telegraph, that the Duluth oarsmen won the national championship, throwing the town into overdrive to plan the welcome-home parades and dances.

A week later, in an exhibition swim at Buckeye Lake, Ohio, Weissmuller lowered his open-water 100-yard time to an astonishing 52.2 seconds, sparking headlines about a "Chicago unknown" and an IAC "prodigy." At the end of the month, at Chicago's Edgewater Beach, he swam on the IAC 400-yard relay team that set a national AAU outdoor world record.

The next month, at the famous open-air Brighton Beach Baths in New York, the IAC was invited to officially challenge the tank century mark. Weissmuller finished the 100-yard distance in 53.02, beating Hawaiian Harold "Stubby" Kruger and besting the fifty-four-second world record held by Kahanamoku and McGillivray. "Bachrach told me to swim for form, not for speed," said Weissmuller. Now he understood why. He didn't need to worry about speed so long as his form was right.

If it seemed Weissmuller was already replacing Kahanamoku as swimming's poster boy, Duke's life seemed more interesting

and naturally grander. That same fall, Duke appeared in a sump-
tuous front-page photo in the Sunday *San Francisco Chronicle*
captioned "Flying to the Sea." The Alfred Gurrey rotogravure
showed him in a death-defying 100-foot swan dive, arms majestically spread, feet extended, face heroically stoic. Gurrey, a
member of Hui Nalu, had taken the photo a decade earlier when
Duke dove from a ship's mast in Honolulu Harbor. Despite
the news of a special young swimmer from inner-city Chicago,
admirers still found their way to Kahanamoku. Even when he
was doing nothing at all — and he wasn't actively competing
in 1921 — Duke managed to outshine everyone, the mainland
boy wonder included.

DURING KAHANAMOKU'S EXTENDED absence from Hawaii following the 1920 Games, a young physical anthropology researcher
received an urgent note. Louis R. Sullivan was preparing to leave
for Hawaii, where he would conduct a massive race survey for
a eugenics conference in New York City chaired by Alexander
Graham Bell and financially supported by the Rockefeller family.
Apparently unaware that Duke was in Europe, Sullivan's boss,
Henry Osborn, the former director of the American Museum of
Natural History, wanted Sullivan to get Kahanamoku's complete
measurements in addition to those of other native Hawaiians.
The standardized procedure involved using measuring tapes and
steel calipers to record height, head circumference, and nose,
ear, and eye length. Shape of earlobe, slope of forehead, thick-
ness of lips, and hair and eye color were also noted.

"Do not fail to make the acquaintance of Duke," wrote
Osborn, excitedly describing him as a model "chieftain" type.
"Ascertain if you can whether [Kahanamoku] is full-blooded . . .

and obtain any data regarding swimming adaptations in the limbs and feet."

Coincidently, the artist and writer Robert L. Ripley, a national correspondent who traveled with the 1920 American team, had published an illustration of Duke's enormous feet and hands. Another cartoon had him playing his ukulele aboard the ship in blackface. "The Duke and his Uke," it was captioned.

Throughout 1920 and into 1921, Sullivan acquired physical measurements and ancestry reports for 11,000 Hawaiian citizens across the islands. With the help of dozens of assistants, he wielded calipers and recorded facial features. A key (if unwelcome) test called for subjects to open their mouths wide so that Sullivan could determine if their molars and incisors had the shape of teeth thought to identify pure-blood Hawaiians. With the cooperation of Honolulu's Bishop Museum his team dug for skulls in old burial grounds. At the Kamehameha Schools they inspected and measured students, took hair clippings, and sometimes drew blood samples. Sullivan personally photographed hundreds of adult Hawaiians, many of whom posed naked.

Sullivan charted the racial makeup of thousands of families, relying on interviews with women, whom he found far more knowledgeable than their male partners. In each region, he traveled with a respected local who could assist him in breaking the ice. In Kona, T. C. White, who looked after the Bishop estate on the Big Island, was granted a month's leave to help handle "the natives."

Sullivan's own health would suffer in the campaign. His physical measurements, though unrecorded, could be gleaned from his photos: pale, gaunt face, thin lips, receding hairline, small ears, wide-set eyes. Characteristic for his breed, he was dolichocephalic, or long headed.

In Honolulu, Sullivan hired Gordon Usborne, whose sculpture of Waikiki surfers was featured at the 1915 World's Fair, to make plaster casts of the faces of Hawaiians he studied. According to Usborne, former Hawaii governor Charles McCarthy had asked Duke and David Kahanamoku to participate as "typical specimens of the Hawaiian race." The census of 1920 recorded 30,000 pure Hawaiians but Sullivan noted that Hawaiians themselves believed that number was wildly inflated. They suspected there might be fewer than 100 full-blooded Hawaiians. The Kahanamokus were regarded as one of the last truly native families.

Usborne used candid photos of Hawaiians to create plaster masks, helping to illustrate what race scientists called the Hawaiian problem: the mixing of races. Eugenicists knew the images would shock white people and lead to fears that interbreeding was rapidly happening in Hawaii as it was poised to do on the mainland. Chinese and Japanese immigrants were already facing restrictive crackdowns in California. An emerging degenerate race could soon take hold across the country.

If Hawaii were a patient, Sullivan said, it was "very sick." Purebreds were dying faster than they were reproducing. They were being outcompeted and outworked by the rival European and Asian races. In seventy years, they could be as good as gone. "It is too bad the teeth of Hawaiians are so badly neglected," he observed. "It is that which is causing them to die of disease, rather than anything else."

In the last weekend of July 1921, the Bishop Museum's curator, H. B. Gregory, invited Hawaiians to view Usborne's masks before they were boxed up and shipped to New York. The Hawaiian community had gone silent about the project when the survey was finally complete. Few came by to see the masks.

———————

SULLIVAN'S "DYING RACE" exhibit at New York's American Museum of Natural History opened that fall as part of the second International Eugenics Conference. The lavish presentation in the Hall of the Age of Man featured Sullivan's hundreds of photos and caliper measurements. Usborne's plaster masks ringed the fourth-floor main gallery and represented the dozens of racial types throughout Hawaii.

At the center of the exhibit was a life-sized sculpture of a "Hawaiian chieftain type," which David Kahanamoku had posed for. He was in the act of spearing a fish, naked but for a primitive style loincloth.

The dozens of exhibits, all of which explored some facet of the eugenics holy grail —better breeding to improve human stock — included a chart by the Eugenics Record Office in Cold Spring Harbor, New York, outlining ten proposed ways of "cutting off the supply of human defectives," and photographs of the brains of fifty "feebleminded" criminals from the Massachusetts State Psychiatric Institute. Book publishers from Harvard University Press to Houghton Mifflin promoted leading authors and titles.

John Harvey Kellogg, founder of the Race Betterment Foundation, displayed a device called the Universal Dynamometer that he used to strength-test subjects, some of them amateur athletes, at his famous sanatorium in Battle Creek, Michigan. His data informed his ardent message, dramatically displayed in the museum's halls, that the incoming stream of immigrants into the U.S. would produce a line of "inferior people that threatens the integrity of the nation." No scientist in America knew the ins and outs of analyzing the idealized human specimen like Dr. Kellogg. Swimmers, and their supremely fit bodies, were a growing preoccupation at his wellness center, where there were plans for a new state-of-the-art competition pool.

The Sullivan exhibit was an enormous success, drawing 10,000 visitors. Sullivan told interviewers asking for his bottom-line appraisal that the Hawaiian man was respect-worthy but inferior to his white counterpart or a mixed-race person with some white blood.

When everything was shipped back to Hawaii — the masks, the statue, the reams of data, the nude photographs, the blood samples — it would be put in storage at the Bishop Museum and, like Hal Prieste's stolen Olympic flag, remain a secret not to emerge for almost a century.

NINE

GREAT WHITE HOPE 1922

"Weissmuller is the fastest swimmer that ever lived."

—Robert L. Ripley, Olympics correspondent and syndicated cartoonist and columnist

BILL BACHRACH KNEW exactly what the 1922 season would look like, and he couldn't wait to get started. His seventeen-year-old superstar — handsome, talented, white — would travel everywhere, drawing attention and huge crowds and answering every event organizer's demand for headline-making records. Bachrach's first big star, Norman Ross, was a war veteran. He was his own man, independent, strong-willed, much more an equal than an understudy. But Johnny Weissmuller was Bachrach's to lead and shape. They would be unstoppable.

Bachrach solicited race promoters, offering a new speed record in return for $100 or more in kickbacks. "They'd wonder if that wouldn't make me a pro," Weissmuller would later tell the Olympics historian William O. Johnson Jr. "But Bachrach'd say, 'No, you're giving the $100 to me. I'm the pro, not Johnny.'"

The hype began on the first page of the New Year's edition of *Tri-Color,* which featured a rhyme describing Weissmuller's first world record of 1922, a 2:19.6 over 220 yards in the IAC tank:

> 'Twas a balmy winter's evening and a goodly crowd
>   was there,
> That well-nigh filled Bill's poolroom to the swell
>   affair.
> The officials looked so very grand with badges of
>   yellow hue,
> While Bill took Johnny to one side and told him
>   what to do.

Throughout that winter, Weissmuller broke records from Detroit and Milwaukee to Philly and New York. Their first stop in the East was Philadelphia's Weightman Hall. The stop was not a coincidence. Weightman was the same pool where Kahanamoku first announced himself a decade earlier in front of George Kistler. It began a yearlong pattern where Weissmuller would race in the same pools Duke had, systematically taking on the legend and, one by one, erasing his records. At the New York Athletic Club's palatial marble natatorium, before the buttoned-up eminences of the sport and the IAC president, S. J. Hitt, Weissmuller set a 100-yard world record; at Columbia University two days later, he set more records.

As Weissmuller performed day and night across the city, the major New York papers published features on him at the urging of Bachrach. The nationally syndicated illustrator and writer Robert L. Ripley told his readers that Weissmuller was the "fastest thing in human form that ever dove into the water." He was born in Vienna, Austria, he wrote, his family moving to Chicago when he was a baby. Now a strapping six-foot-one and 167 pounds, Weissmuller was a typical boy who adored hot dogs. He was a bookkeeper but planned to return to school and might attend Yale.

Another paper, the *Brooklyn Eagle,* featured a caricature of Weissmuller with a tiny head juxtaposed against a vee of a torso, beam-straight shoulders, and gargantuan feet and hands flopping from long, rubber-band arms and legs. It was the era of athletic phenoms, and some said that Weissmuller, even at seventeen, belonged with the four greats: Babe Ruth, Jack Dempsey, Charley Paddock, and the racehorse Man o' War.

When Weissmuller and fellow IAC swimmers returned to Chicago aboard the *20th Century Limited* out of Penn Station, they had set eight individual world records and three world relay records and won a national AAU title. Days later, Bachrach announced that he and Weissmuller would travel to Honolulu for the biggest headline-grabber of all: a potential showdown with the aging champion himself, Duke Kahanamoku.

———————

KAHANAMOKU'S new manager, Oscar Henning, settled into his suite at the Plaza Hotel in San Francisco. He had invited the city's top newspapermen to his rooms so that he could introduce himself and make an announcement: Kahanamoku had signed a five-year contract with him, and their goal was to make Hollywood films.

Henning said that he and Duke had become friends when he first visited Honolulu a decade earlier. He had been a champion breaststroke swimmer in Sweden who won a medal in the 1912 Games.

Henning offered up his nickname, "Honest" Oscar. He had

a wife, a young child, and a breathless story of past adventures. He accompanied Jack London in Fiji and traveled around the world five times. He had multiple academic degrees and lost a 172,000-ruble fortune during the Russian Revolution, when the Bolsheviks destroyed his medical practice and imprisoned his wife for sixteen months.

The future, Henning told the reporters, was film. Duke's future was film. He said that if plans continued apace, it was possible that Kahanamoku might rival other athletes-turned-adventure-actors like Douglas Fairbanks and Tom Mix. Their proposed $750,000 production company would be based in Hawaii. One of their first films would tell the heroic story of King Kamehameha, the uniter of the Hawaiian Islands. Kahanamoku would play the leading man opposite a "famous woman screen star."

Nobody seemed to know what to make of Duke's dramatic change in plans or his antic manager. Few of the newspapermen were impressed. Regardless, Henning assured them that the many bright prospects for Duke's future would be finalized once he was back in Honolulu.

From February to April 1922, Henning blew around the Waikiki waterfront with fervent purpose. He pitched business leaders on converting Kapi'olani parklands in Honolulu for use as a private studio. Later, after the city and county attorney ruled against the idea (and skeptical local investors asked Henning to "show us something"), he announced Kahanamoku as the star of a surf-riding exhibition tour of Scandinavia. Henning claimed that a Copenhagen newspaper had agreed to fund this surfing safari, which would be filmed and shown in theaters. As the tour took shape, Henning scheduled vaudevillian performances in which Duke swam fifty yards with his hands tied, then his feet tied, and then he posed as a living statue. Henning also filmed "Duke in Action" segments which would be shown at Liberty Theatre Palace of Pictures every day during the last week in April. The boxed ad in the *Advertiser* read, "In holding up the ancient world / Friend Atlas has no snap / But 'twas Kahanamoku put / Hawaii on the map!"

At the same time, controversy raged about Kahanamoku's amateur status. The stories the New York reporters wrote after meeting with Henning caught the attention of the AAU, which immediately launched an investigation. The problem wasn't just his contract with Henning but a *Saturday Evening Post* advertisement in which Duke endorsed a surfboard varnish. Sportwriters got a laugh at Kahanamoku's association with a product that promised in its tagline never to turn white.

"The AAU still picks on him," wrote the Honolulu sports columnist Doc Adams. "They will probably claim he had a job of 'greeter' because when the launch was busted he sometimes swam out to meet the arriving tourist boats."

The Hawaii AAU chapter also defended him, and Kahanamoku himself pointed out that fellow amateur athletes Norman Ross and Charley Paddock wrote newspaper articles for which they were paid. "What's the difference?" he asked.

Bill Bachrach, always happy to divert attention to himself, chimed in. "I don't care if the national AAU declares him a professional," he said while en route to Hawaii. "I will race Johnny Weissmuller against the Duke over any distance, any place." He said he greatly looked forward to his man's "acid test of competition in a *foreign* country."

———

FROM THE MOMENT Weissmuller and Bachrach arrived in Honolulu aboard the *Wilhelmina,* Duke Kahanamoku was conspicuous for his absence. He wasn't part of the on-deck greeting committee. He didn't swim against Weissmuller in a pool or in the harbor. He wasn't in their regular company at the Pleasanton Hotel. In fact, amidst the growing hoopla over the affable seventeen-year-old, he simply left altogether, shipping out to Los Angeles two weeks into Weissmuller's stay. Kahanamoku said he had recently been sick and lost more than ten pounds, and though he wanted to race Johnny, he clearly couldn't. Though no one would have suspected it at the time, Kahanamoku and Weissmuller would never race each other in Honolulu.

Future biographers saw Duke's leaving for L.A. as a calm, orderly act, conceived and planned months earlier when he first hired Henning in advance of a probable retirement. But the tumult of that spring hastened his departure. Staying felt increasingly impossible. And when he did go, the newspapers expressed surprise.

Weissmuller and Bachrach, though disappointed not to have a showdown with Duke, nonetheless carried on with gusto. They managed to rack up $20,000 in expenses in today's dollars. They surfed, they fished, they canoed. An illustration in the IAC magazine shows Bachrach in a bathrobe beneath palm trees, playing a ukulele while Weissmuller, drawn as a creature with a sleek fish tail, wriggles to the water's edge. In a kind of developing vaudeville act Bachrach, in a snug-fitting bathing suit, futilely attempted to tandem surf with David Kahanamoku, his weight sinking their board. Weissmuller went on a picnic to Pearl Harbor and posed next to an eight-foot shark David speared. At Liberty Theatre, he watched newsreels of himself setting records at the new outdoor pool at Punahou Academy.

Weissmuller was plainly starstruck by Hui Nalu and the Kahanamoku brothers. How could he not be? During one of their outings, he witnessed David, Sam, and Dude Miller unveil an entirely new sport — aero surfing. The trio rode their surfboards behind a military seaplane, holding a sixty-foot tow rope and flying through the Pearl Harbor waves at forty-five miles per hour. The heroic wipeouts, the bravery, the pure fun of it all captivated the young Weissmuller, leaving him with a permanent if unrequited wish to be part of the same tribe.

During his first workout in the Punahou pool, Weissmuller gamely tried to teach himself *lele kawa,* the feet-first jump of Hawaiian royalty. During his first swim in Honolulu Harbor, only his sixth time ever in salt water, Weissmuller was similarly unfazed, pronouncing the seawater easy to move through. He was comfortable in *any* water, Bachrach told reporters. "They're all just tile and water to him. The boy's a wonder."

At the Hui Makani Punahou 50-yard sprint, where tankside tickets cost $1.50, Weissmuller had a bad start and lost by a hand to Duke's 1920 Olympic teammate Warren Kealoha. The local crowd was delighted, standing in applause for two minutes. Weissmuller was stunned, and said he suspected he had been cursed in a Kahunaism rite Bachrach had told him about. He confronted a small Hawaiian boy who had touched his shoulder before the heat. "Why did you do you that?" he asked.

"Getting beat by a hand in the 50 must have angered Weissmuller," the *Honolulu Star-Bulletin* story began, "for he set up a killing pace in the 220-yard race to win by ten yards." Weissmuller broke his own world record at a distance swimmers regarded as the hardest. He was utterly spent when he was pulled from the tank.

Confusion broke out the following night. A judge awarded Weissmuller the win in the 100-yard backstroke despite all the timekeepers having clocked Kealoha as faster. When the decision was announced, the boos rained down. Whoever won, both smashed the world record. For older Hui Nalu members and other Hawaiian swimmers, the dispute echoed past decisions involving Bachrach teams, especially Hawaii's rigged defeat at the 1915 World's Fair.

Bachrach said the Hawaiians had tried to steal the race with the "customary kanaka practice of beating the gun a yard or two." The controversy threatened to derail the good feelings between Bachrach and Weissmuller and their hosts, but the matter was set aside for national AAU officials to assess.

In the open-water races in Honolulu two weeks later, Weissmuller was electric. Those watching from Moana Pier noticed that he seemed to take a breath at every stroke, flipping his head from side to side, which was unusual. He also was a little high in the water and splashed some. But it was incidental; he seduced everyone with his speed. He shattered three middle-distance records and beat Duke and Pua Kealoha's shared fifty-three seconds flat in the 100-yard, finishing in 52.4. Duke had been world champion in the open-water 100 since 1911; it was the premier event in the Hawaii swimming world. Now the Honolulu papers announced, "The King is dead! Long live the King."

The open-water events coincided with an influx of Shriners to Honolulu. The Chicago chapter was covering Johnny and Bachrach's expenses through a seemingly endless entertainment budget. For one week they took over the city in what was called the greatest overseas pilgrimage in Shriner history. Before arriving at the Waikiki waterfront, they paraded in Arab costumes past 20,000 onlookers as Imperial Potentate James "Sunny Jim" McCandless rode a camel that was borrowed from the city zoo. Dances, tours, and surfing followed.

The last day of the open-water meet featured the 100-yard backstroke, the 220-yard freestyle, and an undercard surfing competition. At Pier 6 the top two nobles from the Aloha Temple, wearing fezzes and dressed in vivid Shriner green, yellow, and red, had seats of honor in the stadium. The "standing room only" sign went up at 8:30 a.m. but still the fans kept coming. The log jam of people on the pier forced delays as racers struggled to access their changing rooms in a specially equipped barge. Spectators closest to pier's edge repeatedly fell into the harbor as the crowd pushed forward to watch the races. The Shrine Chanters, backed by the San Francisco Shriner Band, urged the racers onward. The *Honolulu Star-Bulletin* patted itself on the back when it was all over, having promoted the visit with the slogan, "Shine for the Shrine."

During his six-week visit in Hawaii, Weissmuller came across as a nice-enough boy, handsome, goofy, and gifted. He wasn't unbeatable, however. As expected, Weissmuller easily won the 220-yard race, but Warren Kealoha countered by winning the 100-yard backstroke, defeating Weissmuller just as many thought he had in the Punahou pool weeks earlier. For this event, the Hawaiian AAU had insisted on eight timers, not the customary five.

Warren Kealoha also defeated Weissmuller at the 50-yard two weeks earlier. The Hawaiians' prideful reign wasn't over yet. It was easy to wonder, as George Center publicly did, what a healthy and motivated Duke Kahanamoku might have done in the 100. He said he liked Duke's chances.

"Comparing the temperaments and 'tricks' of the two champions, Duke and Weissmuller, is interesting," observed Norman Ross, anticipating a head-to-head meeting soon despite Kahanamoku's move to a film career. "They both have slow, powerful strokes; they both make a slow start, usually leaving the board after everyone else is in the water, and each man is known to pace his opponent, and the Chicago swimmer claims that he has never been hard pressed. It is safe to say that they are as equally matched a pair of swimmers as has been seen in Honolulu or anywhere else."

On June 27, 1922, Weissmuller and Bachrach sailed out of Honolulu Harbor. Like every visitor to the islands, Weissmuller declared his age, marital status, and birthplace for the ship's manifest. On the *Wilhelmina*'s passenger list in May, he was seventeen, single, and born in Hungary. On the outgoing

Ventura, he was eighteen (his birthday was June 2) but the rest was the same.

Nobody seemed to comprehend a glaring fact about the world's most dominant U.S. swimmer: He was foreign born. He wouldn't be able to race for America in the coming Games, which was shaping up as the most important Olympics in history. He would have to represent Hungary, or Austria, or wherever in Europe he came from.

Eventually, in the coming months, the conflicting facts of his birthplace would be aired in public. He might have hoped the situation would be easily fixed and that his father had followed through years earlier with his promised naturalization application, but he likely knew Peter hadn't. Weissmuller felt the hole at the heart of his story. He had just left the warm, close-knit Hawaiian community to return to Chicago, where he remained at his boyhood address with an absent and scandalous father banging around up the street. Weissmuller had the records, but he wanted more. He wanted a home.

TEN

DREAMS
1922 – 1923

"It seems to be a celestial event that bobs like an emperor's zeppelin above reality. It seems untouched by social troubles. It seems unstained by man's proclivity for sin and folly. Mainly it's very serious. Even sacred."
—William O. Johnson Jr., in his
1922 book about the Olympics,
All That Glitters Is Not Gold

PIERRE DE COUBERTIN felt the uplift in his mortal bones when he first heard Spyros Samaras's swelling cantata "Hymne Olympique" at the 1896 opening ceremonies in Athens. He and 60,000 others at Panathenaic Stadium stood awestruck as nine bands and 150 choir singers heralded the first Games to take place in fifteen centuries. When they were done, the applause pounded so loudly and for so long, King George I had them play it again.

Coubertin was breathless as he heard the lyrics written in honor of his creation: "Ancient immortal spirit, pure father / of beauty, of greatness and of truth / descend, reveal yourself and flash like lightning here / the glory of your own and sky." It would be of little surprise when, forty-one years hence, the baron would be granted his final wish to have his heart buried in Greece, at Olympia.

And yet the Olympic spirit seemed a world away in 1922. The Games' planning was not going well, and the headwinds in Coubertin's native Paris were brisk and chilly. There was determined insistence to continue the ban of enemy nations — Germany, Austria, and Hungary. And there was pushback against the large public subsidies needed to erect a grand stadium in the city. The left-leaning paper *La Petit Bien* argued that France's war debts should be paid before expending Fr 20 million "to see a lot of young men run themselves off their legs in front of an empty grandstand and bare benches."

The main debate was over Coubertin's plan to build a magnificent *grand stade* to accommodate 100,000 people. The stadium, he said, would signal France's rise from the ruins of the Great War. A design contest was held, and the winning submission featured classical archways, sculptural figures, and columns soaring high above the fields of play.

The plan was rejected, so Coubertin and his advisors proposed a renovation of the city's original *grand stade* from the 1900 Games, Parc des Princes. This was also the venue where the Black American cyclist Marshall "Major" Taylor faced French champion Edmond Jacquelin in a 1901 race that drew 30,000 spectators and high-stakes gamblers from New York City and Pittsburgh. Though wan and neglected, Parc des Princes could suffice, Coubertin said, if top-to-bottom improvements were made.

This plan was shot down, too. Opponents countered by suggesting the drab Stade Pershing, built hurriedly for the 1919 Inter-Allied Games, that would accommodate only a quarter of the anticipated spectators. Leftist critics called the organizers' proposed luxury stadium for 100,000 a "criminal distraction" with no social benefit. The opposition was gaining.

Coubertin's stadium setbacks were symbolic of a greater problem: He lacked respect. Outside his inner circle, he was rudely ignored. In 1896, Greece refused to acknowledge his role in bringing back the Olympics, then held him in contempt when he refused to make Greece the Games' permanent home. The domineering director of the 1900 Paris World's Fair, Alfred Picard, refused to let the concurrent Games be referred to as the Olympics in advertisements or anywhere on the fairgrounds. Only when competitors received medals did some of them realize they had competed in the Olympics. And in 1904 and 1908 Coubertin was undermined by the perpetual American schemer James Sullivan, who attempted to form a U.S.-British alliance to oust him.

And yet the tidy, now-elderly aristocrat — more moustache than man — gamely battled on. He maintained nothing was out of reach. A brand new technology, radio, would broadcast the Games in real time across France. Parliament would approve a Fr 6 million bond, and an Olympic Village — which he unsuccessfully proposed for the 1900 Games — would be built this time. There would be medal competitions for literature and the arts as well, he promised.

Late in 1922, an Olympic stadium compromise was finally reached. The new site was Colombes, a sprawling industrial suburb five miles northwest of Paris. What it lacked in Parisian élan (smokestacks belched acrid black clouds into the air above the town's aging sports arena) was made up for in practicality.

The Racing Club of France, whose members ranged from soccer players to cricketers, agreed to renovate the grounds in exchange for fifty percent of ticket sales.

In the end, virtually all of Coubertin's stadium proposals were rejected. But somehow, he got exactly what he wanted for the swimming venue. The stadium, first planned for the Seine, then Colombes, was now being built at Porte des Lilas in Paris. At a cost of Fr 10 million, Piscine des Tourelles would be the most expensive, state-of-the-art tank ever constructed for an Olympics. It was the "greatest swimming pool in the world," Coubertin declared, a monument to sport that would stand long after the 1924 Games were forgotten.

Located in the twentieth arrondissement, the hillside pool would be near Père Lachaise Cemetery, eternal home to the most famous souls in the city. Frédéric Chopin, Honoré de Balzac, and Camille Pissarro resided there, along with many other timeless legends. Coubertin could rest easy knowing his watermen athletes would be competing in Paris's most exalted cultural company.

———

WITH HIS FUTURE OLYMPIC standing in jeopardy, an unrealized surfing tour to Europe, and a can-do-no-wrong Johnny Weissmuller still in his proverbial living room, Duke Kahanamoku unexpectedly steamed away from Honolulu on May 31, 1922. He was going to make California his new home. Perhaps he was fed up. Or he was racing to get to Hollywood before Weissmuller did. Or both. "Aloha Duke!" wrote the *Honolulu Advertiser,* which had defamed Duke in 1919, resulting in a jury-awarded $1,500 in damages. "May his familiar face long smile down from the silver screen, bringing the clean joy of the open water and the fragrance of Hawaiian valleys to the countless thousands of the cinema theaters in Hawaii and throughout the world."

He arrived in San Francisco on June 6 to begin the "Tour of the Americas," a series of swimming exhibitions up and down the coast, concocted by Oscar Henning. Charley Paddock, a Southern California native who now wrote regular newspaper columns, helped with the promotion. He and Duke had met in 1920 as Olympians and had reunited two months earlier when Paddock visited Honolulu for a series of exhibition running races. Son-in-law to a publisher and an international sports celebrity, Paddock was surprisingly frank and insightful in his writing, especially about Duke and how he was perceived at the time. An icon himself, Paddock had uncommon weight with Duke and was free to speak his mind. In his columns he tried to explain his friend's recent history of eluded challenges, perhaps hoping readers would be sympathetic once they had a better understanding of Duke's psychology.

Paddock discounted Kahanamoku's declarations about never swimming competitively again. He believed he was one of those tortured and temperamental elite athletes who needed to be frightened into his best work. "Duke loves competition; he cannot live without it — and he knows it better than anyone else," wrote Paddock. "If matched against Weissmuller, he would make the latter swim as he never swam before, though the Duke no doubt would protest against swimming him clear up until the starting gun was fired."

Paddock made a compelling case for his friend, detailing his royal connections and the comparisons to King Kamehameha. He noted the history of older athletes taking on young phenoms and putting them in their place "from whence they sprung, unhonored and unsung."

In the florid style of the time, Paddock expressed this in a poem:

You may talk about your Johnnys
And your Rosses and the rest,
But there's a name that time will never dim;
Kahanamoku, the Duke, he's the greatest and the best.
To the end we will stand pat for him.

Befitting his reputation as "the greatest and the best," Kahanamoku bought a new automobile, a Cadillac Phaeton, customized with a Hawaiian flag on a side panel and a gold hood ornament of his likeness riding a Waikiki break. He and Henning set off in it for their Tour of the Americas. The trip started with promise, with appearances along the coast and exhibitions at the Los Angeles Athletic Club. Duke was photographed with film comedian Harold Lloyd, the two of them swimming in Lloyd's Hollywood pool.

But the tour ended almost as quickly as it began, and Duke's promotional opportunities vanished. His manager vanished, too. Henning appeared as an extra in Goldwyn Studio's *The Strangers' Banquet* and was complimented in a gossip column for his marvelous water feats. He was still in Los Angeles late in the year, staying at the Hotel Astoria, but abruptly left for New Orleans in early 1923, touting an unknown local swimmer named Buddy Smith as the "new Weissmuller" and announcing his import business to bring Airedales to the South. In early 1924, Henning was hired as scoutmaster of Troop 75 in Birmingham, Alabama. It was later discovered that his real name was Oscar Verner Hellstrom and no record existed of him competing in any Olympic Games. He had appropriated the identity of Thor Henning, a Swedish breaststroker who won medals in the 1912 and 1920 Games and would compete in Paris in 1924.

What Duke knew of his manager's actual identity is impossible to say. The two Swedes were close enough in appearance and age (and Hellstrom *was* a good swimmer) that he could have been fooled. For his part, Hellstrom was asked, upon arriving in Alabama, what had happened to his bright partnership with Kahanamoku. "Duke didn't take," he told the *Birmingham Times*.

Duke was left in sad limbo, with no film projects and the vaunted Kahanamoku-Henning Film Corporation lifeless.

His amateur status was hanging on by a thread, but Kahanamoku found a temporary safe harbor with Leslie Henry, an affluent bank president and bond dealer and amateur sports official connected with the Los Angeles Athletic Club. Duke had met Henry a decade earlier when he visited the club after his first gold-medal victory. Delighted that the champ had relocated to L.A., Henry invited him to live with his family in their large home on South Rimpau Boulevard, a stucco Italianate with a red-tiled roof, elegant archways, and balcony columns that swirled like rotini. Kahanamoku swam and raced five miles away at the club, which featured the first pool in the nation to be built on an upper floor. With its dazzling, domed skylight, the pool was the next best thing to being in the ocean.

WEISSMULLER'S TEAR didn't end in Hawaii. It lasted a sensational eighteen months, during which he broke some fifty records in oceans, lakes, and pools, including Duke's sole remaining record, the 50-yard freestyle. His 22.8 time in Columbus, Ohio, sliced off a full second. Bachrach boasted that his IAC swimmers now owned ninety-five percent of all world records. In San Francisco and Los Angeles, Weissmuller completely overshadowed Kahanamoku's recent arrival, shattering marks and dominating local sports pages.

In early 1923, Bachrach was hoping to arrange a massive, coffer-filling European tour as a Weissmuller Olympic preview of sorts. The idea was unprecedented, as professional a concept as there had ever been. England was lined up to host, along with other countries, and Bachrach had even received full expenses for the trip. Ultimately, it was too much for the AAU, which nixed the idea.

The cancellation left a sudden gap in Weissmuller's schedule, which Bachrach filled by signing a quick deal to appear in Decatur, Illinois, for a July 4 carnival. Also in the offing was a headline-making event with Duke Kahanamoku to take place in Chicago in August. Paddock had already laid the groundwork for the match, sizing up the combatants the way newsmen described a prize fight. The young Weissmuller had records — he now held all swimming records up to a half mile — but Paddock claimed that Kahanamoku had a far superior body. Duke was a huge man, Paddock wrote: six-foot-three and 200 pounds with a forty-six-inch chest and thirty-one-and-a-half-inch waist, almost identical measurements to the boxing great Jack Dempsey. "[Weissmuller] hardly typifies the Strong Man as he always has been pictured," he argued. Duke, on the other hand, even at thirty-two, "resembles a bronze statue in physical perfection."

Expectations ratcheted even higher when, in a surprise, Kahanamoku took back his 50-yard record that summer, swimming a stunning 22.6 seconds at the Los Angeles Athletic Club. Fred Cady, Duke's new coach, thought the credit belonged to his competition, a sixteen-year-old comer named Buddy Smith who pushed him every inch of the way. He set personal bests in 100 yards (52.6 — two tenths off Weissmuller's record) and a week later set a world record at an exhibition at Yosemite, a 10.0 flat for twenty-five yards. Paddock was right; Duke still had it. "Add the name of Duke Kahanamoku to those of Jess Willard, Exterminator, and Babe Ruth," reported the *Los Angeles Evening Post-Record,* citing the year's other famous comebacks in boxing, horse racing, and baseball.

"Kahanamoku's Latest Record Doubted in the East," was the *New York Daily News* unsurprising headline. "Swimming experts cannot make themselves believe that Duke Kahanamoku, who has been out of competition for more than a year, can make the remarkable time that has been credited to him. Duke is no youngster."

As negotiations for the Kahanamoku-Weissmuller showdown progressed, Johnny traveled to Decatur, where gala celebrations were underway for the christening of Lake Decatur, a ten-mile-long artificial lake created from the damming of the Sangamon River. The weather was unseasonably nasty for the four-day celebration. Still, spectators made the best of it. Traffic jams to and from the lake were treated with good humor, and the rain and leaden clouds didn't prevent the evening fireworks display, the 300 clowns marching down Washington Street, the boat parade, and the first of five appearances of the Chicago golden boy Weissmuller. In abysmal, wave-tossed conditions, Weissmuller, as expected, set a new middle-distance mark at 500 yards, beating the runner-up by seventy yards. His sub-seven-minute time, the first ever, beat the old record by eleven seconds. For his efforts he was awarded an eighteen-inch-tall silver cup valued at $200. After four more races the same afternoon — all wins — he returned home with Bachrach and the rest of the team aboard the Wabash overnight sleeper train.

The next day Weissmuller was rushed to the hospital.

The press converged on Chicago's West Side hospital, fishing for scoops. Finally, Weissmuller's physician, M. H. Wilkinson, came forward with a statement: he cited high blood pressure and exhaustion, which caused a heart murmur "relevant to the aortic valve." Headlines roared across the country: "Is He Lost Forever?"; "Weissmuller Menaced by Heart Trouble"; "Weissmuller, Swimmer, Victim of Overexertion"; "Johnny Weissmuller May Be Through." Dr. Wilkinson put him on forced bed rest with no timetable for a return to swimming or racing. "Johnny Weissmuller, the greatest swimmer that ever splashed the water, will never swim again," began an Associated Press story.

Observers were quick to seize on the cause. Weissmuller was the victim of relentless record hunting. "Encouraged to swim in race after race, beyond all bounds of reason, he was now confined to his bed with a tired-out heart at the age of eighteen," editorialized the *Spokane Chronicle*. It blamed his trainers and the IAC and called for an investigation: ". . . true to the color of those who have gone mad in the twentieth century scramble for 'records,' they did not care [about Weissmuller's health]."

In 1922 Weissmuller had traveled more than 12,000 miles, visiting dozens of cities, including Detroit, New York, Philadelphia, Duluth, Los Angeles, Kansas City, San Francisco, Honolulu, Sacramento, Columbus, Indianapolis, Louisville, Peoria, Milwaukee, and Atlanta. In the first half of 1923, he went to Buffalo; Cincinnati; Brookline (MA), and Pittsburgh. Often he raced the moment he pulled into a city; this is what he did in New York, where he set his first East Coast mark at Brighton Beach. At each stop, he was expected to set a record, sparking wagers that added to the trip's financial bottom line.

Transportation was grueling, accommodations mixed. Sometimes the hosts would be local clubs, sometimes area families. The venues were uneven, the distances or conditions rarely uniform. At Lake Geneva, Wisconsin, he was mobbed by hundreds of starstruck girls on a school retreat. In many places, such as Lake Decatur, inclement weather brought a chill to the bone, especially for an exhausted teen dressed in a cotton singlet.

And there was no end in sight. Bachrach had plans for a monthlong trip to Europe that included stops in at least seventeen cities. Bachrach's appetite for more — more dates, more records, more money — was insatiable.

There were other rumors, too, about the cause of Weissmuller's abrupt breakdown. There were suggestions he had lost his way in training. George Center said a friend in Chicago told him that Weissmuller had "not been observing training rules as rigidly as he should." That strain was as harmful as the swimming-meet overload.

There was also a stressful situation concerning Weissmuller's younger brother, Peter, who seemed to be on a star-making trajectory almost as dramatic as his brother's. Though smaller and a year younger, Peter was a gifted sprinter, winning junior races and eventually being called up to the senior team. He was second only to Johnny at the 100-yard distance, and he joined the other aces on the 4-by-400-meter relay team, setting a series of records throughout the year.

Peter's picture had been prominent in *Tri-Color,* when an article came out in spring of 1923 that was witheringly critical. In trying to pinpoint what it was that set Johnny apart, the author compared him to one who did not have this quality — his brother. "This something is hard to define," wrote the author. "He has a brother who is a fine swimmer but lacks this 'something.' His brother's name is Peter . . . . Johnny is a little larger. Maybe he is a little stronger, a little longer geared. But the real advantage Johnny possesses is that intangible something. Here are two brothers, a year apart in age. Johnny has the goods that makes a champion, and Peter has not." Never had the magazine published such a cutting story about one of the club's own athletes.

The criticism of Johnny's kid brother was like the infamous *Advertiser* story about Duke Kahanamoku's cowardice, meant to inflict the kind of emotional damage no physical injury could match. Bachrach had patiently handled Johnny, building his confidence early on until he was ready to compete and win. But Johnny's brother, at a similarly crucial point in development, had his knees cut out from beneath him.

By the time of the July 4 carnival in Decatur, Peter — who Johnny fondly called "punk" and who seemed to be headed for the same Olympic team Johnny would be on — had been relegated to the B team. Later in the year he was nowhere to be found, no longer a meaningful part of the IAC squad.

Peter's slide was sad and perplexing. But his value to his brother remained, especially a year later as the Games beckoned. Peter had "something" after all.

ELEVEN

GONE
1922 – 1923

"Corpses piled on bridges, corpses blocking off a whole street at the intersection, corpses displaying every manner of death possible to human beings. When I involuntarily looked away, my brother scolded me: 'Akira, look carefully now.' When that night I asked my brother why he made me look at those terrible sights, he replied: 'If you shut your eyes to a frightening sight, you end up being frightened. If you look at everything straight on, there is nothing to be afraid of.'"
—Film director Akira Kurosawa on walking
through Tokyo in the aftermath of the
1923 Great Kantō Earthquake as a middle
schooler

AT 9:30 A.M. ON APRIL 12, 1922, Edward, the Prince of Wales, arrived in Yokohama aboard the British battleship *Renown* to begin a highly anticipated state visit. A fleet of Japanese battleships escorted the boat into the harbor, which teemed with thousands of people hoping to get a glimpse of the world's most eligible bachelor. A special train transported Edward to Tokyo's Central Station, where he was received by his counterpart and dear recent acquaintance Prince Regent Hirohito. The two led an elaborate processional to the emperor's palace. A welcome arch, a replica of London Tower Bridge, had been built outside the station.

The princes commenced with the expected courtly activities: a performance at the Imperial Theatre, a banquet at the prime minister's residence, a welcome from thousands of college students at Hibiya Park. Amidst the countless goings-on, one aspect of the visit increasingly captivated the public's imagination — a relentless side schedule of exercise and sporting contests. The twenty-one-year-old Hirohito was reported to have gone swimming with his royal friend, a bit of gossip that the Japanese found especially thrilling.

The times were changing. The reign of Prince Hirohito's father, Emperor Taishō, was nearing its end. He was terminally ill, inactive, and largely shielded from public life. The prince was officially named regent in November 1921, shortly after he had spent six months in Europe, most of that time in England. On his first day at Buckingham Palace, Edward introduced him to golf. Later they toured Eton and its famous sculling course.

That 1921 visit had left its mark, leading Hirohito to return the favor during their days together in Japan. The prince regent, showing what the *Japan Times* described as his "democratic tendencies," indulged the twenty-eight-year-old Edward's love of tennis but also introduced him to the sport at which Hirohito excelled, jujitsu. At the Hama Detached Palace Gardens, on the shore of Tokyo Bay, they stalked wild ducks with billowing hand nets, a traditional Japanese hunting technique. The most reproduced photo of the trip, snapped during the young princes' final day together, showed them at Tokyo Golf Club, casually standing side by side in similar tweed jackets and plus fours tidily accented by plaid woolen socks and caps.

"How the matches on links and court turned out, none outside the inner circle know, as spectators and reporters were carefully excluded from the Games," reported the *Japan Times.* Scorecards weren't turned in.

Yet it did not matter. The mere news that the young prince was game — churning through water and scrambling on courts — gave a symbolic lift to Japan's budding physical-culture movement. Hirohito displayed the vitality expected of the next generation.

By the end of his visit, Prince Edward pronounced Hirohito the driving influence of sports in Japan. Soon afterward, the Japanese government pledged to subsidize the country's Olympic teams, with the goal being a medal-winning turnout at the 1924 Games in Paris.

But when it came to swimming, ambition outpaced reality. In 1922 there was just one indoor pool in Tokyo, a small tank at the YMCA. Den Sugimoto's scrappy Ibaraki school team attempted to train there, aiming like everyone else to qualify for the 1923 Far Eastern Games the following spring. But Sugimoto was told the university swimmers had priority and there was no room for his squad.

The impasse gave him an idea: He would retool the outdoor swimming pool at Ibaraki, partitioning it by building a strong wooden dividing wall and, more challengingly, temporarily heating and enclosing it. During the school's early spring break, his swimmers, in addition to dozens of other students (one of them was the future Nobel Prize winner, novelist Yasunari Kawabata), went to work. Barefoot and wearing identical white school uniforms, they erected the partition wall, then drew water from the

Ibaraki River, heating it with an old boiler borrowed from the bath house. "We lit a fire for three days, day and night," said Sugimoto. By encircling the smaller-sized pool with a tent-like fabric shell, they were able to raise the chilly forty-six-degree river water to a near optimum sixty-eight degrees on the surface. He had his students jump into the pool en masse to mix the warm surface water with the much colder bottom layer. By March 10, 1923, the training pool was ready, giving the Ibaraki team two months to prepare for the Far Eastern Games.

Sugimoto and his fellow educators saw the pool as embodiment of the school's mission — a unifying project requiring thrift, diligence, and hard work. The students, almost to their surprise, were swept up in it. When they looked at photos of themselves years later — in one, they're shoulder to shoulder in ankle-deep mud, standing against the long retaining wall — they had to laugh. They looked ridiculous in their traditional white shirts and short pants and bare legs. The "perfect outfit for dirt workers," joked Shigetaka Suzuki, one of Ibaraki's top swimmers. But they were also proud. "We dug and built that pool, which could be said to be the mother body that nurtured future athletes," he said. "We gave up all of our time to do it."

Katsuo Takaishi, or Kacchan, as his teammates fondly called him, excelled in the new setup. Because he boarded at the school, he could swim constantly — student housing was next to the pool. "From the physical chemistry classroom I could see the swimming pool right outside the window," he would recall. "Athletes were swimming in the pool, and I could see Mr. Sugimoto glancing at his stopwatch. Suddenly I was shocked to hear Mr. Inaba's [his teacher] words: 'Takaishi, you are looking at the pool all the time, aren't you?'"

His single-minded determination allowed Takaishi to progress quickly at Ibaraki, from a boy who once dog-paddled in a nighttime river to an emerging elite athlete learning the modern crawl. He grew physically. By 1922, Takaishi was increasingly seen as the best of Sugimoto's mentees, bypassing several swimmers initially evaluated as better. Swimming fast was hard work, but, like his samurai forebears, Takaishi made it seem effortless. When Western coaches first saw him they couldn't understand how his "nonchalant" arm stroke propelled him so fast. Tadaichirou Iritani, one of the first of Sugimoto's students to adopt the crawl and win with it in competition, remembered how Takaishi kept pushing ahead. "As Takaishi got older, his swimming skills dramatically improved, and I felt disappointed when I lost to him," said Iritani in a eulogy given at Takaishi's funeral. "He had been my good rival."

Once the Ibaraki pool renovation was complete, Takaishi stopped competition and practiced endlessly in the ensuing months as the Far Eastern Games approached. It promised to be the biggest swimming event in Japan's history. He trained despite having punctured his eardrum in a high dive. The injury resulted in a lifelong disability; whenever he flew in an airplane, the pain was so acute he would roll in the aisle clutching his ears, trying to find relief.

Sugimoto's plan was not only for his swimmers to win the hometown Osaka event but also to record dazzlingly fast times like their brethren in England, Australia, Hawaii, and Chicago. When Japan's swim team for the Far Eastern Games was announced, one-third of them came from Ibaraki. All used the crawl stroke. The ingenious and ever-resourceful Sugimoto was the talk of the country's swimming world.

———————

THE FIRST JAPANESE teams to compete in the Far Eastern Games were not teams at all but enterprising private citizens who showed up alone or in pairs, having paid their own way. The general disinterest reflected Japan's conflicted feelings about participating in Western-oriented competitions.

The 1923 Japan team, by contrast, was, in the words of Elwood Brown, "fully aroused." The country fielded a powerful squad with 175 athletes competing across all disciplines. Emperor Taishō had promised a magnificent silver cup for the overall winner, and his son, the tennis-playing Prince Chichibu, was the Games' official patron. The prince wouldn't be just a figurehead, either. He was spotted at the baseball park, at the infield of the running track, and underneath the high dive, earning him the nickname Prince of Sport. He held a stopwatch as an unofficial timer at some events and was beaned by a wayward spike in a volleyball game.

The Far Eastern Games' most anticipated contest was swimming. Elite times comparable with those of the world's best athletes weren't expected in track and field or other disciplines, but there was hope for the Japanese swimmers. Not much was known about them other than they seemed unusually confident. And unlike the defending champions from the Philippines, they were uniformly using the crawl stroke.

The teams started streaming into Osaka in early May. Each squad was enthusiastically welcomed in separate city-hall receptions, the fifty-car Filipino motorcade stopping en route to the first ceremony as the mayor led the large crowd in well-wishing banzais. (The occasion was slightly marred when a motorcade collision with a trolley left the concussed second baseman and center fielder doubtful for the opener.) At the event stadium, there was another welcome ceremony, this one in English and featuring flower-bearing students from the Ichioka Girls' Higher School.

On the citywide celebration day, houses were decorated with Rising Sun flags, per officials' requests, and all grade schools had lectures on Olympic history and physical culture before dismissing students to go to the Games in the afternoon. An evening lantern procession wound through the city on the way to Prince Chichibu's quarters at the Osaka Hotel, where he acknowledged the tribute with a brief appearance.

Because the new fifty-meter municipal pool needed final preparations, dozens of swimmers took trains to Ibaraki Station, followed by a short drive to the middle school, where they practiced in the pool Sugimoto and his students had built. Hundreds of Ibaraki students fanned out to greet them and the town donated and delivered 1,000 eggs for snacks. In a group photo taken the day before races began, two long rows of foreign swimmers pose on the rudimentary deck, another row of officials behind them. Their deferential Japanese hosts, Katsuo Takaishi included, stand neck-deep in the pool itself, smiling. If there was one photo the peace-through-sports ideologues Elwood S. Brown and Pierre de Coubertin would gladly take to their graves, it might have been this one, showing teams in arm-in-arm unity, some hailing from nations, such as Japan and China, that habitually wished to destroy one another.

The elaborate opening ceremonies on May 21, full of song and thousands of adorable schoolchildren, would be dampened by monsoon rains that drew attention to an oversight on the part of the stadium builders: no sheltering roof. Even the indefatigable cheerleader Prince Chichibu would be chased away for a time. As a result, the epoch-making sight of 100,000 spectators watching Asia's best athletes parade in the stadium wasn't as telegenic as wished. Most of the opening-day rituals would be repeated a few days later for photographers and film crews.

The swim trials started the following morning with the 200-yard relay, a highly anticipated, crowd-drawing event due to the rivalry between the two competing countries, Japan and the Philippines. Spectators were ten deep around the pool, and the bleacher section above the starter blocks was sold out. Pipes connected to a boiler in the grandstand blew steam into the pool to raise the water temperature to sixty-four degrees. The swimmers wore dark, tight-fitting racing suits with no identifying markings.

The Japanese relay team was comprised of two Tokyo swimmers, Kazuo Onoda and Denmei Suzuki, both from Meiji University, and Takaishi and Iritani from Ibaraki. They obliterated the Filipinos, cutting ten seconds off the old Filipino mark and hinting at what soon would be viewed as the relay-team model for the world.

The result set in motion Japan's victory march. They swept the top three spots in each of six races, notching records in all. A second was cut in the 50-yard sprint, four seconds in the 100, thirty-six seconds in the 440, and 2:36 from the mile. Throughout the three days of swimming finals, office workers in downtown Osaka gathered at lunchtime to read times and scores sent via wireless telephone from the swimming stadium and posted on bulletin boards. The skies had long since brightened.

Seventeen-year-old Takaishi, performing in front of friends and family, felt the pressure of being a favorite. Throughout his entire career, despite disciplined preparation, he would feel the same thing prior to the starter's gun: knee-buckling self-doubt. He rarely slept the night before a competition. He didn't race the shorter distances at the Games — his stern-looking Tokyo rival Onoda won both the 50 and 100 — but he dominated the longer ones, taking the 440 and the mile. Takaishi was mentally well-suited to the grueling endurance distances, but it was still undecided what his best event would be. He surprised coaches with his burst of speed during his 50-yard leg of the relay.

The Japanese records were still some distance from European,

American, and Australian top times, wrote Brown in his summary of the 1923 Far Eastern Games, but Japan's wholesale cut in times boded well for the future. "The Japanese had bent their whole energy to building up as an aquatic team that would be invincible in the Far East," he concluded.

On the final day of competition, the top women swimmers competed in their open-exhibition event. It was likely the first time Takaishi glimpsed his future wife, a teenaged Mineko Nagai, a future Far Eastern women's champion in the 400-yard freestyle.

Takaishi stayed in Tokyo with a friend of Sugimoto's as he prepared for the Olympic trials to be held in the city in late August. He had a decision to make about where he would attend college. Most expected him to go to Meiji University to join Onoda and Suzuki on an imposing and most likely unbeatable swim team. On the advice of his host, he instead decided to enroll at Waseda University, a school that pioneered Western sports and fielded championship baseball teams that travelled to the U.S. as part of a cultural exchange program. But Waseda was also a school in turmoil. The same week as the Far Eastern Games, the campus erupted in riots as enraged liberal-leaning students heckled and fought with faculty and student supporters of the Society of Studying Military Affairs, a new initiative on campus that critics saw as a dangerous extension of the military clique vying for national power. "Who admitted the fellows carrying man-killing sabers inside this school?" yelled a protester as a professor attempted to read the society's oath of allegiance. It was a pivoting direction for the proudly independent school, and it wasn't yet clear which side Takaishi would choose: the rising militarists or their alarmed student counterparts.

———

ALL THE RECORDS set in Osaka were reset in the national meet at Tokyo's Shiba Park. Shiba's new pool, finished only months earlier, was one of fifteen built across Tokyo as part of the nationwide sports craze inspired by the young princes, Hirohito and Chichibu. Takaishi's upset of Kazuo Onoda in the 100-meter was the shock of the finals. Ibaraki, swimming as a team with Takaishi as anchor, won the 200-meter relay.

Takaishi's overnight adaptation from endurance grinder to flying fish was unheard of in Europe, mainland America, and Hawaii. You were one or the other. Everything was different about distance and sprint races: the breathing, the aerobic systems, and the type of muscle fibers required. But in the space of three months, Takaishi transformed himself from a one-mile to a 100-meter champion. It was extraordinary, shaking Onoda's confidence and mystifying observers. Takaishi didn't have a sprinter's body: He was five-foot-six and 154 pounds with a thirty-six-inch chest and tiny feet and hands. His schoolmate Iritani, always viewed as the number one Ibaraki prospect because of his early developing physical gifts, said it felt like Takaishi had no ceiling, while he and others did. Within a year Takaishi would cut more than five seconds from his Shiba Park time, becoming the first Asian athlete to swim the 100 in under a minute.

In the blink of an eye, the Japanese champions of 1922 were too slow to compete. The innovations, most of them driven by Sugimoto and his team of outliers, were too rapid and too profound.

With his 100-meter title Takaishi accepted the Japanese Amateur Athletic Association silver cup and a place on the Paris-bound steamship that would leave Kobe the following spring.

Three days later, Shiba Park and much of the rest of metro Tokyo was either aflame or buried in rubble. Thousands of refugees huddled without food or water where Shiba's brand-new pool and famous temples, built in tribute to past shoguns, had been. Robert L. Ripley had presaged the disaster on his travels the previous year. Each time he stepped foot in Tokyo, he wrote, he was reminded of an old saying about the country's frequent calamities: "Fire is Tokyo's flower."

The magnitude 7.9 Great Kantō Earthquake, centered eighteen miles away in Yokohama, was one of the biggest seismic events in Japan's long, devastating history of them. It lasted two seconds, striking at midday. The flames from open fires lit to prepare lunchtime meals quickly spread across the city landscape of densely clustered structures. Panicked people raced from burning homes and headed for the bridges crossing the Sumida River. But seemingly no place was safe. Superheated wind and encircling high smoke created a rare, destructive phenomenon at Sumida River — a 300-yard-wide and 200-yard-high fiery tornado swept the riverbank, reducing everything to ashes, including thousands huddled in apparent safety at the Army Clothing Depot.

Power lines were down, the water supply ruined. The subways, the YMCA building, Meiji University, and the Kabuki Theater were all destroyed, along with hundreds of railway bridges and thousands of homes. A tsunami roared across Sagami Bay toward the Izu Peninsula at 600 miles per hour, creating a forty-foot wave that destroyed hundreds of buildings around Atami, a coastal town only miles from where Takaishi first raced at Heda. More than 130,000 were feared dead. Thousands of Koreans living in Tokyo and Yokohama, falsely rumored to be setting blazes and poisoning wells, were massacred by vigilantes and the Japanese police.

When the composer Nakao Tozan stood in Shiba Park a short time later, he said he felt nothing but emptiness. Everything that was once there — gardens, temples, ponds, ancient trees — was gone. The famous lotus pond, where aesthetes would gather in summer to hear the soft pop of great blossoms opening, was choked in ash. His resulting piece, "Kogarashi (The Chill Winter Wind)", is haunting. It begins with a solitary woodwind that rises like an alarm, then trails off in ghostly silence.

Who lived or died would not be known for days and weeks. The whereabouts of Katsuo Takaishi, his teammates, and everyone else living in Tokyo and Yokohama at the time of the earthquake were unknown. Kodokan, Kanō Jigorō's legendary school of judo, was reported gone. Its founder — the man responsible for Japan's first Olympic teams and as famous in his country as Teddy Roosevelt was in the U.S., according to Robert Ripley — was missing, too.

TWELVE

THE DANCE
1923 – 1924

"If you accomplish anything you must have patience. It is the greatest thing in swimming. This means persistence, but it means something more. It means a cool head; it means reason at the helm."

—Bill Bachrach

JOHNNY WEISSMULLER sat in a poolside wicker lounge chair at the IAC, abiding by his doctor's orders, which were to do nothing. He had just awoken, clambering down from room 806 on the club's fifth floor wearing a checkered, knee-length robe. It was 10:30 a.m. The days rolled together. He couldn't eat hot dogs in customary volume, and he was told to cut out acidic foods like tomatoes and grapefruit, an edict advocated by sanitarium nutritionists like John Harvey Kellogg. He claimed to be enjoying books. "I have read *Tom Sawyer* and *Huckleberry Finn* since I have been laid up," he said.

Reports continued to describe his condition in gravely inventive ways — he had a "stretched heart," "leakage of the heart," "faulty valve action." Factoids were trotted out. The human heart does about one-fifth of the mechanical work of the entire body, expending enough energy to lift its own weight as high as Mount Everest every two hours, explained one of dozens of news articles.

The writer Clarence Bush attempted to illustrate Weissmuller's aerobic apparatus in action, offering his readers an imaginary seat above the zooming swimmer as he raced through the water: "You would see transparent fluids rushing under him in a torrent, a rapids, a cascade. You would see water jet, spirt, trickle, spout, splash, and gush from under his arms. Spreading out from the churning of waters in his wake you would see riffles, ripples, billows, waves, swells, and surges. Under his thrashing feet you would see an oozing, purling, bubbling, gurgling, percolating whirlpool; and when he really stepped on the gas, you would see a regurgitating maelstrom."

Weissmuller said overexertion didn't cause his condition because he never tried all that hard, doing just enough to set a record then get home. He never had to be fished out of a pool, wrung out and exhausted like lesser swimmers. Bachrach agreed, and maintained that Johnny's diagnosis was sensationally overblown. *Tri-Color* magazine, always a slick and smart mouthpiece for him, began publishing satire about the will-he-or-won't-he survival saga. In a cartoon captioned "Bach helps Johnny recover from his illness," the coach, dressed in his ballooning robe with a Red Cross patch on the breast pocket, dispenses a spoonful of medicine.

A photograph in the same issue shows Bachrach and Weissmuller, both in bathrobes, looking into the distance from the twelfth-story roof of the IAC. Bachrach, right arm raised, points eastward across the lake, as if gesturing to Europe and the next big payday, the Paris Olympics.

Six weeks after his collapse, Weissmuller, apparently healed, made his successful return to racing in front of 5,000 spectators in DeKalb, Illinois. His appearance in the 100-yard sprint overshadowed his time, which was slow and several seconds off his personal best. Within days, Bachrach, swagger fully restored, was proposing a Labor Day race against Kahanamoku at a Long Beach, California, resort.

The two superstar swimmers had been circling one another since Kahanamoku left Hawaii for San Francisco in 1922 (when Weissmuller and Bachrach were in Waikiki). Not a month went by without a rumored head-to-head event in the works. Weissmuller fans wanted the race to be on the East Coast, where pools were shorter than in the West and thus gave strong turners an advantage. Weissmuller had one of best turns the world had ever seen, said Norman Ross. In the early summer of 1923 they had finally reached agreement on a date when Weissmuller was hospitalized. The dance continued.

Throughout the rest of the 1923 outdoor season, Weissmuller made a handful of mostly local appearances. A notable exception was a September date at New York's Madison Square Garden, but the competition wasn't first-rate, and his victory came without a record despite Bachrach's promise that Weissmuller would cut his 100-yard time to fifty-four seconds. That was pure fantasy, one reporter observed.

Weissmuller's full comeback finally began to take shape during the indoor season. By the end of the year, he was again recording top sprint times, which for Bachrach meant they were fully back in business. A *Tri-Color* cartoon showed the swimsuited men and women of the IAC, led by Bachrach, goose-stepping in formation and wielding mallets labeled RECORD BREAKER.

The regional indoor meets in January and February would

be followed in April by a swimming, diving, and water polo competition hosted by the IAC and held at the club and at the larger Loyola University pool. It was a novel event in an Olympic year and would bring together the nation's best swimmers, promised Bachrach. The headline visitor, he announced, was none other than Duke Kahanamoku. General admission for the long-awaited showdown was a steep $2.20, almost twice the normal price.

At the same time, Bachrach was putting the finishing touches on a two-week-long spring-training trip to Miami Beach. A range of performances, exhibitions, and novelties were planned (including a race pitting Weissmuller against a girl's relay team from a local club), most of them at the Roman Pools at the Miami Beach Casino. If it sounded like professional paid entertainment Bachrach assured everybody it wasn't; his swimmers were still in high school and therefore should be considered amateurs. Of course, Weissmuller hadn't been in school for years. Bachrach also announced that he would swim against rival coach "Big Bill" Edwards in the Fat Men's Swimming Championship, despite having dropped fifty pounds in anticipation of the Paris Games.

In March, Bachrach published a book detailing his theory of all things swimming; excerpts were nationally syndicated. His star pupil, Weissmuller, was featured front to back in photographs that showed the latest swimming techniques. "All my family thought I was cuckoo," Bachrach wrote, about choosing to spend his life as a swim coach. When he was asked how one could get a copy of *The Outline of Swimming*, he replied, "Everybody is to have an equal opportunity to get my book. That opportunity is to pay cash." The cost was $5.00, his autograph included.

Alas, Kahanamoku didn't agree to the Chicago match, which severely undercut the IAC card and required Bachrach to do some postevent spinning. It was spectacular, the *Tri-Color* gushed, the best field ever assembled. In truth it wasn't very competitive and the IAC trounced everyone.

Diminished as the event was, Weissmuller was on form. He was clocked in the 200-meter at 1:59.2 seconds, the first time a swimmer had broken the two-minute barrier for that distance. There was little doubt that he was still capable of pushing the sport into unknown areas of human performance, despite his illness. "The boy's future is bright," wrote Norman Ross, now in semiretirement. "If nothing goes wrong he will be the next world champion."

———

BUT THAT SPRING, a month before the Olympic trials in Indianapolis, Indiana, something did go wrong. An Illinois congressman announced that he had asked the Department of Labor to determine whether Johnny Weissmuller was a U.S. citizen. Henry Riggs Rathbone, a Yale man who had started his first term a month earlier, said he didn't want the U.S. to be embarrassed if it was discovered that Weissmuller wasn't a citizen and the news broke in Paris.

Rathbone was a tireless worker; he wished to be known not for his sensational family history but his diligent legislative labors, such as cracking down on popular but harmful medical serums. It was a tall task. He was the son of Henry Reed Rathbone Sr., the Union Army officer who was with Abraham Lincoln at Ford's Theatre on April 14, 1865, when John Wilkes Booth fatally shot the president. Booth then stabbed and seriously wounded Rathbone before fleeing the box. Rathbone's inability to prevent the assassination was later cited for his deteriorating mental condition and eventual commitment to an asylum for the criminally insane after he murdered his wife, attacked his children, and stabbed himself five times.

It was common knowledge — at Yale, alma mater of a long line of elite swimmers; in Honolulu; and in the Hungarian town where the family came from — that Weissmuller wasn't born in the U.S. Any number of immigration and travel documents, one as recent as the ship manifest from Weissmuller's trip to Hawaii less than a year earlier, said as much. It wasn't as if Weissmuller had a cloudy notion of where he was from. When he was a boy his mother had twice taken him and his brother to Freidorf, the village where he had been born. A Hawaiian columnist conceded it was the biggest open secret in sports, saying it had been "hanging fire" in newspaper circles ever since Weissmuller began breaking records. "There were many sport writers who knew about it but refrained from publishing anything," he wrote.

The Rathbone announcement, for its timing and for it coming from a home-state congressman, was a shocker. Some suspected it was officials from the Hawaiian AAU who tipped him off. George Center was president; maybe this was his ploy to get another Honolulu swimmer on the Olympic team. Others said it was officials from Europe or Australia, or the IAC's rival from a block away on South Michigan Avenue, the CAA.

The question of citizenship seemed to hinge on whether Peter Weissmuller, Johnny's father, had been naturalized, a process that many German immigrants didn't bother to complete for an assortment of reasons. During the war, as enemy aliens, they were prevented from naturalizing. The family said that Peter had gone before the naturalization board twice but was denied because he didn't speak English.

Rathbone didn't elaborate on his sources nor deliver a personal judgment, but on April 13 he provided evidence to the labor department's assistant secretary, John Henning. One of the desperate work-arounds from the Weissmuller camp was the proposal that a wealthy IAC family quickly adopt Johnny for him to acquire Olympic eligibility.

On April 15, in another surprise, Weissmuller and his mother, Elizabeth, explained there was a giant misunderstanding. Johnny was born in the U.S. The Weissmuller boys' names were so close — Peter John and John Peter — they had had their birth dates mixed up. Peter John Weissmuller, or "Johnny," the superstar swimmer, was born on September 3, 1905, in Windber, Pennsylvania; his older brother, Peter, was born on June 2, 1904, in Freidorf. It was Peter who made the passage in steerage to Ellis Island, not Johnny.

As if a mother's testimony wasn't enough, the family provided the baptismal records from their Roman Catholic Church in Windber, where an entry confirmed the birth of Peter John Weissmuller. The "John" was squeezed between the two other names and appeared to be in different handwriting and ink.

"I was born right here in Chicago twenty years ago," Weissmuller told a *Chicago Tribune* reporter at the IAC pool deck with fellow swimmers crowding around. "Can't Bar Weiss From Olympics; Was Born Right Here," blared the headline. Later, he would correct himself: Technically his birthplace was Windber, where the Weissmullers briefly lived before settling in Chicago. In an emotional interview with Chicago newsmen, Elizabeth defiantly supported her son.

In Weissmuller's passport application filed on May 16, another supporter threw his weight behind Johnny and Elizabeth's assertions. "The affiant bases his knowledge upon the following facts: that he was present when John Weissmuller was born and that he is the father of John Weissmuller and that he gives his consent to John Weissmuller's departure to France and England." The affiant was Peter Weissmuller of the Foreman Machine Shop on 226 West North Avenue, a man the family claimed had been dead for about six years.

The passport was stamped the next day. Any case files created by the Department of Labor or Congressmen Rathbone's office weren't publicly disclosed. There is no surviving record of any investigation.

This fixed everything for everybody except Peter Weissmuller Jr., the true younger brother, whose identity was sacrificed for his Olympics-bound sibling. It was the beginning of a life of troubles for Peter, whom his nephew remembered as a good guy but one who was tripped up repeatedly by substance abuse and bad decisions. An early marriage ended in divorce; an acting career in Hollywood got him stuntman work but never a big part.

He and his brother remained close throughout their lives, according to Johnny's son, John Jr., who wrote warmly about his tortured uncle in a memoir. When his dad was with Peter, often a long night of drinking followed. Pete sank deeper and deeper into a "shady" lifestyle until it finally consumed him, wrote John. He died in Los Angeles on September 4, 1969, a day after his true birthday.

Peter never told his brother's secret, and if he sometimes used his real birthdate, it was done without thinking, not with the hope someone would find out. Over the years both brothers made a hash of their birth dates, repeatedly reverting to their actual birthdays, not the ones claimed in 1924. When Johnny returned to Windber in 1950 for a day named in his honor, the church pastor presented him with his brother's baptismal and birth certificates. Weissmuller never told anyone the truth. When a *Sports Illustrated* investigative reporter, Arlene Mueller, revealed the lie after Weissmuller's death, John Jr. said it was the first he had heard of it. "I'm stunned," he said.

A century later, the confusion persists. A request for photos of Johnny Weissmuller at a history museum in Chicago turned up an image of Pete — young, athletic, and wholesome in his tricolor IAC swimsuit. It was taken at the beginning of what some thought would be a brilliant Olympic career.

And perhaps there was something more. The timing of Johnny's 1923 collapse coincided with Pete's dramatic fall from grace, when he slid from top status at the IAC to the anonymity of the second team, and when he was harshly described as competitively weak. It is plausible that Pete and Johnny had run into trouble. George Center had said Johnny had fallen off on his training prior to his hospitalization. He didn't say anything more specific but whatever was going on, maybe Pete blamed himself. It might help explain why a man would give up everything, including his identity, to another.

Much later Elizabeth Weissmuller, during divorce proceedings, would offer a window to the chaos and terror of her household in the spring of 1924. She testified in an Illinois court that her husband, while intoxicated, struck her on the face and body in repeated incidents, causing "severe pain and anguish." He later threatened to kill her.

It was something else that neither Johnny nor his brother ever talked about.

———

ON AUGUST 8, 1923, Duke Kahanamoku found himself in court facing speeding charges. The judge, perhaps feeling a news opportunity was at hand, told Kahanamoku that he may be a "fast boy in the water" but Santa Monica Boulevard was dry land and hence different rules applied. He sentenced Duke to ten days in jail, then suspended the sentence when appeals were made saying that Kahanamoku was scheduled to face Johnny

Weissmuller in Chicago on August 15 (an event that was subsequently canceled due to Weissmuller's illness).

At the time, Kahanamoku had made plans to return to Hawaii to headline the winter carnival in October and to train with his 1920 Olympic coach, George Center. In a local story about Duke's return, Center held out hope of Weissmuller coming, too. Duke's presence alone would create some much-needed excitement and help the money-strapped Hawaii AAU, which didn't have enough funds to send more than a couple swimmers to the Olympic trials. But more than that, Duke's Hawaiian fans saw his return as proof of him coming back for good. "Word was recently given out that a Honolulu firm would make him an offer if he would come back and make Honolulu his home again," reported the *Star-Bulletin*.

But on September 19, Duke reversed course and canceled his trip. The wired message to Center at the Hawaii AAU was curt: "Impossible Come. Kahanamoku." The lack of explanation felt like another body blow to his ancestral home. It even felt disrespectful. "It was the Hawaiian AAU which financed Duke's trip over to compete for the last Olympic team," the *Honolulu Advertiser* complained in an anonymous column. "And when stranded in New York [when Kahanamoku was hospitalized with influenza in 1918] it was the Hawaiian AAU which came to his assistance and brought him home."

The reasons for the snub could only be guessed at. Some thought Kahanamoku's coach at the Los Angeles Athletic Club, Fred Cady, was afraid he wouldn't return once back in the islands. Cady, a former Barnum and Bailey strongman, was famously territorial, even paranoid. (Though his new wife, Viola Hartmann, had qualified as a diver for the 1924 Games, he wouldn't let her go to Paris because he was sure she would fall in love with someone else.) Others thought Cady feared the young Waikiki challengers were too fast for the aging champ. "It is quite possible that Cady fears for Duke's reputation if he should come here and get beaten by local men," the *Advertiser* theorized.

Whatever the case, Duke stayed silent. He would not see fellow Hawaiian swimmers, including his brothers, Sam and David, until they arrived on the mainland for the Olympic trials in May 1924.

In the autumn and early winter, Duke performed in exhibitions at his L.A. club, but did not approach his blistering sprint times from early summer. His big comeback seemed a "false alarm," in the words of the Honolulu papers. He was spied on golf courses and sailboats and at beaches and was increasingly a fixture at the many social events taking place in a city swooning with Pacific Island mania. He was invited to be the celebrity chef at a luau fundraiser hosted by a wealthy Los Angeles doctor. He attended a Thanksgiving Day football game at the Rose Bowl between Pomona College and the University of Hawaii, staying around after Hawaii's defeat to soothe disappointed fans and players with "Sweet Lei Lehua," a love song composed by David Kalākaua, the islands' last king. The Los Angeles sportswriter Maxwell Stiles couldn't believe what he was seeing. "Led by Duke Kahanamoku, the best-known Hawaiian in the world, and a trio of ukulele players," he wrote, "the plaintive strains of the song made us aware that the Hawaiian rooters were still there, waiting for the members of the team to dress, waiting to serenade them when they should appear. Above them all stood the proud figure of the Duke, and then 'Aloha nui oe' (Love you so much)."

Los Angeles, newly connected to Honolulu with direct luxury steamship service, was fast becoming a sister city. The 500-foot *City of Los Angeles* delivered 400 first-class, lei-bedecked passengers weekly, and the *City of Honolulu* brought them back. Hollywood performers and traditional Hawaiian bands alternated as shipboard entertainment. The weeklong passage quickly became famous for reckless romantic affairs and the ships' "libraries," speakeasies offering hard liquor.

Like Hawaii, Los Angeles was aggressively touting itself as a sunny and fun destination, an oasis of health and wellness in a dirty, disease-riddled world. Kahanamoku, Olympic sports star and the chief reason the islands were on the minds of millions, was evidence of Southern California's rising profile. Duke wasn't simply a visitor; he had chosen to stay, apparently finding something in the potent mix of Hollywood, society, and athletics he couldn't find back home. He was one of several famous athletes now living in California, including boxing champion Jim Jeffries, sailor Tom Sharkey, and a litany of baseball players, golfers, jockeys, tennis pros, and race car daredevils. A few on the list, like Duke, had seemed to find a proverbial second life. California promised not just renewal but rebirth.

But amidst the good times and booming economy, there was a growing problem. The race question, it was called.

The Ku Klux Klan was in ascendancy across the nation. A few years earlier a reporter embedded with a Chicago chapter wrote that 2,376 men were initiated at a single meeting, the biggest Klan recruitment day ever recorded. The Klan had recently organized in L.A. and claimed new adherents from the highest strata of Southern California leadership.

An uptick in racial intolerance was reflected in segregation at the beaches and swimming pools. Unlike most of America, there were abundant places to swim in Los Angeles, but what troubled the Klan, and the city leaders they controlled, was bathing in the same waters as dark-skinned folks. Black designated swimming beaches were few — one was called Ink Spot — and pools were fewer. Black access to public pools was limited to a day or two a week because pools had to be drained then refilled before the city's white population could use them.

The racial tension was raised to boiling in the summer of 1923 when the city shuttered a popular Black-owned beach resort in Santa Monica and took the land for a park, citing eminent domain. The park was never built. When Black activists defied the Jim Crow ban and went swimming, they were pulled from the water and arrested.

It was a tortured time to be a minority in Los Angeles, but Kahanamoku existed with an exemption. He was well-known enough not to be targeted by racists, and even if he wasn't recognized, he was frequently in the company of privileged white friends.

His relationship with the Henry family deepened; he called Leslie Henry's wife, Madge, "Ma" and was close to the couple's two sons: Thomas, their adopted fifteen-year-old, and William, eight. He joked about living and working around so many white people, he had become "haole-fied" he said, using the island euphemism for nonnative colonizers. He was baptized in the family's Episcopal church, and for reasons he never explained and which mystified others, was entertaining the possibility of the Henrys formally adopting him.

Leslie was president of the Bank of West Hollywood and a stakeholder in the L.A. Athletic Club, the local AAU chapter, and a leader of the organizing group trying to lure the Olympics to Los Angeles. Most thought it was a fanciful dream; even if the money could be raised it was doubtful top athletes from Europe would come because of the cost and inconvenience of oceanic travel. But right up to the last minute, Henry, a third generation Californian, and his fellow believers pressed for the 1924 Games. A U.S. Olympics would signify that the host city had arrived, and for L.A.'s dreamers and schemers it couldn't come fast enough.

Duke was torn. Go back home, and he would please Hawaii. Stay, and he might rise as Hollywood rose. His friend, the native Hawaiian waterman George Freeth, had stayed in California. Freeth became famous in the early 1900s as one of the surf riders bringing the sport back to prominence in Hawaii. Jack London described him as "Mercury — a brown Mercury. His heels are winged, and in them is the swiftness of the sea." But Freeth went to the mainland in 1907 to promote the ancient royal sport and never looked back. For the next twelve years he earned a living at Southern California resorts and later launched the country's first elite corps of ocean lifeguards.

His example was comforting to Duke when he moved to Los Angeles, but there were differences. Freeth had mixed heritage and the lighter complexion of his English father. He came from old money and had more options.

Kahanamoku attempted to refocus. On December 12, in the first indoor event of the winter season, he was featured in a 220-yard race at the L.A. Athletic Club. Cady billed it as his first serious attempt on the road to the 1924 Games, and the probable occasion for a new world record. Duke's competition, the talented prodigy and club teammate Tom Blake, was also fashioning a comeback after several years away. Blake was the surprise winner. Duke had struggled to get second.

Exactly a month later, on January 12, the LAAC found itself with a new intercity rival when the Hollywood Athletic Club opened its doors on Sunset Boulevard. The nine-story building — a bachelor's hotel whose twin towers framed a two-story clubhouse — was just seven miles away. It had all that the older club had and much more. It was the tallest building in Hollywood; the gym was one of the largest, best equipped, and best lit in the country; and a rooftop sundeck beckoned for massages and tanning. The interior draperies copied those from Florentine palaces, and the game rooms echoed Pompeii. The tiled pool would be home to record making, the founders promised.

Philosophically, the raison d'être was fitness, minus the evangelical YMCA conceit. Vanity needn't come with remorse. The club's audience, and its calling card, as the name said, was Hollywood. Its first resident was Charlie Chaplin, the number one film celebrity in the country. Its first athlete was Johnny Weissmuller, a surprise founding member having at that point barely set foot in Los Angeles. Fellow founders and A-list stars included John Wayne, John Ford, Humphrey Bogart, Rudolph Valentino, Bela Lugosi, and Douglas Fairbanks Sr. and Jr.

———————

DUKE'S LONG ABSENCE from Waikiki magnified a malaise with swimming that seemed unthinkable in the years when locals were flinging hats and themselves into the water to celebrate his victories. There were continuing problems in getting the Hawaiian people behind another costly fundraising campaign to subsidize native Olympic aspirants. The enthusiasm had been missing since the summer of 1922, when Duke sailed away and Weissmuller took over. The 1924 spring swimming carnival in Waikiki had featured the international sensation, Sweden's Arne Borg, along with hotly competitive races to determine Hawaii's next crop of Olympians, but attendance was still down.

Bill Rawlins came out of retirement to try to get people back, naming George Center the coach of Hawaii's Olympic hopefuls. In the *Honolulu Advertiser* the paper's owner, Lorrin Thurston, pleaded for the $8,000 to $10,000 needed. "The surf riders on the beach at Waikiki and the Hawaiian swimmers are our great calling cards," he wrote. "We must recognize this fact and capitalize on it. We must send a swimming team to Paris."

Duke's name would have brought in donations, but he was not mentioned, in part because nobody knew what he was doing. Was he even trying out?

On May 1, 1924, the seven-person Hawaii team, still short of money, departed Honolulu for San Francisco. (The one female member, Mariechen Wehselau, traveled separately with a chaperone.) The first of three Olympic trials for them — they were expected to compete in Western, Middle West, and Eastern qualifiers — kicked off at Stanford University. The team included Sam Kahanamoku, Duke's nineteen-year-old heir apparent, and David Kahanamoku. Sam came despite a near deadly bout with influenza a few months earlier, and David, the team trainer, came despite trepidations about leaving his community. When he departed a young boy clung to him, presumably a nephew or a beach tutee, refusing to leave his side until he was ordered off the ship and the gangplank was pulled. The *Advertiser* reporter made fun of the mutual show of emotion. The head of Waikiki's beach lifeguards, who was recently described in newspaper headlines as Hawaii's "champion saver of lives," David Kahanamoku was a homebody. He was the last man aboard. "David has steadfastly refused offers in the States," a friend told a local reporter, "because he fears he will grow hard, lose his native warm sympathy."

Duke didn't join the team at Stanford but sent word that he planned to try out after all. He reunited with David several days later at a qualifying event at the Brookside Park Plunge in Pasadena. When the pool opened in 1914, it barred nonwhite swimmers except on a solitary weekday called "International Day," after which the pool was drained. Later the city council prohibited non-white swimmers entirely. Kahanamoku would be forced to break the municipal pool's ten-year-old exclusion rule. Baseball great Jackie Robinson, a native of the city, recalled years later in his autobiography that Pasadenans looked at people of color as intruders. "[They were] less understanding than Southerners and even more openly hostile," he wrote.

Despite brother David's reassuring presence — the family nicknamed him Juke Box for his volubility — Duke could only manage a tie with an unknown Venice high school senior in the 100-meter sprint. One report said the race was held behind closed doors, as if to limit the public outrage of a person of color sharing pool water with a local white boy. The tie was good enough to qualify Duke for the second qualifier, the big meet in Indianapolis.

With swimmers competing at different sectionals in California, the whole Hawaiian squad didn't get together until May 29, when they stopped in Chicago en route to Indiana. Most of them had traveled on the *Pacific Limited,* disembarking during a brief stop in Sherman, Wyoming, 8,000 feet above sea level, to hurl snowballs at one another. "I looked for shelter when the battle started," said Warren Kealoha. "That snow may look soft, but it is not so soft when made into a snowball."

Reuniting with his brothers in Chicago seemed to lift Duke's spirits. They shared a laugh about the newspapers that mistakenly assumed the teenaged Sam was Duke's son and about assistant coach Harvey Chilton's San Francisco training no-nos: no dancing, no late hours, and no poi. They were united in their anger that Charles Pung, a shy nineteen-year-old teammate of Chinese Hawaiian descent, had been delayed in San Francisco by immigration officials pending an investigation of his visa eligibility. Months earlier, California had passed legislation limiting the number of Asians allowed to enter the state. Honolulu papers called it a "conspicuous instance of discrimination."

In recent weeks those who saw Kahanamoku swim believed he was slowing down, finally yielding to his age. The caveat, though, was what could happen if he felt motivated. Reporters recalled a 1922 race at the University of Hawaii where he sleepwalked to a slow win in the 50 yard in an unchallenged heat, then a day later reeled off an unofficial record in a relay when he had yards to make up to catch his rival. He won by two yards in 22.4 seconds. "Competition is always necessary to make Duke paddle fast," wrote *Honolulu Star Bulletin* columnist Mike Jay, previewing the upcoming trials.

During their stopover in Chicago, the Hawaii team gathered at the IAC, where the gregarious Bachrach had invited them to take a swim and freshen up before reboarding the train for the final leg to Indianapolis.

Bachrach eyed the Hawaiians appraisingly during their brief workout. In 1916 he almost landed Duke Kahanamoku when the swimmer was wavering in his allegiance to the Hui Nalu. Kahanamoku visited the IAC and consented to a photo session wearing the team colors. Bachrach had him swimming in tight briefs with the club crest and lounging on the pool deck strumming a guitar. But Duke didn't go through with it, and instead got the better of Bachrach's swimmers in almost every race over the ensuing six years.

Now that Duke was here in the flesh, Bachrach would finally have his chance. As coach of the U.S. team headed for Paris, he could lay claim to the country's best swimmers, including Duke. The showdown about to happen in Indiana, he told reporters, wasn't merely the Olympic trials. It was the "Battle of the Century."

Duke Kahanamoku in the canvas practice pool rigged to the deck of the ship taking the U.S. Olympic team to the 1920 Summer Games in Antwerp, Belgium. A harness tied to an overhead rope allowed him to swim in place. *Outrigger Canoe Club Historical Committee*

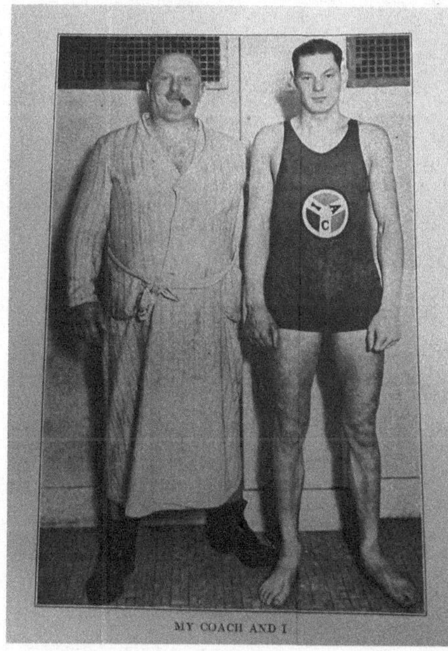

Johnny Weissmuller and his longtime coach, Bill Bachrach, famous for always wearing a bath robe on the pool deck. Bachrach was known for playing fast and loose with Amateur Athletic Union rules and was rumored to place bets on his swimmers. *Swimming the American Crawl* by Johnny Weissmuller

Katsuo Takaishi and his wife, the champion swimmer Mineko Nagai, at their home in Osaka. The first Asian swimmer to win an Olympic medal (using the soon-to-be-famous Japanese crawl), Takaishi had a bronze bust and a university swimming pool dedicated to him on his return from the Paris Games. *Courtesy of Takaishi Family*

Duke Kahanamoku in the New York City ticker-tape parade celebrating the U.S. Olympic team following the 1920 Games in Antwerp, Belgium, where he won two gold medals. He had told a reporter, "My training consists of going out and swimming around." *Library of Congress*

Baron Pierre de Coubertin, founder of the modern Olympics. Determined to have the Games proceed with order, dignity, and exalted purpose, he was perpetually dismayed by the carnival atmosphere American athletes in particular brought to the event. *Library of Congress*

An American newspaper cartoon depicting Duke
Kahanamoku and fellow Hawaiian swimmer Vincent Genoves
in anticipation of the 1912 Olympics in Sweden. The caption
reads, "Hawaii has two athletes to send to Stockholm."
Honolulu Advertiser

The Hawaii contingent of the 1924 U.S. Olympic swim team, including Duke Kahanamoku (back row, third from left), Warren Kealoha (to the right of Duke), David Kahanamoku (back row, far right), Sam Kahanamoku (seated, far left), Charles Pung (seated, second from left), Mariechen Wehselau (seated, third from left), and Pua Kealoha (seated far right). *Outrigger Canoe Club Historical Committee*

Members of the 1924 Japanese Olympic team, including Katsuo Takaishi (back row center, with white pocket handkerchief) and his coach, Den Sugimoto (front row, second from right), at their quarters in the Olympic Village in a suburb outside Paris. *Bibliotheque nationale de France*

Johnny Weissmuller's younger brother, Peter, who for a time was considered a promising up-and-comer on Bill Bachrach's famous Illinois Athletic Club team. *Chicago Daily News Collection, Chicago History Museum*

Three future stars of the 1924 Games—Johnny Weissmuller, Aileen Riggin, and Duke Kahanamoku—on the deck of the ship taking American athletes to Paris. Kneeling is David Kahanamoku, the swim team trainer. *International Swimming Hall of Fame Archives*

The 100-meter freestyle final at the 1924 Paris Games.
Twenty-five meters from the start, Duke Kahanamoku and
Johnny Weissmuller are neck-and-neck, followed by Katsuo
Takaishi, Arne Borg, and Sam Kahanamoku (left to right).
United States Olympic & Paralympic Committee

Johnny Weissmuller poses for a portrait in Manhattan after winning three gold medals at the 1924 Games. His talent and physique made him attractive to eugenicists who argued that the future of the white race was threatened by immigrants of different skin color. *National Portrait Gallery*

Duke Kahanamoku teaches the crawl stroke to actress Shirley Mason during the filming of the 1925 movie *Lord Jim*. Though he had bit parts in a number of Hollywood films, he never hit it big like Johnny Weissmuller. *Hollywood Museum Collection, Margaret Herrick Library*

Katsuo Takaishi and Johnny Weissmuller in Osaka during Weissmuller's final international competition before retiring in 1929. Takaishi was never able to beat Weissmuller in a race, saying, "He stands in a class by himself." *International Swimming Hall of Fame Archives*

Duke Kahanamoku and Johnny Weissmuller at the 1932
Olympic Trials in Cincinnati, where Duke, at age forty-two,
attempted to make the American team for the fourth time.
Bishop Museum Archives

Duke Kahanamoku and Johnny Weissmuller dance the hula at a 1950 Swimming Hall of Fame event in their honor at the Helms Athletic Foundation in Los Angeles. Despite their age difference and the tensions leading to the Paris Games, the two men became lifelong friends. *Bishop Museum Archives*

THIRTEEN

SPIRIT
1923 – 1924

*"It's the morning after my defeat. My heart is
aching with regret for the rest of my life. If people
want to laugh, laugh. To wipe off this shame,
I will work with all my strength to raise the
prestige of our country."*

—Shizo Kanakuri, Japan's first Olympian,
writing in his diary the day after he
dropped out of the marathon during
the 1912 Games

PROFESSOR KANŌ JIGORŌ's lecture drew a full house at the Los
Angeles Athletic Club, where he stopped on his way home from
the 1920 Games in Belgium. The Japanese team he directed
had failed, adding to his country's unfortunate track record at
the Olympic Games. The stereotype of the Japanese people as
a physically weak and backward sporting race persisted.

From the first Games Japan attended, in 1912, there had

been disappointment. At those Games, Japan's favored marathon runner, Shizo Kanakuri, whom Jigorō personally trained, disappeared at mile sixteen and was reported missing before he showed up weeks later at a nearby farmhouse, where he had been recuperating from exhaustion. So bitter was the memory and the feeling of shame, Kanakuri returned to Stockholm in 1967 to complete the race he started. His finishing time was fifty-four years, eight months, six days, five hours, thirty-two minutes, and 20.3 seconds.

Jigorō, too, had the feeling of unfinished business. The next Olympic chapter had to be different.

The lecture at the LAAC wasn't about any Olympic sports but about judo, the school of self-defense he founded. Jigorō was not a master, he humbly told his audience, but a perpetual student. He was an able showman, too. The audience was rapt throughout his presentation, especially when the five-foot-two, 100-pound, sixty-three-year-old academic took to the demonstration mat against one of the club's coaches, a man half his age. Jigorō lifted him over his head and, with a graceful, sweeping movement that seemed to defy everything the people in the room knew about strength and force, launched his opponent halfway across the floor. A beautiful thud reverberated. The dramatic throw was more than a party trick. It was personally satisfying, given his recent frustrations at the Games. More than that, it was a show of prideful strength to a white audience. Judo, declared Robert Ripley, was "the greatest physical science in the world."

Jigorō would survive the September Great Kantō Earthquake in 1923 though the great arenas of Japanese sports — his own dojo, Kodokan, and the Madison Square Garden of sumo wrestling, Kokugikan — would not. Japan's Olympic team was again in limbo as reconstruction took hold. Tokyo was rebuilding roads, railways, and thousands of collapsed buildings, including the YMCA, where only remnants were left of the ground-floor pool. Tokyo's champion swimmers, with months to go until Paris, were without a winter facility to train.

Meanwhile, politics had intruded on the Games, with anti-American sentiment and protests raging across Tokyo. The U.S. Congress was in the process of passing national immigration policy that would deny entry to all Japanese citizens. As a friendly nation with a long-standing gentleman's agreement with American legislators, Japan, unlike China, had never been turned away from U.S. borders. The key architects of the new legislation were eugenicists and "yellow peril" alarmists who said they wanted the race-based law to stop "a stream of alien blood." California had already passed legislation preventing Japanese immigrants from owning land. In San Francisco and elsewhere across California, nativists objected to Japanese-born students attending American schools, "sitting next to little American girls." For a supposed ally to be placed on the exclusion list was viewed across Japan as hostile and discriminatory. In later years, a historian at the U.S. State Department would concede, "In all of its parts, the most basic purpose [of the act] was to preserve the ideal of U.S. homogeneity."

As student protests spread in Tokyo, Japan's intellectual leaders debated a response. Some sought to aggressively fight back. Rash Behari Bose, an Indian revolutionary who fought against British rule before fleeing to Japan, wanted to create a rival block of Asian nations to "civilize the white race and remold them into men of justice." He said the historic superiority of the "Orientals over the Occidentals" needed to be acknowledged, at which point their adversaries could be taught and converted.

Others, like Abe Isoo, a Waseda University professor and founder of Japan's socialist party, believed the nation had to review its own imperial aggressions in China, Russia, and Germany and address mistreatment of its labor force.

Despite the international tension, Isoo continued the work for which he would ultimately be remembered: nurturing the growth of baseball in Japan. In 1910 he began a pioneering series of exchange trips with the University of Chicago baseball team, and in May 1924 he and team coach Amos Alonzo Stagg announced a fourth visit of the Maroons to Tokyo. Stagg's inclusionary stance was unusual for the time and for a person known to oppose Blacks hoping to cross the athletic color line. He didn't want them on his teams, something he wasn't shy about stating. Stagg also had attended prominent eugenic conferences, including one held at Battle Creek by John Harvey Kellogg's Race Betterment Foundation. There, he would have heard lectures on the "degenerative tendencies actively at work in America" and the need for immediate action to prevent the passing of the "Great Race."

Stagg's benevolent views of the Japanese was likely thanks to a former student of his, Heita Okabe, who enrolled at the University of Chicago in 1918. Okabe was a sports fanatic who had taught physical education at Tokyo Higher Normal School, where Jigorō was principal, before heading to America. He was already a black belt in judo and a competitive sumo wrestler, but while studying sports management under Stagg, Okabe tried boxing, basketball, baseball, grappling, swimming, and football. He started as a twenty-six-year-old left tackle on the University of Chicago team in 1919. A *Chicago Tribune* story chronicling Okabe's boxing debut said he didn't know how to hold his hands when putting on gloves, but it didn't take him long to learn.

He and Stagg would become lifelong friends — Okabe would become a football missionary back in Japan and a forceful advocate for the character-building influence of amateur sports. Stagg in turn would become an ardent supporter of sports exchanges and a vocal critic of U.S. exclusion policies. Later, he would decry the criminal mistreatment of Japanese Americans imprisoned in camps during World War II, even telegramming his protest to Henry Stimson, the secretary of war.

In mid-January 1924, it was Stagg's friend Okabe who would be called upon to rescue Japan's Olympic fortunes. Japan had announced it would attempt to send a team to Paris despite, in Okabe's words, "the sorrow she has suffered over the recent earthquake." The goal was to send about ten athletes, nowhere near the thirty-five which were anticipated before the disaster. The Japanese government had reluctantly agreed to pay half of the $60,000 cost to finance the team; the rest would have to come from public contributions. Beginning in March, Tokyo Athletic Association volunteers stood on street corners, appealing for ten-yen donations. "The love of our university students for sports made them refuse to give up hopes of winning international honors," said Okabe.

Okabe was capable, resourceful, and a gigantic help with fundraising and logistics. He successfully wooed donors in San Francisco and New York, then traveled to Paris, where he oversaw team registrations, inspected venues, and secured accommodations. The team would stay in the two- and four-room Olympic Village cottages to be built for athletes along the recently named Avenue Pierre de Coubertin.

Ultimately, twenty-one athletes boarded trains from Tokyo to Kobe on April 26, then reported to the elegant, 500-foot ocean liner *Katori Maru* bound for Paris. A small crowd of well-wishers gathered on the deck hoisting an enormous national flag donated by Prince Chichibu. Unlike the circuitous travels of the 1920 Japanese team, the *Maru*'s route was direct to Europe.

They hoped to be in Paris in six weeks. For their send-off, the team wore dark blazers with a rising-sun patch over their hearts. Shizo Kanakuri, who followed his 1912 disgrace with a strong finish in Antwerp in 1920, was back, at thirty-four years old, for his third consecutive Olympiad.

Also on the team was Hiroshima native Katsutoshi Naito, an intercollegiate wrestling champ and senior captain of the Penn State team. Naito had trained at Jigorō's judo school before accepting a scholarship to Penn State, where he quickly came to the fore by merging his martial arts skills with wrestling. Naito, who had lost both parents as a small child, earned the nickname Tiger. His familiarity with American athletes would prove helpful throughout the Games.

The swim team was notable for who *wasn't* on board. Sugimoto's students at Ibaraki had seemed to win the majority of the six coveted team spots, but at the last minute, their Tokyo rivals, two of whom were either absent or pointless at the Far Eastern Games, secured four of them. Only Ibaraki's Takaishi and breaststroker Tsunenobu Ishida boarded the *Katori Maru*. (Naito was also added as a swimmer at the recommendation of Japan's ambassador to the U.S. but politely declined the slot.)

Whether the Ibaraki swimmers were rejected because of the strong bias for Tokyo swimmers or personal travails associated with the Kantō earthquake is unclear. Before the earthquake hit, some twenty-five swimmers were going to be sent to Honolulu for a final selection. That didn't happen. Personal hardships were overwhelming, with families trying to rebuild from loss. The roster changes could be attributed to something as simple as athletes being called to take care of their families and communities.

Class was a new and shifting factor in Japan's overall athlete selection. Like the British hierarchal model, Japan's organizing body traditionally imposed restrictions against athletes with working-class backgrounds. Among the family occupations considered disqualifying were rickshaw driving and postal work.

But with the eleventh-hour decision to send athletes to Paris came pressure to loosen restrictions. Some argued for a more American model in which merit was considered, especially in the case of candidates who could be entrusted with bringing home a medal. Black- and brown-skinned athletes like Howard Drew, Jim Thorpe, and Kahanamoku were part of the changing Olympic landscape. They were social and racial examples of what might be possible in Japan if the athletic pool was expanded. In the end, Japan's effort to get to Paris spread its own aftershock. In one devastating shift, the privilege of class had, at least in one arena, been swept away. Beating their opponents, the Japanese officials announced, was all that mattered.

For a curious and amiable person like Takaishi, the voyage — complete with milk and mail delivery to his cabin — was an adventure. Like Duke in 1912 and Weissmuller now, Takaishi had never been abroad. He wasn't an English speaker yet and had just completed his first year at Waseda University. Sports excellence preceded Takaishi at Waseda, and many athletes who competed in the Far Eastern Games and the Olympics were fellow students or alumni. For years the school was embroiled in a baseball rivalry with Keio University that got so heated the teams had to discontinue their games because of fights between fans. But swimming didn't have a big name yet. Takaishi had nonetheless decided on Waseda over Meiji or the academically superior Tokyo, the country's first imperial university. Takaishi would later acknowledge he was being groomed to become a successful merchant like his brother, who had founded a steelmaking ironworks in Osaka. But his Ibaraki education, punctuated by Sugimoto's enigmatic midnight mountain climbs and river-water raids, changed his orientation. He would duly follow the executive training his family expected and he would do so within an environment that was as crazy about sports as he was. (In 1925, in the aftermath of the Games, Waseda would build an indoor pool in his honor, Japan's first at a university.)

Takaishi trained onboard the ship in a tiny canvas tank strung to rigging with heavy ropes. He was comforted by Sugimoto's presence but wondered about his place next to the world's foremost crawl swimmers: the Kahanamoku brothers, the Swede Arne Borg, and, most of all, Weissmuller. Sugimoto would later admit he wondered, too, especially when he saw Takaishi on the pool deck in Paris surrounded by those tall trees. His star pupil looked to be miscast, more fodder for the amused foreign coaches than a true contender.

Still, many in Japan had wildly high hopes for Paris based on what happened at the Far Eastern Games in Osaka, where they had established absolute sporting supremacy in Asia. Despite the initial disinterest in the Far Eastern Games, the Japanese were more than quick studies; they were becoming masters. Though reports emerged boasting of talented Japanese track-and-field athletes as medal contenders, some team officials, including Jigorō and Okabe, thought the breakthrough would come from swimming, the sport that was always their own.

The *Katori Maru* was halfway across the Pacific when word came that the man who had set it all in motion, the indefatigable sports missionary Elwood Brown, had died suddenly. While taking a break from the arduous, ongoing process of writing his report about the 1923 Far Eastern Games, he had dropped to the pavement with a fatal heart attack as he played handball in New York.

FOURTEEN

THE RACE OF THE CENTURY 1924

"Records are induced by keen competition, a sustained effort to overcome an opponent's lead, a desperate effort of nerve and energy induced by the desire to conquer. But you get that only when you see an opponent in front of you or feel him breathing his challenge on your neck."

—*New York Daily News* sports columnist Paul Gallico

"Athletes of the 'cool' type always seem to stay in the game longer than the 'nerves' type. A million dollars at stake would not get [Duke Kahanamoku] excited at the start of a race."

—Mike Jay, *Honolulu Star-Bulletin*

INDIANAPOLIS'S BROAD RIPPLE PARK — "Sixty acres of good times" — was a worthy venue for the race of the century. The concrete pool, the world's largest, was 450-feet long by 207-feet wide, which was big enough to fit almost eight IAC pools.

Continuous water circulation and chlorine — a relatively new sterilizing agent for pools — meant you could swim next to a person with contagious disease and be perfectly safe, park pamphlets assured. If you wanted to drink the water you were swimming in you could do that, too. The sheltered grandstand accommodating 3,500 spectators looked comparatively small against the expanse of water, like a cottage on the bank of a lake.

For Indianapolis, the largest inland city in the U.S., Broad Ripple was its White City, a *grand stade* on an audacious Pierre-de-Coubertin scale that made you look and marvel. "Drive out and check your cares outside the gates," the promoters beckoned. "Come out and let yourself go, for Old Man Gloom has been exiled from this Joyland forever."

And now came the spectacle of the much anticipated, relentlessly advertised June 6 opening of the 1924 U.S. Olympic swim trials. If you timed it right, you could glimpse the races from the apex of the 100-foot-high roller coaster or adjacent Ferris wheel.

Bachrach came as more than an American coach, he was *the* American coach, with a nationally syndicated swimming column often graced by a photo of him or his star pupil, Weissmuller. "Here is shown a man who, single-handedly, has turned out the majority of the world's champion swimmers during the past decade," read one caption. Bachrach explained to America everything from the dog paddle to the hydroplaning principle to breathing to the "fish-tail slip," a kicking innovation for the breaststroke. Except for his friend Amos Alonzo Stagg, no amateur coach in the country was more visible or better recognized. His salary, always high, was now far beyond the $300 a month he was making in 1921. It seemed to some, including the Hawaiians, that this Olympic team was intended to high-light one great swimmer, Weissmuller, and advertise one great club, the IAC.

The Hawaiians, thousands of miles from home and facing some of the biggest races of their lives, tried to adjust. Warren Kealoha had had a son born in Honolulu in his absence. The chilly weather was bracing. In a long letter to a coworker in Honolulu, Kealoha, the favorite for the 100-meter backstroke, described their first look at the water they had to swim in. "On Decoration Day we went to see the pool in which the trials are to be held and found the temperature of the water to be fifty-eight degrees," he wrote. "Our pores were sticking out all over just looking at it . . . believe me the place is sure cold."

Photos Charles Pung sent to his dad showed the team in thick V-neck sweaters with a large "H" on the front, Sam Kahanamoku in a bow tie with a guitar in hand. The Hawaiians' music making — a tribute to their heritage and to their hosts — was constant and a way for them to stay connected to home. The reciprocal nature of Aloha — *O ke aloha ke kuleana o kahi malihini* ("Love is the host in strange lands") — was second nature. Their music was wildly popular, too. Sam could play anything. Pua Kealoha, who won gold along with Duke in the 1920 Olympic relay, was a gifted guitarist and composer who would play for years in the Royal Hawaiian Hotel orchestra and aboard the tourist ships that sailed between the islands and the mainland. The original Hui Nalu skipper, Dude Miller, played piano and several string instruments in the Bird of Paradise Orchestra, which received nine curtain calls following one New York performance.

Duke's postcard to the governor of Hawaii was brief but enthusiastic. All is well, he wrote, and they were continuing to promote the islands. Duke good-naturedly posed at the pool for photographers. He had raced under different banners the past five years, even swimming for the Outrigger Canoe Club to boost his career, but this Hawaiian team brought him joy. He was back in the company of those who knew him best.

Weissmuller and Kahanamoku were increasingly character-ized as championship prizefighters. Their stark age difference seemed to favor the younger swimmer, but one fellow swim-mer thought otherwise, saying Duke had apparent advantages. He was never nervous at a race's start and had a better burst at the end. Weissmuller had never lost a major race, but it might work against him. "I think Weissmuller will be nervous," wrote swimmer J. W. Kreuttner in the *Honolulu Advertiser*. "It is rather disconcerting for a natural nervous youngster over six-feet tall to have to look up at a taller competitor who is as calm as a May morning and has a reputation fifteen-years long."

Norman Ross saw it differently. He believed his teammate was a lock, poised to achieve the sport's biggest milestones, like swimming 100 yards in less than fifty seconds. Ross openly doubted the recent times that Duke's coach Fred Cady claimed for him. Ross saw Duke as indecisive about competition; nobody was sure if he would show or not show, race for real or simply produce a respectable time. Maybe Duke now thought of it all as a necessary evil since he didn't have a clear fallback plan. Ross, the ex-champion, knew the allure of a comeback. A guy like Duke with questions and self-doubt swirling inside him didn't have a chance.

There was drizzle to start the first day of trials, cold down-pours in the afternoon. Thanks to a rain delay, officials lost some of the paying crowd for the feature race, the 100-meter. Well after the 3:00 p.m. start the final qualifiers emerged. Johnny was in the middle lane, with the Kahanamoku brothers on either side. One surprise IAC entrant had been Norman Ross, who had perhaps come to steady the young Weissmuller, but he failed to qualify for the final heat. In the earlier qualifying round Weissmuller had irritated the Hawaiians when he loafed on the home stretch, teasing his closest challenger, Pua Kealoha, before turning on the speed to win. Glancing now at Duke and his brother Sam and anticipating they might collaborate to beat him, Johnny wished he had been more circumspect.

As the five men nervously crouched and readied to let fly, someone prematurely jumped ahead of the gun, and the rest followed. The false start exception was Duke, who remained on the pool deck, composed and poised. Decades later the basketball superstar Kobe Bryant would display a similarly unshakeable front, not even flinching as a rival forward bluffed rifling an inbounds pass at his exposed face. The viral video remains one of the most memorable moments of Bryant's Hall of Fame career. To some, the image of Duke standing at the starting blocks as Weissmuller and others climbed out of the pool was what they came for and what they would remember. *How did he do that?*

At the restart, Duke was first in the water and Weissmuller got off late, immediately having to play catch-up. At the halfway mark he seemed to overtake Duke but at the turn, one of Weissmuller's strengths, Duke popped up right beside him. On the final straightaway, as the rain-drenched spectators crowded the rail, Duke was in front when he suddenly slowed up at the eighty-meter mark. Weissmuller started to pull away but veered off course and clattered into the lane divider. He regained his bearings and touched the wall first, followed by Duke, then Sam. Johnny's winning time was 59.4, a second faster than Duke's gold medal time in Antwerp.

Bachrach called the showdown the greatest race ever run in the U.S. Privately, he was concerned by a couple of things. Weissmuller had swum a fast heat in abysmal conditions but had made mistakes — a bad turn and start, and a near disastrous tangle with the divider. Early in his career, Weissmuller often lost his way when swimming in pools other than the one at the IAC, which had a line of black tiles at the bottom to guide him. Bachrach would put a hat at the end of a swim lane and tell Weissmuller to steer to it, trying to teach him not to rely on the tiles. But he had gotten nervous and forgot his lesson. Paris would be even more fraught.

Duke was clearly slower from carrying a few extra pounds — his training had been erratic over the previous months — but he could be expected to get into top shape for the Games. He had made no mistakes in his heat. Technically, he was superior. It seemed implausible he could crack the 100-meter one-minute barrier at his age (much less the sub-fifty-second mark that Ross predicted for Weissmuller in the 100 yard), but his aura and peerless experience gave pause. Nothing that happened at Broad Ripple led observers to count him out. His difficulty over the last twenty meters wasn't stamina related. It was a cramp which made his legs "give way," wrote Charles Pung in another letter to his father.

In an exhibition race that same day, Duke swam the 50-meter in 25.3 seconds, the fastest time recorded outside of competition. And he had let up in the final stretch. "Duke is still good yet," wrote Pung.

How the two stars felt about each other was hard to say. Weissmuller had been groomed with an overtly competitive American mentality. Duke hadn't. For two years, Weissmuller had been the challenger and Duke the challenged. Though they had met in Hawaii during Weissmuller's 1922 trip, they hadn't spent much time together. Swimming against a person you don't know and may dislike was a delicate game.

U.S. swimming legend Aaron Peirsol, an Olympic gold-medal

winner in the backstroke — sprint distances in 2004 and 2008 — recalled his first duels with Lenny Krayzelburg, then the popular reigning champ. Peirsol is a thoughtful and generous man who would later move to Hawaii, where he avidly researched the life of Duke Kahanamoku, drawn to his rare, competitive grace. But as an impatient seventeen-year-old, he ached to unseat Krayzelburg, stoking the rivalry with brash quotes to reporters. He knew he would soon be faster than his much older U.S. teammate but he wasn't there yet. After losing to him at the Sydney Games in 2000, Peirsol couldn't pin down Krayzelburg for a race. Peirsol tried to remind himself, when he did see Krayzelburg in the adjacent swim lane two years later, that it wasn't him against the champ so much as him and his own race. It's just another race, he told himself. Relax. And yet it was hard. The race was unexpectedly tight. Krayzelburg, some two years out of racing, came within three-tenths of a second of beating Peirsol. On that occasion and later ones, Krayzelburg was nothing but magnanimous, Peirsol said. In their relationship, they seemed to mirror the earlier rivalry between Weissmuller and Kahanamoku. Johnny was desperate to get on with it. Duke was coolly removed, as if he already knew how the story would end.

———

THE 200 COMPETITORS, dozens of officials, and a few fans posed for a panoramic photo at the conclusion of the trials. Standing in the back row is a robed Weissmuller looking away from the camera, no smile, shoulders sloping. He is a skinny boy-man. Next to him, looking straight at the camera, is Duke, still in his racing suit. He is impressively muscled across the chest and shoulders, his keen gaze looking like he can't wait for the rematch.

The following day, June 9, Bachrach announced the Olympic swim roster. All the Hawaiians made the team, proving wrong the many AAU experts who felt the islanders' run was over. The Hawaiian contingent would include David Kahanamoku, who was said to be invited at Bachrach's insistence. He had experienced David's bodywork and saw how the athletes, including Weissmuller, had responded to his soft-tissue massage. "He is more important than I am," Bachrach cracked. David was said to produce miracle cures with his mastery of lomilomi, an ancient Polynesian massage technique. The secret ingredient, which the team would have to do without, he said, was Hawaiian moonlight.

In addition to the Hawaiians, who made up almost half of the men's team, the sprint roster included Weissmuller and two of his fellow IAC swimmers. It was a motley crew, wrote one East Coast reporter, comprising "white boys, golden-skinned Hawaiians and a solitary son of the Celestial Empire." In a stunner, Duke had been relegated to a single event, the 100-meter. Bachrach had not selected him for the relay team despite Duke being the anchor on the winning team four years ago. Many had also expected him to be named to the water polo team, given his recent starring role at LAAC matches. But he was left off. Weissmuller, Bachrach announced, would compete in four events, including water polo and the relay. Kahanamoku was upset but left the protests and calls of favoritism to the Hawaiian columnists.

One week later, the team boarded the *20th Century* for New York. They attended team fundraisers at Rutgers College and the Long Beach Olympia Pool and swam in gimmicky exhibitions: Weissmuller doing a high-dive comedic routine with teammate Harold "Stubby" Kruger, and Duke swimming twenty-five yards in sixteen seconds using only his legs.

At the last event before the team set sail for Europe, an

East versus West four-person mixed relay came down to Weiss-muller and Kahanamoku as the respective anchors for the final forty-yard leg. They both reached for something extra, exhibition be damned. Weissmuller didn't quite catch his new teammate, who had recently won more votes than him for the honor of team captain. In the spirit of team unity, the U.S. officials publicly declared the race a dead heat. Maybe the win meant nothing — Weissmuller had easily won an earlier exhibition — but maybe it was the psychological edge Duke was looking for. He felt the old strength returning.

On Monday, June 16, some 250 athletes and almost as many officials, coaches, reporters, and friends boarded the SS *America* in Hoboken for the nine-day passage to Cherbourg and then Paris. Hundreds of self-described "essential" personnel appealed to go but had to be left behind, including a thirty-piece brass band, a twelve-year-old mascot, an American waiter, and a "pep" stimulator who told the U.S. Olympic Committee he was as necessary to American victories "as is salt to the manufacture of ice cream." Newspaper photographers swarmed the deck as exhibition wrestling and boxing matches took place, to the delight of 1,500 dockside onlookers. Groupings of club athletes and regional AAU chapters dutifully posed for pictures, including the "mermaids" of the women's team, wearing skirts and double-breasted blazers embroidered with the U.S. team crest, and floppy, flapper-style white sun hats.

On hand was the famously jaded *New York Daily News* columnist Paul Gallico, who on this day was uncharacteristically moved. "Picture that deck with its white painted railings and shining brass work, black with people, alive with color," he wrote. "There was real romance in the thought of these handsome, healthy youngsters drawn from all walks of life, crossing the ocean to match their athletic skill for the country."

The Hawaii swimmers, eight strong, posed for their picture, as did the IAC contingent, led by Weissmuller and the almost unrecognizable Bachrach, who now had shed at least 100 pounds and looked like a new man. He had bought a Ford in Chicago and told his swimmers that he intended for it to be in New York when they got back to transport them to Michigan Avenue along with the medals they won.

At some point another picture would be composed, its intended target not the club magazines with names like *Mercury* or *Winged Foot* but young people looking for generational heroes. Spread along the railing of the SS *America* is a quartet of swimmers — the charismatic and petite diving champion Aileen Riggin, the imposing brothers Duke and David Kahanamoku, and the young superstar Weissmuller. Riggin, sitting on the rail, is camera center, her head tilted slightly, her gaze stylishly disaffected. David kneels below her. Duke, to their right, wears a light-colored suit and tie, his large hands clasped in front of him. Opposite him, on the left, is a cool, matinee-ready Weissmuller, wearing white slacks and the dark tank top of his club, the tri-color IAC emblem on his chest. His posture is slouched, a cowlick shades his eye, and his careless and cocky expression calls to mind the Chicago Nord Seite street kid he once was. The Olympic image of wholesome, Christian values and clean-living amateur endeavor it is not. It is Hollywood; it is new.

FIFTEEN

CITIUS, ALTIUS, FORTIUS
PARIS 1924

"Paris, I can assure you, is one of the best places in the world to be a hero."
—Norman Cleaveland, 1924
U.S. rugby gold medalist

"Johnny Weissmuller's next swimming race will have to be against some fish at catch weights."
—Grantland Rice, *New York Herald Tribune,* July 18, 1924

EVEN BEFORE THE AMERICANS ARRIVED, they were irritating Baron Pierre de Coubertin. Their all-in athletic attitude discounted the Games' loftier ideals, he felt. But there was more. In April the U.S. Olympic Committee had instituted a citizenship rule barring any foreign athlete from competing in American trial races, arguing that foreign teams would benefit from the stiff competition America provided. Arne Borg, the Swedish swimming phenom thought to offer a major challenge to the American sprinters, was in North America at the time, criss-crossing the country from race to race. His plans were suddenly sabotaged. Foreign entrants to the Boston Marathon were told to stay home. A wire-service story began, "America refuses to aid European nations in discovering Olympic athletic talent."

The pledge of chivalry among participating countries — the sporting fellowship the baron yearned for — absorbed more hammer blows. Some members of the U.S. soccer team who were questioned over the validity of their amateur standing threatened to take it up with their foreign accusers as soon as they got off the boat. The U.S. rugby team, forbidden to disembark in Boulogne because of a visa snafu, charged off the ship anyway, scattering the gendarmes. "You watch us," team member Norman Cleaveland remembered saying to one of them, "See if we get off this boat!"

The U.S. contested the French Olympic Committee ruling that awarded exclusive photo rights to French firms. They contested the process by which team points were given, complaining that it favored tiny Finland, whose track-and-field star, Paavo Nurmi, was expected to clean up. They adopted a resolution demanding that bars serving spirits near their athlete quarters be shuttered and signs pointing the way to the pubs be removed. And back in the States, *LIFE Magazine* published its Olympic preview issue featuring a satirical essay about a "Better Olympics." Proposed new events included the Tar and Feather race, in which "groups leave Klan's headquarters, secure a lone victim, carry him five miles beyond city limits, apply a coat of tar and feathers, and return." Points would be deducted if the victim survived.

Even without the long-dead James Sullivan rising from his grave, the Americans were haunting Coubertin.

There were practical worries, too. Though the new electric timing system was tested at the French swim trials, the committee still had not yet made up its mind to use it. The new cork-and-rope lane dividers had their critics, some fearing entanglements and others doubtful they would help reduce water turbulence to produce faster times, as the French organizers promised. Even worse, Piscine des Tourelles, with its basin of steel and a finicky water filtration system, was still not complete.

Though the official opening of the Games wouldn't be until July 5, the rugby and soccer competitions got underway in May. Rugby was chosen to start the Games because of the likelihood of a French victory. On a stormy day, with 40,000 fans in attendance, the gold-medal match between France and the U.S. turned riotous when a free-for-all broke out in the grandstands. Two American students were knocked unconscious when French partisans beat them with walking canes. (*Canne de combat*, or combat cane, was a self-defense demonstration sport in Paris.) "The only way they could get the injured Americans into an ambulance was to bring them onto the field," recalled Cleaveland. "We thought they were dead, and we thought that it was only a matter of time before we would be dead, also."

The heavily favored French lost the match, and the American team was booed during the medal ceremony. Their valuables were then stolen when thieves ransacked the locker room.

A few days later, the U.S. soccer team was jeered mercilessly during its match against Estonia at Pershing Stadium, a site picked as a nostalgic nod to the Yanks who built it in the aftermath of the Great War. The Estonians insisted that the Americans were English professionals, a rumor fueled in the French press. The fans were irate, hurling refuse onto the pitch and grappling with the gendarmes trying to restrain them.

Frustrated shouting matches and fisticuffs reportedly erupted at the Gare Saint-Lazare railway station. As witness to much of the mayhem, Coubertin perhaps understood why his royal parents pined for the order and decorum of the monarchy and prerevolutionary France.

If Coubertin found a shred of hope for the events to come in July, it was in his cherished Contours d'Art, a medal competition among the world's foremost writers, architects, composers, and artists whose submissions had to be inspired by sports. "There is only one difference between our Olympiads and plain sporting championships, and it is precisely the contests of art as they existed in the Olympiads of Ancient Greece, where sport exhibitions walked with equality with artistic exhibitions," he said.

Coubertin had entered the inaugural Contours d'Art in 1912 as the fictitious German duo George Hohrod and Martin Eschbach. He did this, he later explained, to boost the quality of the writing submissions. His "Ode to Sport," a nine-verse prose poem, won literature gold.

The 1924 medal winners included a drawing of a rugby tackle, a sculpture of a discus thrower, and an expressionist painting, *The Liffey Swim*, by Jack Butler Yeats, brother of the famous poet. The painting shows a sprawling Dublin crowd collectively leaning forward to catch sight of swimmers sprinting down the River Liffey. Yeats and literature bronze medal winner Oliver St. John Gogarty would become the answer to the trivia question, who were the first Irishmen to win Olympic medals?

Perhaps the highlight of the Contours d'Art was the Hungarian architectural student Alfréd Hajós, whose rendering of a sports stadium (a subject that continued to preoccupy Coubertin) earned a silver medal. It was the same Hajós, the so-called "Hungarian Dolphin," who barely survived Greece's frozen Bay of Zea to win the first ever 100-meter Olympic swim sprint in

1896. Only one other person would double medal before the arts competition was discontinued in 1948.

———————

WHEN THE U.S. TEAM landed at Cherbourg on June 25, they were in good spirits and relatively healthy. The exception was the coxswain of the four-man rowing crew, John Kennedy, who in an unexpected roll of the boat was grazed in the neck by a wayward round fired during modern pentathlon target practice. His readiness for Olympic competition was questionable. (Another pentathlete, Sidney Hinds, would shoot himself in the foot when a Belgian marksman absently knocked into him. Despite the wound Hinds scored a perfect fifty in the 400-meter event.)

In the excitement of the U.S. team's arrival at Gare Saint-Lazare station, the world record holder in the breaststroke, John Faricy, broke an ankle in an overeager leap to the platform from the still moving train. His IAC teammate Weissmuller jumped off as well, to grab a baguette from an attractive girl selling them, but struck the landing without incident. For the rest of his life, Faricy, whose injury kept him out of the Games, would say the sight of French bread made him ill.

The team suffered another unexpected blow when diver Thomas McKee had to be dropped from the roster after getting in a shipboard altercation with Henry Latham, vice president of the American Olympic Committee.

The Paris correspondents from *L'Auto* and other publications were there to record the American invasion, most of the ink devoted to Duke and Sam Kahanamoku, who serenaded reporters with a quiet and nostalgic song with old country memories "we know nothing about," one wrote. Their ukuleles "filled the air with weird strains of unalloyed jazz and the more subtle

Hawaiian melodies," reported the English language *Paris Times*. Duke looked ageless, the reporters gushed. Weissmuller was likened in appearance to Maurice Chevalier, the handsome French entertainer. He lit up when he saw an American car parked on the street. "I traveled 3,000 miles only to see a Ford on the other end," he said.

The U.S. athletes split up to settle into their lodgings. About 100 of them, including the swimmers, were assigned to Spartan wooden huts at the experimental Olympic Village. "This was decided upon in the interest of goodwill, showing that the United States is not boycotting the official Village," the *Los Angeles Times* reported. After a single night, the rowers from Yale — among them James Rockefeller, athletic scion to the oil magnate John D. Rockefeller — packed up and left for the Hotel Ritz.

Most of the team stayed at the Rocquencourt estate of Prince Joachim Murat, whose great-grandfather fought with Napoleon. The beautiful, wooded grounds and château on the Seine were nine bumpy miles from Colombes stadium and eighteen from the natatorium. American Olympic Association president Robert Thompson, who had secured the rental, stayed in the white colonial main house, with views of Versailles. The rent for two months was a reported $27,000.

Some 200 athletes were housed in wooden barracks erected on Rocquencourt park grounds, which slept two to a room on hard cots. To the annoyance of the veteran athletes, the camp was run military style. A bugler sounded reveille at 7:30 a.m. and lights-out was at 10:30 p.m. Permission had to be granted to leave the camp, and in case an excursion went awry, the athletes had tags hanging from the lapels of their coats that read in French: "I desire to go to the Murat estate at Rocquencourt."

The biggest concern for everyone was water. Fearing illness from the local water, the Americans traveled with their own supply, but it was deemed tainted and U.S. officials had to scramble for a solution. Craems Hammond, head of the medical team, conducted tests to see if the artesian well water at Rocquencourt was safe. On the plus side, the huge crates of shredded wheat and cornflakes had arrived intact. America's hungry athletes were duly photographed tearing into the boxes.

On the first night at Rocquencourt a fire broke out in the surrounding village, the emergency bells and whistle blowing rousing the American camp. The athletes had overwhelmed the electric grid and caused a short circuit that sparked the blaze. Sprinter William Richardson raced to the power station — his fastest 800-meter ever, he said — but a local man had already died trying to cut a live wire. Instead of blaming the athletes for the tragedy, the villagers thanked them for their help and for the $200 donation they made to help the widow. "When the hat was passed everybody gave," said a U.S. coach. The French sporting public, feeling only grievance after the rugby and soccer matches, were chastened.

The American team was led by Lawson Robertson, a Scottish-born athlete and coach who was once celebrated in a Ripley's *Believe It or Not* newspaper column for finishing a 100-yard, three-legged sack race in eleven seconds flat. He wrote his own syndicated column during the Games, providing color commentary on the events and outlining his theories about training. In his most interesting dispatch, he wrote of how he barred athletes from "swimming places" when their contests neared and mandated lumps of sugar as a performance enhancer. Hot baths were verboten ("A hot bath can take more energy and vitality out of a human than six punches on the chin," he wrote.) as were croissants and coffee.

All of the U.S. coaches and officials were on edge about discipline. Rocquencourt was chosen in part because it was far removed from Paris's seductive array of diversions. "I was greatly surprised to see many of the boys smoking during the trip," fretted the Hawaiian team manager, D. L. Conkling, "and drinking was added to smoking as soon as Paris was reached."

The U.S. team's biggest rival, joked Olympic correspondent John O'Brien, was the renowned nightlife district of Montmartre. Olympic-themed events were scheduled at the clubs from midnight to 6:00 a.m., featuring girls in flimsy silk togs racing across dance floors and swimming contests held in tanks filled with champagne instead of water. "Montmartre insists that any athlete who thinks he can play Montmartre's game must play it under Montmartre's grounds, under home rules," wrote O'Brien. "There is no AAU control of the activities on the hill but if one must have initials, Montmartre offers three which are just as formidable as any ever discovered — W.W.S., which is the local abbreviation for wine, women, and song."

All the Americans were forbidden to enter downtown Paris without permission. The track-and-field athletes, whose events were among the first, weren't much of a concern, but the swimmers had weeks until their preliminary heats and would need extra watching.

Duke was only four years removed from his triumphant swim in the Seine. Back then, gossipy Parisian chefs had been agitated when he and Norman Ross had gluttonously eaten through the menu at one restaurant and washed the meal down with beer instead of wine. "Why do they drink beer with all this food?" the maître d' told an AP reporter. "And what's more, right in the middle of the meal, they drank a big bowl of sweet chocolate!" Weissmuller, always eager to do everything Duke had done first and already known for rascal tendencies, was considered a prime risk the moment the lights were turned off.

As if to forestall trouble, the swim team joined most of the

American contingent and thousands of tourists at the Auteuil racetrack on June 27 for the high-fashion event of the season, the Prix des Drags steeplechase. Parisian fashionistas shone in the midday summer sun. Rapt spectators followed female attendees who arrived in horse-drawn carriages that rolled along a carpet to deliver the women to a private gathering at the track's Roman Pavilion. The race was an afterthought. "Translucent gowns revealed the fact that the women were wearing nothing except slip gowns, chemises . . . molded themselves over the figure as though they were painted on, betraying every line and curve," wrote *Chicago Tribune* correspondent Henry Wales, seemingly happy to be off his political affairs beat.

As much as Paris disparaged their American visitors, it held only love for the Japanese, whose art and aesthetics had influenced their own for a half century. The affair dated back to the Paris exposition of 1867, the first time French designers and the public saw the expressive woodblock prints and paintings of *ukiyo-e* masters. A decade later the Japonisme movement was all the rage in Paris. It was "no longer a fashion, it's infatuation, it's insanity," wrote the French critic Ernest Chesneau. In the 1920s the assimilation of Japanese art was everywhere, in Hermès tea sets and handbags, Coco Chanel kimono-style capes, and Louis Vuitton steamer trunks. The city's most famous bohemian artist was the painter Tsuguharu Foujita, the son of an Imperial Army general, whose free-flowing lifestyle and outrageous getups made him and his Montparnasse studio at no. 5 rue Delambre a place of pilgrimage. Foujita neither accepted nor rejected Western art but liberally borrowed from it while maintaining the essence of the Japanese aesthetic. In a way, Sugimoto and Takaishi, consciously or not, mirrored the approach in swimming. The modest concrete confines of a pool didn't have the sexy allure of a studio occupied by a slight, bespectacled painter in a tank top and surrounded by voluptuous nude models (often holding fluffy calico cats), but athlete and coach knew their crawl interpretation would soon cause a sensation.

A Japanese visitor to Paris just off the boat and taking even a short walk about the city would have felt more than welcome. They belonged, and the pop cultural love affair was mutual. (French music and movies had a grasp on young people in Tokyo and Osaka, inspiring inventive Japanese interpretations.)

The Japanese community in Paris — embassy attachés, artists, students — came out in force to greet the team when they arrived on June 7. A chef from the Ris Japanese Club was hired to prepare their meals. The team settled into quarters in the Olympic Village, a photo from one of the rooms showing a quartet of athletes seated on a cot below a portrait of a French actress. An American wire-service correspondent strolling around the village seemed to possess a wary attitude about the Japanese that was prevalent in the U.S. He expressed surprise that the team hadn't made their corner of the village into a nationalistic Little Japan as everyone supposed they would.

By the time the six Japanese swimmers started training, they had a two-week head start on the U.S. contingent. They had morning and afternoon sessions in Piscine de Tourelles, and dry-land workouts. Once all the teams were in town, the swimmers numbered 400-plus, and the congested daily schedule allowed for a single one-hour training session per team in the week prior to the early eliminations. Aileen Riggin recalled that divers and swimmers trained simultaneously. "Every time I took a dive," she said, "I was afraid of landing on Johnny Weissmuller."

When the U.S. team arrived, Takaishi and his teammates gravitated to the Hawaiians, led by the Kahanamoku brothers, who brought their ukuleles to the pool deck, singing and playing between their heats. The wrestler Katsutoshi Naito, who attended Penn State but would compete for Japan, noticed the uneasiness the Japanese felt around the rest of the U.S. team. On July 1, Congress had passed the Johnson-Reed Act, which tightened the visa quota system and ended the gentlemen's agreement that allowed Japanese immigrants to naturalize in the U.S. Ongoing anti-American protests in Japan intensified. On July 2, an Osaka man targeted the U.S. Embassy in Tokyo, stealing the American flag that flew outside the building. "Japan must never forget July 1 when America inflicted an intolerable insult," read a popular placard distributed across the country. "Hate everything American," the populace was told.

By contrast, Sugimoto, always open-minded, looked at the American contingent with admiration. He loved the old cars that delivered the U.S. swimmers to the stadium, dozens of male and female athletes in white robes spilling out to commandeer the pool deck. "Two thirty-seater vans with as many as sixty American swimmers arrive and it is astonishing," he recalled. "The head coach Bachrach is wearing wooden shoes [a trendy fashion item in 1920s New York]. The athletes are swimming beautifully. In particular, Weissmuller's swimming is indeed superb. His hand pitch is slow, but his swim leaves a single white line like a boat would leave behind. Kahanamoku, on one side, swims with a ferocious look. It is a spectacular scene to see a dozen or more swimming side by side behind these two swimmers."

Sugimoto was also impressed by the confidence of the Swedish. The middle-distance gold-medal favorite, Arne Borg, caught him by surprise when he asked, point blank, who his fastest swimmer was. Borg said he'd like to invite that person to an impromptu 800-meter training race. Sugimoto was too stunned to answer but Borg spotted Takaishi in the pool and said, "Must be him." Borg was coming off a celebrated worldwide exhibition tour during which Bill Bachrach offered him a spot on the

IAC squad (which Borg would take after the Games). Takaishi had been swimming for forty-one days in a shipboard canvas tank with a rope harness tied to his waist. Still, he took Borg's challenge. Somebody said "ready, set, go!" and the two were off. The duo swam stroke for stroke for two lengths of the pool, then the next 100 meters and, remarkably, the next. "The two swimmers fought a close battle as if they were weighing each other's abilities," said Sugimoto. At the 600-meter mark, and still even, Takaishi pulled up. "Okay enough, I'm tired!" he said. This pioneering breed of Japanese crawl swimmers will be factors in the Games, Borg declared. Louis Handley, the women's coach, also noted the change. "They have made enormous strides since the Games in 1920 at Antwerp, when their obsolete methods were a matter of amused comment," he said, adding that the Japanese had mimicked the American crawl stroke.

From the first sighting of champion swimmers at the Olympic pool, debate swirled among onlookers, media, and coaches about what the athletes were doing and why, and who was responsible for the crawl stroke that made men and women into torpedoes and flying fish. There were chats about starts and turns and the beat count of fluttering feet: Was it six per stroke, or could it be eight or ten or even twelve?

And what about breathing? Bachrach had recently published a column about a breathing method used in the crawl stroke and employed by Weissmuller in which four breaths were taken every three or four strokes instead of one. In photos accompanying the article, Weissmuller posed with inflated cheeks then with lips pursed, pushing out the air. He looked like Chaplin in gag mode. Bachrach said Weissmuller proved his theory that the more air you got, the stronger in the water you would be. Also, the Bachrach Breath had a nice alliterative ring to it.

The cognoscenti theorized about starting blocks, first used at the trials in Indianapolis. Bachrach's hunch was that the launch angle provided by blocks would result in faster times, though the innovation wouldn't be introduced at the Olympics until 1936. They speculated about starts. A prominent San Francisco swim instructor had recently unveiled a starting technique that involved windmilling the arms before diving. Whether done from the pool deck or a raised block, the motion was claimed to generate kinetic forces that propelled the body forward before it hit the water. The momentum created by the dive could keep a racer in underwater glide mode for some thirty feet. The trick was to start whirling the arms at "ready" and have them extended forward at "go." It took some practice.

Theories differed about optimum water temperature and lane dividers. Some doubted the French assertion that the rope dividers, which were suspended with cork, helped to dissipate water turbulence that slowed swimmers. The utility of dividers made pragmatic sense but the snafus at the U.S. trials, where multiple swimmers, including Weissmuller, got entangled like fish in a net, made everybody nervous. Swimmers who failed to qualify because of their collisions with lane dividers futilely lobbied for an exemption.

Eventually, the long days at the pool and longer nights at the cafés led to the one topic nobody could agree on: Who was responsible for where the swimming world stood in 1924, on the cusp of breaking records once thought to be beyond human possibility? It was a highly partisan conversation dominated by the acclaimed Western triumvirate Britain, America, and Australia.

In an article Bachrach wrote for the *Tri-Color*, Weissmuller had credited Handley, coach of the New York Athletic Club swim team, for his winning crawl stroke. The timing raised eyebrows. Handley was a well-respected, much-published coach primarily credited for developing champion female competitors. The article came out in late 1921, which was shortly after Bachrach returned from the Belgium Games he had not initially been invited to. Was it a quid pro quo; a thank you to the East Coast power brokers who had finally agreed to add him to the Olympic coaching roster? They would have cared deeply about getting credit for the revolution in swimming.

Lulls in the various swimming debates were likely filled with local gossip. Amid the inflated prices and tourist mobs, some French residents fled Paris until the Olympics were over. Ernest Hemingway, then a short-story writer and correspondent for the *Toronto Star*, was one of them. He went to Pamplona, Spain, for the running of the bulls, where he and fellow American expatriate writer Donald Ogden Stewart managed to get into the ring and were subsequently gored and hospitalized. Stewart had intended to mimic the native bull riders who played leapfrog and other daring games with the beasts, telling Hemingway beforehand he planned to blow smoke into his opponent's eyes before he rode him. But while he collected the toreador's red cape in the infield prior to the ride, the bull caught sight of scarlet and madly charged Stewart, throwing him high and far and cracking several of his ribs.

———————

AT THE START OF OPENING CEREMONIES on the morning of July 5, a duo of French flyers piloting a biplane and a rattling floatplane zoomed down on sunny Colombes stadium. It was an ode to the modern aviation age and the adventurous strivings of the great republics. Aeronauts were crossing continents seemingly every day, each setting records for duration and speed. The French held many of them. American flyers had just touched Japanese soil for the first time. But crashes were also commonplace, the public knew.

When the planes, with "motors crackling like machine guns," in the words of the *Chicago Tribune*'s Henry Wales, strafed the packed arena, the taller athletes on the infield wheeled around to corral lost straw hats, and others let out half screams. The planes came in so fast and so low — at the request of motion picture cameramen — a fiery crash looked inevitable. Douglas Fairbanks was said to have held Mary Pickford a little tighter as the planes dive-bombed. In boxes nearby sat the Prince of Wales; the new French president, Gaston Doumergue; and Ethiopia's Crown Prince, Haile Selassie, wearing a flowing white robe and a look of apprehension.

The Parade of Nations that followed settled the crowd. Some 3,000 athletes from forty-five nations (up from twenty-nine at the 1920 Games) strode in alphabetic order past the dignitaries' box, the overflowing stands, and hundreds of photographers and foreign correspondents, the redoubtable Grantland Rice of the *New York Herald Tribune* chief among them. Great Britain entered with its women's delegation in white flannel skirts, leading the main body of men and the kilt-wearing Cameron Highlander pipers. The United States, twice as big as any other delegation, spooled out in endless ranks before some 5,000 screaming American fans. Wearing blue blazers and crisp white slacks and skirts, the Yanks stretched the full length of the straightaway on the quarter-mile cinder track, plus a turn. The coaches, trainers, and masseuses alone dwarfed the tiniest delegations, such as the two-person China team.

Japan's small group, in silk hats and waving Prince Chichibu's imperial flag, entered the stadium to approving nods from the French spectators. That very day, the prince had criticized the Tokyo police, who had barred the public from seeing Rodin's *The Kiss*, part of a French exhibit at the National Museum. Chichibu viewed the work as beautiful, he said, and Japanese moralistic censures as silly. The French now had one more reason to love all things Japanese.

The long ceremony continued. Three 200-piece military orchestras, along with French and Czechoslovakian choirs, launched into the "La Marseillaise." "Automatically, your hand goes to your hat and you rise to your feet," wrote the *Outlook* magazine correspondent Elon Jessup. "Standing at attention, a little shiver runs up and down your spine. How could it be otherwise?"

The white-bearded president of the French Olympic Committee, Count Justinien de Clary, stood at a high podium draped with the Olympic flag and emphatically welcomed the world to Paris. President Doumergue, in a tidy fifty-one words, then declared the Games of the VIIIth Olympiad open. Artillery fire from French 75 field guns boomed, the smoke remnants floating into the hot summer sky like wispy doodles in a dreamy student's notebook. Minutes later the thud and boom were replaced with giggly merriment as athletes bent over wicker baskets to release 2,000 carrier pigeons that were dispatched to their respective home countries with news that the Games had begun. With a whoosh, the birds rose in a flapping cloud, then re-oriented themselves and headed in every direction at a streamlined fifty miles per hour. Georges André, a French fighter pilot in the Great War and a champion hurdler and rugby player, earnestly read the Olympic oath to clean sport and high-minded behavior, written by Coubertin. The French applauded politely, apparently now brimming with goodwill after the rugby and soccer debacles.

However, when competition began the following day, it did not proceed with the order, dignity, and exalted purpose Coubertin had hoped for. Fights broke out in the stands, and defeated athletes refused to respectfully doff their caps when opposing flags flew at award ceremonies. Players threatened walkouts over suspect judging and, in the case of the tennis players, who wore all white, the absence of laundry service and shower facilities. The nastiest display came when members of the Italian fencing team, convinced they had been robbed by partisan French officials, stormed out of the stadium, madly gesturing, singing a nationalistic hymn and raising arms in a fascist salute. Later, Italy's Oreste Puliti, a saber medal favorite, challenged the Hungarian judge who disqualified him to a duel. *The Times* of London pronounced the whole Olympic experiment a failure that exacerbated "international bitternesses instead of soothing them." After an altercation at the boxing ring, Britain hinted it might not return to the Games in 1928.

There were glimmers of magic, especially from the brilliant collection of American and British sprinters. The voluble Charley Paddock made an unexpected return to form after a disastrous 100-meter race, finishing in a near dead heat with teammate Jackson Scholz for 200-meter gold, his desperate leap for the tape falling just short but earning stadium-wide applause as he was helped off the track with a broken ankle. The Scotch Presbyterian minister Eric Liddell, who scratched from his favored race, the 100-meter, because he refused to compete on a Sunday, waged a storybook, against-the-odds comeback in the 400, where he said he felt the glory of God in every stride. Those types of stories sang to Coubertin and American YMCA officials like Franklin Brown, who cheered in his late brother's absence. But each tale of character and spirit was overshadowed by the baser, more regrettable side of human nature.

Gambling was rampant. Some of the American rugby players — Norman Cleaveland and others wouldn't say who — took the five-to-one odds in their title game against France. A Berkeley gentleman who had put $5,000 on the Americans to win left cases of champagne in their locker room as a thank you. As Cleaveland said, there was nothing like being in Paris and being a hero. He, for one, was having such a good time, he stayed when his teammates sailed home, chopping wood and doing odd jobs at the American camp at Château de Rocquencourt. Like most everyone else, he fell in with the Hawaiians, especially Duke, with whom he would stay close.

By the time the swimming preliminaries began in early July, the chaos had died down. Coubertin would remember those days fondly because nothing went especially wrong, and the crowds, including his fellow Frenchmen, were mostly well-behaved. He could almost forgive the Americans their gaudy take of nine of eleven swimming gold medals.

———

AS JOHNNY WEISSMULLER AND DUKE KAHANAMOKU'S qualifying events approached, the buzz intensified over who would prevail. The cartoonists had a field day. Feg Murray, a former swimmer and a Los Angeles–based illustrator who was friendly with both men, sketched furiously throughout the spring, at one point posing the question, "Another job for Mr. Solomon: Weissmuller or Duke, which was it, how could anybody decide?" He imagined the two matched against each other on the golf course. Duke made a hole in one, Johnny did not. Another cartoon depicted Fred Cady and Bill Bachrach at loggerheads beneath a text bubble that read, "The greatest swimmer the world has ever known."

Magazines and newspapers were obsessed with the swimmers' physical numbers — height, reach, and chest size. Weissmuller had smaller feet: size ten and a half to Kahanamoku's thirteen. The defending Olympic champ had larger hands, too. At nine-and-a-half inches long, they were bigger than a much taller man's. Future high-flying dunkers like Wilt Chamberlain and Dr. J had similar sized hands but were seven-foot-one and six-seven, respectively. Kahanamoku was barely six-two. The fascination with Duke's hands was such that an avid memorabilia collector considered a hastily drawn outline of them on lined notebook paper his most cherished Kahanamoku artifact.

Both Weissmuller and Kahanamoku shared the perfect body proportions of long upper torsos and comparatively short legs, which made for less water resistance. Their wingspan, commonly the same length as a person's height, exceeded the average. Longer arms equated to longer distance per stroke. People were still not clear on what truly governed speed — early crawl adoptees mistakenly emphasized a fast, windmilling stroke — but it eventually would be apparent that stroke length, along with stroke frequency, produced momentum.

At the Battle Creek Sanitarium in Michigan, John Harvey Kellogg created a series of shadowgraph images of Weissmuller and proclaimed he had never seen a more perfectly aligned body, with hips and shoulders on the same parallel line. On one image, taken in profile, Kellogg drew a head-to-toe vertical line and relational degree angles to show Weissmuller's flawless posture, pelvic obliquity, chest ratio, and head tilt. God couldn't possibly make a better example of a human being, he announced. As if to prove Kellogg's point, an illustrator in Chicago drew Johnny as a heroic sculpture, like Michelangelo's *David*.

Kellogg observed another trait that distinguished Weissmuller: a playfulness, a lightness about him that he didn't see in other test subjects like Amos Alonzo Stagg's bulky football players. "He takes his work as a skylark, he spoofs it, kids it, jokes with it," said Kellogg. After one record-setting performance that

Kellogg saw, Weissmuller celebrated by fooling around in the water like a sea otter for a delighted audience. At Battle Creek, he romped around the cavernous campus gymnasium playing indoor baseball, running bases and lunging for ground balls. "The capacity to be happy is perhaps an art, but any rate is a tonic, and no doubt in Johnny's case it has a good deal to do with his success," said Kellogg.

How fast the two swimmers could push each other was the question. It hit upon a larger question that pervaded all human exploits, from running to flying to auto racing to mountain climbing: What was the limit of possibility? At that very moment, British alpinists George Mallory and Andrew Irvine were clawing their way up Mount Everest, the world's tallest peak, despite the prevailing belief that no one could survive the upper reaches where life-sustaining oxygen was scarce.

Anything was possible in the record-setting age, and pools were where some of it happened. Twenty years earlier, before the crawl was universally adopted, the barrier to be broken was 100 yards in one minute. Weissmuller was threatening to break fifty seconds, slicing through water at a rate of speed akin to runners circling a park. Running and swimming were interchangeable. Humans had been land animals but they were something else now.

The wild card in the coming showdown was Weissmuller himself. Could he stay out of trouble? On the team's first day in Paris, shortly after stepping off the train, Weissmuller had heard an anti-American jeer from a passing bicycle rider. He chased after the man, dragging him to the ground and badly beating him. He was called before U.S. Olympic Committee officials the next day, and only because of Bachrach's persuasive defense did he avoid being sent home. General Douglas MacArthur, overseeing military members of the U.S. team, wasn't pleased. Just before they had disembarked the SS *America,* he had sternly reminded everybody aboard: "Now remember you are ambassadors of the United States, and we expect you to behave accordingly."

Idle time was nobody's ally. Château de Rocquencourt was far from anywhere. The Olympic Village, "an army cantonment without any soldiers," in one writer's words, looked like a dusty Old West outpost — a smattering of shacks, roads without sidewalks, dirt yards. Every day the swim team left the Piscine des Tourelles for lunch at Gruber's American Café, where they returned for dinner following the afternoon training session. Rarely was the team happy with the food or the service, and in the kitchen, the waitstaff grumbled, too.

To pass the time, the Americans bet on wrestling matches. The favorite pairing was the champion swimmer Gertrude Ederle (soon to become famous for being the first woman to swim the English Channel) and the runner Joseph "Joie" Ray, who drove a cab for a living. The U.S. officials eventually found out and put a stop to the matches. Aware of the urgent need of more positive distraction, a subcommittee headed by Robert Thompson's daughter, Sarah Pell, arranged motion picture shows and small concerts for the athletes.

There were numerous formal events where the swim team was expected to be polished representatives of their country. They were feted at the Place de la Concorde and did water stunts at the Sporting Club. There were hundreds of ways for a twenty-year-old star to make the wrong kind of news. Bachrach and company simply held their breath.

The Hawaiians didn't cause the same anxiety, though Duke did raise eyebrows when he expensed the team for guitar strings and $7.50 worth of flowers sent to a "Mrs. Henry." Mistaken for a paramour, Madge "Ma" Henry had come to Paris with her sixteen-year-old son Thomas, hoping to cheer their adoptive family member to victory.

IT WAS NOT WHAT the French paying public expected, but judging by their reactions they couldn't get enough. It was mid-July, a few days after the preliminary qualifying swim heats had gotten underway. This early in the competition, the stands weren't full. Loudspeakers directed eyes to the man on the diving board: It was Weissmuller, long and supple in his club bathing suit, pantomiming to a passerby to encourage the man to clamber up and join him. The man, with a cane and a rheumatoid hobble, was wearing a convict's striped uniform with a ribboned medal pinned to his chest. It was Weissmuller's good friend and Chicago teammate Harold "Stubby" Kruger, the backstroke world-record holder. In their slapstick act, introduced months earlier in exhibitions in the States, Stubby pretended to faint, fell off the board, then sank to the pool bottom as the hero preened above him, oblivious. When Weissmuller breezily looked down, Kruger was nowhere to be found; when he looked away, Kruger was back up, dog-paddling for his life. Asked about his act, which he would reprise thousands of times in his career as a performer at water carnivals, Kruger explained, "By watching people at the beaches, the ridiculous things they do without realizing it, that's how I get my stuff."

The crowd was in hysterics, and Johnny and Stubby were instantly the most popular act this side of the Negro dance review at the Folies Bergère.

It was hard to know what their competitors made of the act, which hijacked the spotlight they'd worked for years to earn. It blurred the crisp line between entertainment and amateur endeavor and could have easily been slotted in at the faux

Olympics at Montmartre, maybe after the showgirls' dance-floor dash and before the champagne swim races. Another coach might have stopped it, but Bachrach wasn't another coach. He was soon fielding offers from across Europe, locking in dates in Amsterdam, Magdeburg, Prague, Vienna, Graz, and Budapest. After the Olympics, Bachrach and his two IAC stars would set off on their vaudeville tour. In Budapest the duo's performance and extended encore went on so long that darkness descended, canceling the scheduled swimming exhibitions. One reporter, anticipating the unceasing demand once the troupe returned to the States, wrote: "Barnum & Bailey please take note."

Pierre de Coubertin, witnessing the distracting sideshow at Tourelles, found himself in the familiar position of hating what Americans were doing with his Olympics. Once savored by the delighted French customers, it was impossible to take this treat off the menu. The act was drawing fans, and the Games hadn't been doing as well at the gate as expected. So the Yanks on stage and the customers in their seats got their laughs, and the baron died a little more. A measure of his revulsion was that this would be the first and last Olympic comedy revue. The prospect of a reprise in 1928 was eliminated when a new IOC bylaw restricted athletes to racing only, barring them from clowning extracurricular entertainment.

In the early rounds of swimming, news wasn't made by the Americans, Swedes, or Australians, all of whom advanced as expected, but by the Japanese and British. Both turned heads but for opposite reasons. The British, the original record setters of modern times, had faded faster than anyone thought likely. The Japanese had reversed their fortunes, having dramatically changed everything in a comparative heartbeat — their anti-quated strokes and breathing techniques, their unshakable belief in the old ways. As they watched the Japanese during training sessions, British experts admitted they were impressed and predicted they would have to look out for them at the next Olympic Games in four years' time. Instead the early results suggested something unthinkable: They had to look out right now.

Kazuo Onoda, the Tokyo swimmer and team captain, was forecasted as Japan's top medal hopeful, having broken all the sprint records in his events at the Far Eastern Games with times, his coaches said, that were not far behind Weissmuller and other leading crawl strokers. In the opening round of qualifiers in the first middle distance event, the grueling 1,500-meter, the unknown Takaishi had not only advanced but swam faster than the favored British. He and his teammates didn't lift their arms out of the water like Westerners did to extend for the "catch" but instead dropped their hands earlier, skillfully pressing against the water and using the movement to decrease effort. They swam lower in the water than the Americans, their backs less arched. Observers assumed the Japanese swimmers, lighter and more agile, had to move their arms and legs faster to keep up, but that theory was quickly dispelled. Westerners moved their arms and feet at the same rate if not faster. They didn't swim in a flat body position, the norm believed to ease resistance. Theirs was a technique that was beyond the bounds of Western how-to books — it wasn't Western at all. There were other noticeable differences: Takaishi's arms stayed closer to the body, his trunk rolled more softly, his shoulders drew perfect ellipses. Years before, Japanese experts asked, How do we teach a new generation to swim faster? Sugimoto pondered the question, contrasting the mechanics of the crawl with the samurai era sidestroke used at the 1920 Olympics. After attending a four-week Ministry of Education seminar in Chiba, Japan, and concluding that the fastest swimming stroke combined elements of old and new, he exclaimed, "Now I know how to teach."

The Aussies watched Takaishi and saw something un-orthodox. One Australian reporter argued that his flutter kick couldn't account for his speed, given he had small feet and hands "of which any woman would feel proud." He was clearly double-jointed, which was an advantage. The Australian news-papers would mix admiration with racist stereotypes when Takaishi visited the Commonwealth two years later. The White Australia policy had long barred immigration of Asians and Pa-cific Islanders. Swimmer Noel Ryan wrote in a coaching bulletin, "[the] Japanese crawl was aided by natural looseness and devel-opment of the thighs and ankles — probably made so strong and supple by centuries of squatting around the communal rice bowl." Japanese swimmers were said to wear a four-inch-wide sheath of black silk hidden beneath their singlets and wrapped mummy-like around their midsections. The Japanese form was a conundrum to students of natatorial knowledge, the Aussies said, contrary to accepted doctrines and born from a place they didn't know.

In reality, Sugimoto was overwhelmed, at least at first. The American presence was powerful — their size, their numbers, and, as he observed, "their matching bathrobes with big Amer-ican flags in the center."

But as his team continued to log impressive times, Sugimo-to's confidence returned. Their work and sacrifice and natural fighting spirit, the flowering of a group project they had col-lectively started, gave him faith, as did the crowd's reaction to Takaishi in particular. His form was marvelous, his agility and flexibility evoking muscle and sinew rather than stiff skeletal framing. He didn't require freakish hands the size of dinner plates and feet like fins. Takaishi, like many Japanese swim-mers to follow, excelled in leg strength, footwork, intuitive feel through the water, and the mental fortitude of "overcoming oneself." The fans threw their support behind the small outlier they couldn't explain but couldn't help but root for.

Years later Kazuo Onoda would himself marvel at his close friend in a memorial poem written after Takaishi's death. "Dear Kacchan, your eyes of a fight . . . the eyes of a friend who speaks to us . . . even now, those eyes are looking at me somewhere . . . ." The nickname Kacchan, a conjunction of Takaishi's first name and the honorific "chan," was one ascribed to a small boy.

At the same time the modernist Japanese swimmers were preparing for the final rounds and Takaishi's likely historic appearance in the 1,500 final on July 13, the old ways continued to prevail a long ocean voyage away. In a circumnavigation of Lake Biwa (the headwaters for the boyhood river where Takaishi first swam), acclaimed distance swimmer Setsu Nishimura used classic martial strokes to softly tread water while blowing a trumpet. Fans onshore cheered wildly.

———————

"NINETY IN THE SHADE IS JUST WHAT WE NEED to boil out the boys and bring them to condition," Lawson Robertson had said when the U.S. team arrived in France amidst a broiling heatwave. The heat was still unrelenting a month later. Temperatures above ninety degrees were expected to continue through the 100-meter freestyle qualifying heats early on Saturday, July 19, and the Sunday afternoon final. Sunday would feature six blockbuster races, from the punishing half mile to the 100-meter sprints. The finals would recognize individual excellence but also determine which locale — Chicago, Hawaii, Sweden, Australia, or the dark horse, Japan — could claim to be swimming's innovative center, the last word on a stroke that brought speed and beauty to a postwar world that was joyously drunk with both.

On the last day of qualifiers, the Hawaiians had come through as usual. Warren Kealoha smashed his own Olympic record in the 100-meter backstroke, finishing in 1:13.2. "When the dark-skinned swimmer came out of the pool someone hurled a wreath over his neck such as the girls of Waikiki are supposed to wear," reported the *Paris Times*.

Saturday's first semifinal heat featured Duke and Sam Kahanamoku along with Takaishi, who had won his quarter-final heat earlier in the day by two seconds. It was hard to not be in awe of the Hawaiians — Duke, tall and muscled, Sam, strong and supple and easy to imagine atop a whipping surfboard. (As a surfer, Sam was said to have no equal.) Their power was magnified by their togetherness. At an earlier heat featuring the Waikiki star sprinter Mariechen Wehselau, all the Hawaiians collected along the pool rail, cheering her on. A rotund, spectacled official in a dark suit stood behind them, gripping a stopwatch on a gold chain. Wehselau, hearing the cheers, didn't do the expected thing and swim just hard enough to qualify, saving herself for the final. She decided to let it go, full gas, like a young Duke performing for his long-ago audience, Queen Lili'uokalani. Wehselau touched out in 1:12.40, a world record, ten seconds faster than the British runner-up. "Congratulations, sausage," wrote her coach, George Center, in a telegram. He later explained that Wehselau hated the nickname, but he didn't want her to get all "puffed up."

The start of the men's 100-meter freestyle semifinal heat was clean, with Duke getting a superb launch, diving low and shallow and already on his first stroke when his brother and Takaishi were still airborne, their feet pressed tightly in perfect form, like drag-resistant fins.

Duke easily held the lead and was the first to qualify for the Sunday afternoon final. But the race behind him was desperately fought, Sam and Takaishi swimming stroke for stroke for second place. Only the top two finishers would advance to the final. Sugimoto, distracted, briefly turned away as he checked his stopwatch. Takaishi slipped off the pace and fell to fourth. But he surged again, taking back third place and reeling in Sam. They hit the wall seemingly together, but Sam was a couple tenths of a second faster. Sugimoto proudly described Takaishi's efforts as pioneering. He said that, for the first time, the Japanese belonged next to the others. Takaishi's time was within 2/100s of Duke's Olympic record in 1920. To the 5,000 spectators, the finish looked like a dead heat. They both deserved to race for the gold.

As it turned out, Takaishi did get another chance. After the six automatic qualifiers, the two fastest times of the three semifinals heats were awarded wildcard spots. Takaishi's 1:02.4 was faster than anyone else's, including the other wildcard winner, Arne Borg, who lost to Weissmuller in their heat.

Whatever happened for Takaishi in Sunday's final, it almost didn't matter. Japan was assured of winning its first-ever Olympic point in swimming, in the premier sprint event, and, more importantly, earning its place as a rising power. None of the other individual Japanese swimmers advanced, including Onoda, but the relay team in the 4-by-200 did and finished fourth in the finals, beating Great Britain by fifteen seconds. In the 1,500-meter semifinal, Takaishi led Borg, the world record holder, at the 600-meter mark and again at the 800-meter. Then Borg came to the front with the Aussie Frank Beaurepaire. Takaishi stayed close. French spectators roared for Takaishi, who kicked past Borg to finish second. The crowd never stopped applauding, Sugimoto would say later. "They filled the swimming pool with cheers of, 'Bravo Japan, Takaishi!'"

Takaishi led his team to do what no Asian swimmers had

done before: perform competitively at the Olympics. Ultimately he would collect eight points and would be shortlisted as a true contender in the next Games, in Amsterdam, something that had once been unthinkable. As he knew well, they weren't even supposed to be here.

When he was asked how they had done the impossible and risen from nowhere, he opted for silence. He shared nothing about what had brought his team here: Yokohama in 1898. Elwood Brown and Kanō Jigorō. The enduring heritage of *Nihon eiho*. The pool dug by him and his fellow barefoot students. The Far Eastern Games in 1923 in Osaka. He said nothing about Sugimoto, perhaps because his coach thought the mystery and mystique might not be a bad thing to let linger. *How had they learned to swim so fast?* They had no coaches, said Takaishi, they only read books.

And the swimming world shuddered. Imagine, one Australian expert wrote, what will happen when they take the next step. Would the next 100-meter milestone fall to Takaishi, not the giant, Weissmuller? Could all that they thought they knew be wrong? Would the most sophisticated form of the crawl not be Aussie, or American, or even Hawaiian? Would the fastest stroke known to man soon be the Japanese crawl?

Back in Japan, the full measurement of Takaishi's achievements would take time to be appreciated since they were briefly overshadowed by the country's lone medal winner, the Penn State wrestler Katsutoshi Naito, who won bronze despite an injured hand. The returning team was celebrated at a slate of formal dinners, and Takaishi readied for a new semester at Waseda. He had new goals, he said, most of which included faster split times in the pool and upcoming benchmark competitive events where he might race against Weissmuller.

But that was not all. Takaishi had another goal, one that

surprised an older colleague, a sensei of the classical noncompetitive swimming arts. "He asked me to teach him *Nihon eiho*," said Kato Ishio. He wasn't always going to be fast, Takaishi told him, but with *Nihon eiho* he was assured he would swim forever.

———

AT 2:00 P.M. ON SUNDAY, JULY 20, the sold-out crowd of 12,000 were in the seats, waiting on the dark-suited French race official to raise his start gun. The lineup of finalists curled their toes at the edge of the pool and assumed a slight crouch. Photographers piled on top of each other in a front-row box beneath the diving platform, and motion picture operators worked the deck. Radio Paris's Edmond Dehorter, nicknamed "Le Parleur Inconnu" (the unknown speaker), was safely set up. He had been banned at the start of the Games when print reporters protested his "unfair advantage" in broadcasting live, but Dehorter would not be denied, squeezing his ample body into a hot-air-balloon basket to produce windy, bird's-eye view commentary of the track-and-cycling events at Colombes. Now free to do as he pleased, the bow-tied Dehorter sat behind a plate-sized microphone mounted on a sturdy tripod. Four large loudspeakers lined the upper stadium wall. The French had reserved the 100-meter race for the last two days of competition for the self-evident reason that "in swimming, as in all sports, speed is king."

Count Clary, his great grey beard spooling to midchest, was in attendance, as was Coubertin, the two Frenchmen having already sat through three renditions of "The Star-Spangled Banner" and three American flag raisings since morning. In one of the most U.S.–dominant days in Olympic history, the Americans had won three consecutive races, taking gold in the freestyle relay, the 100-meter women's backstroke, and the 100-meter women's freestyle and winning all but one of the other six medals.

"Looks like an American holiday," said Clary to the American VIPs in attendance. Many of the track-and-field athletes who competed in the weeks earlier had gone home, glad to leave their austere army cots behind, but some had stayed to see the reprise of the battle of the century. The American camp-maintenance guru and rugby gold medalist, Norman Cleaveland, had stayed around with the apparently unrealized dream of a midnight journey up a Paris flagpole to swipe an Olympic flag.

The French literary set continued to furiously write, inspired by author and fellow countryman Henry de Montherlant, who rhapsodically asserted that the Games represented something beyond physical skill. "Performance satisfies the mind," he wrote in his essay collection *Les Olympiques*, "style does good in the whole being, in its fabric, in its channels, in its roots. Style is the caress of sport."

If Bachrach was concerned that the Kahanamoku brothers would race as a team to defeat Weissmuller, someone had taken care of it by putting Sam in lane one. Johnny and Duke were next to one another in lanes four and five. There was no evidence that the brothers would have engaged in cynical tactics if the trio were clumped together — for example, Sam and Duke squeezing Johnny by boxing him in and disrupting his stroke. There was no history of such behavior by either brother — or any of the Hawaiians — but having Sam unavailable to help his brother was a boon to Weissmuller's positive race psychology. Nervous by nature before a race, Weissmuller could relax knowing the biggest doomsday scenario was erased.

There was a bigger concern, though. Exhaustion. The 400-meter final on Friday had required a Weissmuller effort few had seen before. He had been taken to the limit by Arne Borg and the Aussie Andrew Charlton. He had gathered himself for a triumphant come-from-behind sprint in the final 100 meters, but at an obvious cost. As he posed for photographers, he needed to clutch hold of the guard rope to keep from falling over. In a photo with Charlton, Weissmuller looks spent, arms limply hanging, shoulders slumped, eyes glazed. Inches away lay Borg in an exhausted heap, surrounded by doctors and officials. For Weissmuller, it was the same feeling he had at Lake Decatur a year earlier that landed him in a Chicago hospital.

Weissmuller was also anxious about how the crowd would receive him. They ran hot and cold, howling at his comedic antics but hissing when he disrespected his competitors. In the 400-meter preliminaries he had drawn the fans' ire when he waved his hands around on the final lap to, in the words of the Paris *Times*, "show how easily he was taking it."

He had no time to recover, given Saturday's 100-meter freestyle prelims and the 4-by-200 freestyle relay final. In the latter he didn't have the strongest team to support him. A core group of Chicago-based swimmers replaced the Hawaiians like Duke who had helped win gold for the U.S. in 1920. Still, Weissmuller managed to swim a blistering anchor leg to record a new world-record time.

The three Americans knew a good start couldn't win the 100-meter race but a bad start could lose it. Duke tended to project more steeply downward, eager to get into the water and begin stroking. Johnny liked to lay out, stretching his long body for as long as it could fly. Moments before he hit the water he didn't appear to be diving at all; he held his line as straight as a pencil, then dropped his head and angled down, smacking the water with hands, arms, torso, and legs in what he and Bachrach described as a "shallow plunge." The pancake landing prevented his body from going as deep as most other swimmers at the start. His slightly bent right leg was poised to kick at the same instant he landed.

He was a notoriously slow starter. Bachrach thought he had slow reflexes, and a fast, gun-beating start was all about reflexes. He didn't want Johnny to try to beat any gun, he said, he didn't have to. Once in the water, his speed would prevail.

When he started his stroke, he arched his back, kicking his feet six times for every full stroke. The widest range of Weissmuller's up and down leg action was no more than eighteen inches. The legs were for maintaining his position; the arms made him go. His head sometimes appeared to be completely out of the water, cocked upward like he needed to see where he was going. But he maintained that his face was mostly submerged, at about eye level. He exhaled through pursed lips, then turned his head to the side to inhale, his lungs expanding to take in almost twice the average person's maximum capacity — almost three gallons of oxygen. He gulped air from the left, and since Duke was in the lane to his left, Weissmuller could check on his form.

When he looked to his left at twenty meters, Duke looked good. They were even. He could see the plume of water that Duke's rapid strokes and kicks produced; it was a kind of exhaust trail, and it was longer than Johnny's, or anyone's. Duke had an immense engine. The rest of the field was more than a yard back. The danger to Weissmuller was falling a yard or two behind and being jostled by the backsplash. It was hard to keep a clean line in the tumult, hard not to tense up just a little, hard to put out of his head the image that Dr. Kellogg had described, of acid levels rising in the bloodstream, robbing his body of power.

At twenty-five meters they were on world-record pace. The

crowd rose on tiptoes, eyes glued to the water line, easily identifying who was who even in the absence of colored caps or club uniforms. One swimmer was white, one wasn't.

Weissmuller tried not to do anything impulsive, which was against his nature, but in the defined arena of a fifty-meter pool, he was surprisingly adept and disciplined. In Friday's 400-meter race he performed magnificently. He had matched Charlton's ferocious pace, then out-touched him to touch first. The margin of the error at the 100-meter was even smaller. An iffy start could be overcome. But at the wall ahead — the race's first and only turn — he had to be perfect.

Duke was starting to worry, despite his good start and the strong opening twenty-five meters. His body didn't feel old, but it didn't feel quite right, either. Sometimes that was okay. After all the races he had done and all the years he had been at it, he knew enough not to get alarmed. One hundred meters was longer than most people realized, and during it, everything could change.

But there was something different this time. His friend Charley Paddock, trying to defend his title as the world's fastest human ten days earlier, was running a perfect race, preparing for his final kick, when something small but crucial gave way. The expected high-caliber explosion was muted; he was shocked to finish fifth.

At the halfway wall, Weissmuller grazed the concrete with his right hand, turned his head down, descending toward the bottom of the tank pool, then explosively pushed off to shoot in the opposite direction. It was a technique that the IAC veteran and onetime Duke nemesis Perry McGillivray had taught him. The terms of his 100-meter playbook were simple: The start was shallow, the turn was deep.

When Weissmuller emerged from the turn, he had pulled ahead. The crowd erupted. Each man had his fans, but what drew the cheers was the knowledge that one of them was driving the other to a record.

The inexhaustible Takaishi, after starting well, was fading, feeling the cumulative effects of racing more disciplines that weekend than any of other finalists. An American coach later said he liked Takaishi's "pluck," but nobody could do what he did — race at three different distances in the same day — and compete for gold. He would finish fifth, behind Arne Borg.

Twenty-five meters from home, from where his brother David was sitting, Duke realized he would come up short. He was probably a half-yard behind Weissmuller. In hundreds of races, he had found that extra gear. His finishing sprint was legendary. People who didn't know him mistook his quiet grace for something deeply Hawaiian, a character trait shared with the beach boys who played in the water and sang in the moonlight. But those closest to him — his brothers and cousins, his Hawaiian teammates — knew better. Duke didn't like to lose at anything.

David had tried to massage away the kinks, but the moment Duke needed his body to respond was the moment it failed him. It wasn't the extra pounds he carried in Los Angeles; they had been shed weeks ago. It wasn't stamina, or strength, or desire — there was nothing he wanted more than to clasp the hand of the French president as the three-time Olympic champion and return to Hawaii covered in glory.

But modern living betrayed him, he would realize. This didn't come to him in the last twenty-five meters, or even after congratulating his rival. It came to him much later. In 1926 Duke was on Catalina Island, where he was interviewed while filming a bit role in the movie *Old Ironsides*. He had grown a beard to play a savage Barbary pirate who is brought to justice by the U.S. Navy.

"You know," he said. "I lost to Weissmuller because my legs

gave out." He had finished a body length's back. All the driving he had done in California had imperceptibly changed his muscles. He theorized that the muscles used to press the gas pedal and ride the brake had overdeveloped, tightening his pliable right leg and reducing flexibility in his ankle. Decades later he did an interview outlining the keys to a championship level performance. "Don't drive" topped the list.

"My wind and strength were fine," he continued, "but my legs, because of their muscles, went dead on me. They meant the difference between the inches [in which] Weissmuller beat me and victory."

Duke had supposedly told Weissmuller before the race that it didn't matter who won, just so it was an American. Indeed that happened and the Americans finished first, second, and third — Johnny, Duke, and Sam. And yet it chronically gnawed. In a 1968 biography by his friend, the author Joe Brennan, he remembered how he "hung on at the edge of the pool for some few winded moments, mute, immobile, void of all discernible emotion." Then he made his way to Weissmuller, extending his hand and saying congratulations. "Thanks," Weissmuller responded. "What was the matter, Duke? You lost your way down that lane?" Brennan characterized the barb as Weissmuller's typical "guying way."

Weissmuller's time was fifty-nine seconds flat, a new Olympic record that displaced the one Kahanamoku had set in 1920. It was the last of Duke's records to be smashed. Weissmuller took home a total of three gold medals in Paris and gained an international following. His post-Olympic tour of Western capitals was similarly successful, especially in Austria. Bachrach told IAC members the Austrians seemed to think Johnny was born there.

Neither Weissmuller nor Kahanamoku made it home in time to join the other athletes for a ticker-tape parade on Broadway. The swim team was by far the most successful of the

American squads, winning thirteen of their seventeen finals. Their 221 total points — the first five finishers in each event earned a designated number of points — trounced Sweden, which had the second-highest score, with 55 points.

"Swimming needed a Weissmuller," wrote Paul Gallico years later. "He was invented, carpentered, and made for the sport which, up to then, had only a Hawaiian beach boy, Duke Kahanamoku, to give a fillip of interest."

When Weissmuller arrived back in the U.S. in September, he went to the Pach Brothers studio in Manhattan to sit for a painting. It was executed on a heroic, life-sized scale, Johnny dressed in a white singlet, hand on hip and face turned slightly away. A striking photo of the scene, later displayed in the Smithsonian National Portrait Gallery, shows the near complete painting on an easel in the background and the actual Weissmuller in the foreground. The diminutive painter in a smock is off to the side.

Coaches, movie men, and race scientists would have looked at the finished painting, titled *Johnny Weissmuller,* and seen a monument to the perfect modern athlete — the thoroughbred of thoroughbreds.

SIXTEEN

GOLDEN PEOPLE
1927 – 1964

"Up through the summer mist that enshrouded the lower bay yesterday morning loomed a great liner. Vague and ephemeral it seemed, almost like a ghost ship until one ray of sun, more venturesome than the others, thrust itself through the veil and glittered in full brilliance upon a giant slogan on the ship's side, 'AMERICAN OLYMPIC TEAMS.'"

—Paul Lockwood, writing in *The Brooklyn Daily Eagle* about the U.S. team's triumphant return from France

IT WAS OPENING NIGHT of the men's outdoor AAU championship, featuring America's top swimming stars and, uniquely, Japan's. "East meets West," blared the banner headline in *Nippu Jiji*, the largest Japanese daily in the Hawaiian territory. The stands of the Waikiki War Memorial Natatorium were crammed with 6,000 fans, many of them Japanese émigrés who swarmed the stadium on Kalākaua Avenue, causing massive traffic jams. Some abandoned their cars in their rush to get through the fifty-foot-high Grecian entrance arch; others climbed the surrounding palm trees for a treacherous bird's-eye view. By the start of the first heat, few trees tall enough to provide a look at the pool were free. Just beyond the tree sitters, and seeming so close they could touch it, was the dark sentinel, the famed Diamond Head.

The occasion was the first joint appearance since the Paris Games of the three kings — Hawaii's venerable Duke Kahanamoku; the unbeatable Chicago superstar Johnny Weissmuller; and the "Weissmuller of Japan," Katsuo Takaishi. Hawaii, roughly halfway between the U.S. and Japan (and influenced by each — at the time, native Japanese made up almost half the islands' population), had hosted several major races since 1924, but this was the first in the new seaside stadium.

The hundred-by-forty-foot pool, in which open ducts provided recirculating seawater, was uncommonly dark below the surface because of its sandy bottom. A donated fleet of Nash automobiles brought all the swimmers for a first look. Rumor had it that there were giant eels slithering among the coral, only a few yards beneath the swimmers' kicking legs. Someone said they saw a hammerhead shark circling beyond the pool walls.

Weissmuller had just returned from a week at Kellogg's Battle Creek Sanitarium, where he went to get race fit. Dr. Kellogg, who outside the lab dressed in a trademark white suit, often with a cockatoo perched on his right shoulder, prescribed strict abstinence from sex and alcohol, bland foods, floggings from circulation-boosting machines, and regular enemas. The purging biologics emptied Johnny's bowels at a dizzying pace.

By reducing the acid levels in his bloodstream and achieving "colonic purity," Kellogg predicted better results in the pool.

Weissmuller swam an atypical 300-meter time trial before a large crowd at the sanitarium's new 120-foot pool and, as promised, reduced his record time by almost two seconds. Afterward he clowned around, barking like a seal as Bachrach tried to thank Kellogg for his wondrous work. In the coming months the publicity from their visit would help Kellogg secure a mammoth $2 million private donation for a "college of the future" at Battle Creek, which he said would greatly accelerate the reach and influence of the Race Betterment cause.

Kahanamoku, now thirty-seven and retired, was on hand to inaugurate the magnificent Waikiki pool with an opening exhibition performance. "Opening the natatorium without Duke would be like having a luau without poi, without the main ingredient," pronounced Hui Nalu's Bill Rawlins, now a circuit judge.

Kahanamoku was just back from Hollywood, where he was still hoping to break through and land a leading-man role in the movies. He was traveling with his adopted family, Ma Henry and twelve-year-old William and nineteen-year-old Thomas, his blue-eyed haole brothers. Thomas, who went to the Paris Games aboard the SS *America*, would have a productive film career, inspired in part by hanging out with Duke. Throughout the 1940s and 1950s, he played stalwart army officers responsible, as one critic put it, "for saving Earth from aliens and bad guys."

The *Honolulu Advertiser*, a sponsor of the AAU championship, had hired Kahanamoku to write a series of articles throughout the meet. "This morning when I sat at the rail of the *City of Los Angeles* and saw familiar faces beam up to me from the tug, my heart simply refused to function in its usual manner," he wrote in his debut column. His extraordinary welcome home laid the groundwork for a return to Honolulu in

1932 as sheriff, a post his father had held before him, and one Duke would hold for decades.

Takaishi was now a full-blown star. He had toured Australia — a first for a Japanese swimmer — and had shocked the world a year earlier when he swam the 100-meter in 59.4 seconds, overtaking the record Kahanamoku had held for ten years before the Paris Games. The fifty-eight-second breakthrough, which Weissmuller dearly wanted, too, was within his reach. At that same 1926 meet, the Japanese relay team shattered the 800-meter mark previously held by the IAC. Months before, in a meet against Americans and Australians at Tokyo's Tamagawa stadium pool, Takaishi had won the 100-, 200-, and 400-meter races. Back home, his elementary school swimming pool was named in his honor, and a Tokyo sculptor immortalized him in a handsome bronze bust.

The team he captained was a bellwether, just as Duke's Hui Nalu squad had been in 1913 when it arrived in San Francisco. In the final night's feature event — the first international four-man relay to be held outside of the Olympics — the Japanese raced the mainland American team and the Hawaiian team, each man swimming a 220-yard leg. The American squad, led by Weissmuller, was too strong to beat and smashed the current Olympic record by an inconceivable twenty seconds. Hawaii seemed guaranteed second place until Takaishi, swimming anchor, erased Johnny Woodd's four-yard lead in the final leg to touch the wall first. The crowd, heavily made up of Takaishi fans, rose as one, flinging off their hats from the stands and trees.

The four-day event was a celebration of swimming and, in a sense, Hawaii's foundational role in the sport. There were up-and-comers from the islands, like Buster Crabbe — who would go on to win two Olympic medals and become a Hollywood superstar — and an exhibition for local kids, in which

Duke pretended to drown and Johnny mooed like a cow. In a poignant memorial service, all the swimmers, along with coaches George Center and Bill Bachrach, walked to the Kawaiaha'o church cemetery to lay a wreath at the grave of Charles Pung, the young Chinese Hawaiian who had swum for the U.S. in Paris. A year earlier, the twenty-year-old Pung had fallen ill with heart trouble after swimming in a college meet in Honolulu and died a day later.

The IAC had angered some when it published an overtly racist cartoon in the *Tri-Color* showing primitive islanders running for cover as the Chicago team prepared its invasion. But the fiery rivalry that had burned for ten years had dissipated. After the memorial, the visiting swimmers were invited to the Kahanamoku family home to pay respects to Duke's aging mother, Julia Paoa Kahanamoku.

Duke had been in Los Angeles for almost six years, and reuniting with his family and the new generation of Hui Nalu swimmers would make him miss what he once had. For young Hawaiian natives, including his youngest brother, Sargent, seventeen, (who barely knew him), he was a revelation, the myth made real. "The old-timers told me, 'Watch your brother Duke,'" Sargent recalled about watching Duke christen the big stadium pool. "'When he swims, he makes waves.' I thought, what the hell do they mean 'makes waves?' So I watched him. He goes down about twenty yards and the waves come and hit the sides of the tank. The waves were big, so big that I could take a 120-pound surfboard and ride them. Nobody else, not even Johnny Weissmuller, could get in the middle of a pool and make waves like that."

Weissmuller, in peak form after his stay at Battle Creek and believing there was no faster water than Waikiki's, beat Takaishi in the opening night's 100-meter race, setting another world record in fifty-eight seconds flat. (Takaishi's 58.6 was a Japanese record.) He had called his shot the day before, predicting not only the new record but the exact time. Takaishi was within striking distance of Weissmuller with twenty-five meters to go but couldn't close the gap. Earlier that summer, at the Detroit Athletic Club, Weissmuller had unofficially swum the 100-yard in just under forty-eight seconds. That time wouldn't be equaled until 1961.

In the 440-yard, Weissmuller pulled off what most thought his finest performance to date, beating the world record by ten seconds. Never before had a swimmer cracked the five-minute barrier for the quarter mile. In the final night, he crushed his third individual world record, in the half mile.

Weissmuller was the most dominant amateur athlete across all sports in that moment. He was one of the "golden people," in Paul Gallico's words. He traveled the world erasing mostly his own records, and when people asked how an amateur could afford to own a fast car or dress to the nines, he and Bachrach smiled and pointed out that he had a nice job in the Chicago automobile repair business.

The AAU championship would be Weissmuller's last amateur meet in Hawaii. His athletic career would be over in two years' time, shortly after he won three more gold medals at the Amsterdam Olympics in 1928.

At only twenty-four, he was in his prime when he walked away, explaining he needed to make a living. Bachrach supported his decision, though he squeezed in one last payday when Johnny agreed to make his final international appearance in Japan, with stops in Tokyo and Osaka. It was the first time a reigning Olympic champion traveled to Japan, and the occasion was treated with all the pomp and ceremony of a state visit. The Prince of Sport himself, Prince Chichibu, still on his honeymoon, arrived at the Tokyo event with his new wife and was greeted by Bachrach and Weissmuller on the pool deck at intermission. The prince was dressed in a gray sack suit, Princess Setsuko in a tan sports coat and cloche hat. Johnny wore his IAC swimsuit.

The next day in Osaka, Weissmuller futilely tried to convince Bachrach to let him sit out the 100-meter race out of respect for his opponent, but ultimately he did race and beat Takaishi again. "He stands in a class by himself," conceded Takaishi.

After Weissmuller emerged undefeated in all races, Bachrach told reporters that he had outfoxed the Japanese plans to derail Johnny's form by using colder than normal water in the pools. Bachrach said he made Weissmuller sit in an ice bath for one hour twice a day. It sounded like a line delivered to grab headlines, not unlike the tale he told about getting Weissmuller in shape by lobbing silver dollars out the window of their hotel room and having him run the stairs to retrieve them, and it largely was. Bachrach's true genius wasn't sports science (his hydroplaning principle proved inaccurate, as did his new breaststroke kick) but astute marketing and an ability to collect talent. He had recently recruited and signed Arne Borg, the Swedish middle-distance Olympic champion, and brought him to Japan as well. In pairing Weissmuller and Borg, Bachrach created an international amateur dream team. Nobody before him had done anything like it.

As a promoter, Bachrach's zealous protection of Weissmuller's unbeaten record knew no bounds. The late William "Buck" Dawson, the longtime director of the International Swimming Hall of Fame, liked to share the anecdote of Bachrach ordering Borg to stand down during a 500-yard race he was winning so as not to mess up Weissmuller's streak. "Borg swam, forged ahead, and coming to a complete stop five yards from the finish he yelled, 'Come on, Yonnie, I let you win!'"

Weissmuller signed a contract with BVD, an athletic-wear company that Bachrach had contacts with, and relocated to Duke's neighborhood in L.A., where he was soon hired to play the biggest, most lucrative film role an athlete had ever been given: Tarzan. He came to adore Hollywood life, with its studio bosses replacing Bachrach in telling him what to do. Like his former coach, Johnny loved the spotlight. He would tell interviewers anything — some of it true, some not. He claimed he was a sickly child who'd had polio; his mother had him swim to get stronger. Another time he said that was bunk, a sob story made up for the newspapers. He said he had another brother, Adam, a professional wrestler with one eye who played the accordion prior to matches. Then later, no, Adam was a cousin. He said he ate everything except fish. "They're my pals," he joked.

Weissmuller made dozens of box office hits. At one point he reportedly earned $100,000 per film. He easily made millions, easily lost millions. He was married five times and built a palace to excess and stardom in the hills of Bel Air. The ruins of the compound, though fenced in, still draw tour groups en route to the Jay-Z and Beyoncé property, guides referring to the former owner as Tarzan and sometimes mistaking his name as Weisman. The 8,700-square-foot pink mansion was built in 1931 by Paul R. Williams, a Black architect who wasn't allowed to visit some of the homes he designed. The main manse, with twenty-foot ceilings and a formal ballroom, was in the faux Italianate style popular at the time. Williams's most difficult challenge was creating the one-of-a-kind pool Johnny wanted. It was 300 feet long, with a 150-foot waterfall, and snaked beneath a jungle-like canopy of trees. The basin was reputedly deep enough to allow for a restless man and his friends to swan dive from the house roof. The parties were endless, including one where Duke and other Hawaiian swimmers were in attendance. In a group photo, Weissmuller grins mischievously, surrounded by guests straddling large inflatable pool swans. He was bigger than life, wrote his son, Johnny Jr., in the book *Tarzan, My Father*. "Man, your daddy was the coolest dude in town," his friends told him.

For all his good times, Johnny seemed fated to gossipy scandals, such as when his mother, Elizabeth, was revealed to owe $254 in back rent in a 1936 court case in Chicago. She was earning $16 a week working in a restaurant as her motion picture actor son lived his lavish life. In 1962 his eighteen-year-old daughter, Heidi Elizabeth, the youngest of his three children and named after his mother, was tragically killed when the car she was driving hit a soft shoulder and overturned. She was four months pregnant. Debt and alcoholism consumed him, dooming his fourth marriage, which could have been a keeper. "When he wasn't drinking — was sober — he was the kindest, most loving person you'd ever want to meet," said his fourth wife, Allene Gates. During World War II, he raised money for the troops and taught Navy recruits at the Long Beach station to navigate around petroleum-fueled flames. He was told the GIs requested broadcasts of his Tarzan yell at the battlefront.

He never did acknowledge his actual birthplace. "It just always was Windber, Pennsylvania," said Gates. "I think he might've thought that his fans that idolized him would think of him as being a liar, not being an up-and-up great champion. Or [he might've thought] they might take his medals."

Weissmuller and Kahanamoku's lives continued to overlap with each other. Sometimes it seemed Johnny had to match Duke's deeds, even those that had nothing to do with records and times. On June 14, 1925, only months after the Paris Games and

Weissmuller's headline triumphs, Kahanamoku was with friends at Corona del Mar in Newport when a sudden squall arose, capsizing a forty-foot yacht about 100 yards offshore. Duke raced into the crashing waves on his surfboard, each time bringing a half-drowned survivor back to the beach. Ultimately, he saved eight men in a superhuman effort a local sheriff said was unlike any he had ever seen.

Later he retrieved the bodies of five who had drowned.

On July 29, 1927, a month before the AAU championship in Hawaii, Johnny did something remarkably similar. He was training in Lake Michigan for the upcoming Chicago River marathon when the *Favorite*, a small Lincoln Park excursion boat carrying almost 100 women and small children overturned in a freak squall. A cruising yacht was first to the scene, loading so many survivors on board it nearly capsized. "Aboard the *Favorite* it was pandemonium," said a first responder. "They were mostly women and children. Everybody was shouting and weeping . . . 'Save my child!' 'Save my mother!' . . . that's all we heard."

Rescue boats shuttled from the wreck to Municipal Pier, where emergency medical workers used oxygen machines and first aid to attempt to resuscitate victims. One of the boats scooped up Johnny and his brother, Peter, along with some friends at North Avenue Beach, to dive for bodies trapped between decks. Of the sixty-five women and children pulled from the storm-tossed water, some fifty survived. Johnny and Peter said they had retrieved more than ten bodies, though it was unclear if any were survivors. The traumatic scene of trapped children and wailing loved ones would have reminded them of another Lake Michigan disaster, the 1915 sinking of the SS *Eastland*, and maybe, far deeper in their memories, the story their mother told about the *General Slocum*.

In later years, Weissmuller and Kahanamoku's relationship

ripened into what would seem an unlikely friendship. They visited each other regularly through the years — Johnny traveling to Waikiki and Duke to Hollywood — and even vacationed together when Duke finally married. Nadine Kahanamoku loved telling of motoring with Johnny and Allene through a long tunnel in the Southwest and Johnny yodeling his trademark Tarzan call from the convertible, the rebounding echo leaving them all in hysterics. They were an odd pairing but had traveled the same paths and shared a love for one thing above all else — water. And while it was clear to see the influence Duke had on his young, impressionable rival in the 1920s, perhaps Johnny brought something to a middle-aged Duke, Hawaii's most unerring ambassador. Duke could act "naughty" with Johnny, is the way Nadine put it to friends. Maybe Weissmuller brought him a little lightness, that skylarking quality that none other than John Harvey Kellogg observed and admired decades earlier.

From his time as a "polu" (a "comer" as Duke called him on *This Is Your Life*) to the cavalcade of shared honors that came with retirement, Johnny respected Duke immensely. He didn't approach the favorite-son legacy of Duke, despite his gold medals and famous film career. Duke was revered and remembered as himself and, increasingly, for what he sacrificed for Hawaii. In 1965, the two were inducted in the inaugural class of the International Swimming Hall of Fame in Fort Lauderdale. Johnny came in a conservative suit while Duke wore creased white slacks and brightly colored floral sneakers, a lei around his neck. Even at seventy-six, he had untouchable style.

———————

A FULL-PAGE PHOTO from the *Los Angeles Times* Sunday magazine in 1929 shows Kahanamoku on a surfboard, sliding down a soft wave with a beautiful female companion, blond and beaming, standing atop his shoulders with arms spread wide. It is images like this that would most be associated with Duke. He made history as a swimmer, but his carefree ease as a surfer cemented his legacy. Before surfing was a competitive sport and a pastime for thrill seekers on the hunt for bigger and bigger waves, it was a source of pure joy and freedom for Kahanamoku and pioneers like him. Once he became famous, photographers chronicled much of it, but there were still moments of private discovery, such as the storm swell in 1917 when he caught a big wave and rode it for a mile, from Castles to Canoes breaks in Waikiki, a monumental achievement that future generations dreamed about but could never equal. One surfer who said he had replicated most of the ride, enough to know it could be done, peeled off a little early out of respect for Duke.

Long after his death he remained an ancestral guiding hand, known by every young native trying to find their place beyond the islands and sticking with it even if they felt they could never belong. He was Joe Louis, Jesse Owens, and Jackie Robinson before integration, said a speaker at a 2005 tribute. He dealt with prejudice at every turn, said another. Kahanamoku was aloha, but he was a warrior, too. "It's like his brother said," said Isaiah Walker, a historian who wrote the influential book *Waves of Resistance*, "Duke was a nice guy but *brudda* had heavy hands." Few knew about Duke's lawsuit in 1922 against Honolulu's leading newspaper, the *Advertiser*. It was not a throwaway gesture. Though the First Circuit jury ruled in his favor and awarded him $1,500 in December 1920, Kahanamoku filed an exemption to the ruling, leading to arguments before the Hawaii Supreme Court on May 22, 1922. Kahanamoku disagreed with the original trial judge and his soft interpretation of the word "slacker," which Leonard Withington used to describe Duke when he was too sick to compete. The lower court didn't believe the term was libelous, pointing to the possibility of more generic usage, not the specific one understood during the Great War, which was a person who cowardly evaded the draft. The higher court concurred. Often historians, and even native admirers, have lamented that Kahanamoku was victimized, or exploited, or both, and he just seemed to take it, but this was an example of him saying enough is enough. Kahanamoku didn't back down. It is hard to find another example in the 1920s of an athlete of color suing a powerful white-owned newspaper company.

Some present-day activists and educators see in his quiet response to many injustices an admirable strength that allowed for him to perpetuate his culture without anyone finding reason to push back. "He was peacefully protesting without even using words of protests," said Duane DeSoto, a longboard champion who played Duke in two documentaries and founded the nonprofit youth school Nā Kama Kai (Children of the Sea). "His grace was a form of resistance."

He was reputed to be the blandest interview in sports because he was all softness, no edge. Quotes of his were regularly dressed up to the point that some bore no resemblance to what he actually said. "We used to say, '*Mehape a ale wala'au*,' and that means, 'Don't talk — keep it in your heart,' and that's what he did," recalled his brother Sargent. For modern champion swimmers and surfers who came after Duke looking to find the truth of who he was, why he competed, and how he hung in for so long, the clues were frustratingly hard to find. "He is more an image than he is a man," said Aaron Peirsol, one of the most decorated swimming sprinters in U.S. history and one who sensed in Duke's relationship with water something to aspire to.

Yet Duke did have a full personality. He was a prodigious sleeper who could shut down anytime, anywhere. He steadfastly preferred poi out of a can to a five-star gourmet dinner, his wife lamented. His younger siblings, even when they were not so young, were forbidden to touch anything of his, not his cars and certainly not his famed eighteen-foot redwood surfboard, which had its own special rack at the Outrigger Canoe Club. When Sargent took it for a ride anyway, Duke found out, gave him a hard look, and said, "Kid, don't ever do that again." Sargent didn't.

Duke had an uncompromising competitive edge, something his undefeated six-man outrigger crewmates felt every day. One of them remembered feeling sick during a preregatta training session and quitting before practice was over. Duke didn't talk to him for a month. Like all the greats to come after him, from Michael Jordan to Michael Phelps, he hated to lose at anything. His silver-medal performance in the 1924 Games would annoy him to his dying day.

He gave nothing away of himself. He let people see him exactly as they wished to and seemed to have no interest in staking a claim to an identity the public imagined for him. He didn't talk about his rich personal ancestry, rarely telling anyone that his paternal grandparents were retainers to royalty. He didn't repeat what Queen Lili'uokalani always said: When royalty is born, those who work for them, the *kahus*, were born, too. Hawaiian children were taught not to share Hawaiian genealogy with haoles. Silence was power.

But he wasn't a recluse. He was everywhere, which made it more remarkable that no one knew much about him beyond his melodious voice, swinging hips, and the opening stanza to the 1936 Sol Bright song, "Duke Kahanamoku, the pride of old Hawaii / Surfing on a nalu, appearing like a manu / You would think a moment, he wore a feather garment . . . *oi a no ika oi.*"

In the 1970s, he didn't join the young natives protesting the U.S. military bombing exercises at Kaho'olawe Island or

demand reparations, but he inspired the Hawaiian pride movement with his resilience and dignity and symbolic actions: the
quiet way he spoke Hawaiian in the company of nonspeakers,
the creation of Hui Nalu, the Hawaiian flag decal on his 1922
Cadillac. In future years the Hawaiian language, which he was
forbidden to speak as a child, would roar back to life in grade
school immersion programs. The rallying cry of the younger
generations — "We're not anti-American but pro-Hawaiian"
— didn't seem incompatible with the way Duke lived his life.

By contrast, Weissmuller seemed to vacillate between the
places that claimed him — Windber, Pennsylvania; Freidorf,
Hungary; and the German American enclave on Chicago's
North Side. He visited Windber on Johnny Weissmuller Day
in 1950, and Freidorf erected a plaque near where his birth house
had stood. Chicago, his true home, floated the idea of a Johnny
Weissmuller pavilion near the Lincoln Park Lagoon and beaches,
but it was never built, and it's hard to find any significant sign of
him in the sports-mad city. The IAC pool, where Bill Bachrach
remained a fixture for decades after Weissmuller's retirement, is
still there, though without water or ruddy, bare-chested members. The building at 112 South Michigan Avenue, including
the room where Weissmuller convalesced after his heart leakage, is now part of the School of the Art Institute of Chicago.
After moving to Fort Lauderdale in the 1960s, he donated his
Olympic medals and ephemera to the International Swimming
Hall of Fame, which he avidly supported.

Among the extraordinary collection of images that chronicle
Kahanamoku and Weissmuller's innumerable joint appearances
in later years, there is one that shines brightest. The two are en-
circled by a small group of admirers as they do an impromptu
hula dance, their sports coats stripped off and tied around their
gyrating hips. Duke's knees are loosely bent, his hand gracefully

stretched outward. Johnny holds his arms high at right angles, like he's in a dance-off, waiting to answer Duke's next move. They are smiling straight at each other, especially Johnny, who is locked onto his friend's eyes, like he belonged once and for all. In Duke's generous company Johnny found acceptance and joy and aloha. The hula, not the swimming pool, was perfect common ground: One man knew the dance innately and one was willing to learn.

The fact that Weissmuller had an easy path to a post-Olympic film career as a white swim star was unavoidably obvious but didn't seem to bother Duke. Nor did he seem to feel he had been cheated out of a gold medal because Weissmuller lied about where he was from. Everyone in Hawaii knew Weissmuller had been born in Europe, but most considered him American regardless, just as the Asian immigrants who had sought a better living in Hawaii, laboring in its sugar fields, were American. Kahanamoku didn't publicly comment on the racist caricatures in American, Australia, and European publications that depicted him as a primitive other. He knew, as Jackie Robinson knew decades later, that speaking out was possible only for those with nothing left to lose.

And yet those around Duke wanted more. After his life-saving heroism at Newport Harbor, the Hawaii Society of Los Angeles formally submitted his name for a Carnegie Medal, the nation's premier civilian award for bravery. Set up and funded by philanthropist Andrew Carnegie, the commission recognized hundreds of people early in the twentieth century for rescues involving mine collapses, apartment fires, trampling horse teams, rampaging livestock, and train wrecks. But by overwhelming margins most had to do with boating disasters and drownings, the scourge of American civilian life.

Kahanamoku was denied the medal on the grounds that he was from a territory not a state, per commission guidelines. This despite inconsistencies, such as the Alaskan who was recognized in 1914 for saving a man from drowning in Skagway. In 1925 the Carnegie winners included Harold Overlin, who saved two lives at the same beach where Duke saved six.

The Masonic Lodge in Honolulu had denied Kahanamoku membership some six times, his first cousin Fred Paoa recalled bitterly at a tribute celebrating the 2002 U.S. Postal Service release of a stamp in Duke's honor. The lodge had been the home of Hawaiian monarchs and received the Prince of Wales in 1920, the same trip during which he had surfed with Duke. He was finally granted membership in 1946. A large scrapbook filled with welcoming letters from Lodge No. 21 and a radio-gram from his wife in which she worried that his Masonic pin had yet to arrive were a measure of how important it was to him to belong.

The U.S. stamp was viewed in Hawaii as a milestone in recognition of all he had achieved. Shortly after it came out, a humor writer for *Smithsonian* magazine ridiculed the stamp as an example of the queer trend of highlighting obscure historical figures. "I'd never heard of Duke Kahanamoku, and now I am licking the man's back?" she wrote. "Who is this man, and how did he get on my stamps? Can I be on a stamp too?"

———

KATSUO TAKAISHI CAME CLOSE to beating Weissmuller — Weiss-muller predicted he would do it — but ultimately that didn't happen, and Takaishi was frustrated that his swimming didn't lead where he figured it would, to a gold medal at the Olym-pics. Instead, he earned bronze and silver at the Amsterdam Games in 1928, becoming the first Asian to win an Olympic medal in swimming. In 1932 he was named captain of Japan's men's team for the Games in Los Angeles. The movement he and Sensei Sugimoto started came to fruition in Los Angeles, where the men's team won all but one event and Japanese Americans feted them with parades, homestays, and tribute dinners.

Japan dominated the 1932 competition in a way that only one other nation had previously done — the U.S. in Paris in 1924. In response to the popular question about how the smaller Japanese swimmers outswam bigger rivals, Coach Ikkaku Matsuzawa, a former rival of Takaishi's, explained, "Look at the aeroplane! The scout-plane has a very small body, but it can fly faster than the heavy bomber." Most aspects of the Japanese crawl were quite like the Australian or American crawl, he said, but the swiftness with which they became global sprint champions was due to the long-standing habit of analyzing and changing strokes across the centuries. Adapting technique to meet the demands of fast swimming in a pool was natural for a culture that developed strokes for every conceivable circumstance. "Japanese as a race enjoys it," said Matsuzawa, and Japanese swimmers were "imbued with the national spirit, and if there be any difference [in their advance] it was this fact."

Sugimoto's memory was kept alive in part by his own lively voice — he authored numerous magazine articles with titles like "My Town Ibaraki" and "Souvenirs from Paris," and in 1926 published a book about his life in swimming which featured handsome portraits of himself and Takaishi in the opening pages. To commemorate the fiftieth anniversary of the Ibaraki pool, he and Takaishi collaborated on a long and colorful history of the muddy pond that was transformed into a magnificent Olympic training ground. To Takaishi, his mentor was the most extraordinary coach in Japan because he coached three different water sports at three different Olympics. He introduced the Japanese crawl in 1924, coached the diving team in 1928, then pivoted to water polo in 1932. Nobody had done that before, and it's likely nobody could have. "It is easy to imitate or improve upon which others have but he pioneered a new path. I'm sure nobody has succeeded in coaching so many world-class athletes," Takaishi said. Sugimoto's passion was limitless, and his mind was agile and always free spirited. When a ceremony to open a swimming pool at Takaishi's old elementary school couldn't happen because there was not enough water pressure to fill the tank, Sugimoto took the group to a nearby river instead, entertaining young and old alike with his picture-perfect dives off a high bridge.

Scholars who would revisit Sugimoto's career thought his biggest impact was bringing rival swimming regions — Kantō and Kansai — into something like sporting harmony. He had started in Tokyo, learning how to teach swimming from renowned coaching experts. In Osaka, he taught the foundational stroke that changed everything: the crawl. He had been the first to teach a true national style, not one that dated back to the clashing fiefdoms of ruling shoguns.

When the large post-Olympics parade coursed through Little Japan in 1932, Takaishi thought this competition — the one he didn't qualify for — was the best he had been a part of. Shortly afterward he married fellow swimmer Mineko Nagai, and their formal wedding portrait — she in traditional matrimonial dress, he in an impeccably tailored Western tuxedo — showed up in newspapers around the world. They had a large family and Takaishi brought his trademark intensity to successful careers as a businessman and then as a swim coach.

Takaishi was the first great Asian hope at the Games, the first of his countrymen to fulfill the uniquely pressure-filled expectation to bring honor to his nation first and himself second. It was not like being an American Olympian. When a *New*

York Times reporter asked about displays of emotional distress at second- and third-place finishes in the 2021 Tokyo Games, one Japanese athlete said, "From an early age, Japanese athletes are not really supposed to think like they are playing sports for themselves."

Decades later, a top Australia swim coach would come across Takaishi's story and write about it in an article previewing the 1996 Atlanta Games. Cecil Colwin wrote of "a tiny, scholarly-looking fellow with a little beard" who brilliantly described the future of speed swimming. "Takaishi had an intuitive feel far in advance of what any program could have developed in him. Sixty years ago, long before the advent of scientific analysis, with uncanny accuracy, he predicted most of the fundamentals of the modern crawl stroke."

Colwin was referring to a highly detailed, technique-laden article written by Takaishi as part of a book published in 1935 by the International Young Women and Children's Society called *Swimming in Japan*. The mission of the Tokyo-based society was the interchange of Japanese culture with other countries. Photos and text illustrated both samurai and contemporary styles of swimming. Takaishi's case study of the crawl was four times the length of any of the other articles in the book. He knew it might be the only opportunity to match, or perhaps mute, the voices that were still the loudest in the swimming world, those of Weissmuller and Bachrach. One of the first photos showed Takaishi from above at the beginning of the crawl stroke, his left arm extended and his small right foot cocked, a slender cotton thong — the traditional *rokushaku fundoshi* — the only demarcation between his body and the water.

He didn't make an overt case for the Japanese method except to say his team had incorporated "various merits of the old Japanese styles into it." With cool academic reserve he explained, step by step, how to efficiently develop the fastest crawl. First, one must master the ability to let the body just float. Then came the proper leg and arm movements. There was a right way and a wrong one for *bata-ashi* (the fluttering of the legs). To test whether a swimmer was ready to move on to breathing, the last step, the swimmer should look at the wake behind him. The ripples should be like those of a fountain, not like water spray.

But he drilled down even deeper, beyond what he called the outline of the crawl stroke to crucial elements of a race: the diving start, the turn, the kick to the finish. He dispassionately pointed out that Weissmuller could have been faster if he had not started the wrong way — with a horizontal plunge, his legs hitting the water first to immediately kick. "The impingement from the water is too great at this time that the speed produced by hard kicking is almost reduced to nothing," Takaishi analytically wrote.

His words describing the Japanese crawl would never be forgotten. In the lead-up to the Tokyo Games in 2021, a short history of Japanese competitive swimming appeared on the Olympic Channel. Titled "How Japan Changed Swimming Forever," the segment chronicled the glorious achievement of the 1932 Games. The narrator concluded by saying, "Eventually the rest of the world caught up with the Japanese — they learned to race the proper way, the Japanese way."

During World War II, Takaishi's ironworks company provided the raw materials for the Japanese navy's warships. Whether he was an ultranationalist or a businessman caught in an impossible situation, it is difficult to say. His politics were private. But after the war he quickly abandoned the steel trade and founded the Ashiya Suiren swim school, where he dedicated himself to teaching generations of young people the "Takaishi-style" beginners' method. For this work he received the Star of the Order of the Sacred Treasure, the government's highest civic award, decreed by the emperor. The medal — "shiju hosho" — was a bejeweled circle with striking gold rays hanging from a wide purple silk ribbon.

More honors would follow. Takaishi Memorial Swimming Pool was built on the Toyama Campus of his alma mater, Waseda University. He was named general director of the Japanese national swimming team that competed in the 1964 Tokyo Games. Takaishi invited his old friends Johnny Weissmuller and Duke Kahanamoku as VIP guests. "The opening ceremonies were beautiful," said Duke with typical reticence.

If all three men were, in their ways, come-from-behind stories, so, too, was the Olympic Games, an unproven concept in 1924. Beloved features of the Games were introduced at Paris, including the athletes' Olympic Village, the three flag raisings at the closing ceremonies (honoring the International Olympic Committee and the present and future host countries), and iconic symbols like the Olympic motto and Coubertin's five-ringed flag. Female athletes and non-European countries got a foothold. It wasn't perfect but the pieces were now in place.

The international camaraderie that Pierre de Coubertin had promised with the Olympic Games — the premise that rival nations playing games might lessen their urge to kill each other on battlefields — seemed possible to Takaishi during the Los Angeles Games, where athletes from Japan and other countries felt welcome and safe. Soon thereafter he joined the military — active athletes were able to forgo service while competing — and the sentiment was dangerously different. Athletic success was propaganda for militarists who wanted to colonize and expand. Japan's alliance with Germany in 1936 was grounded in many disagreements it had with the U.S., the first of which were the laws Congress passed in 1924 barring immigration.

Weeks after atomic bombs were dropped on Hiroshima and Nagasaki in August 1945, Takaishi's whereabouts were unknown. A former rival swimmer, the Hawaiian Johnny Woodd, now an army lieutenant, tried to find him. The two had raced each other repeatedly during their swim careers, including the 1927 meet in Waikiki when Takaishi chased down Woodd in the thrilling relay final. Torrential rains made it hard for Woodd to get around, and the only address he had for Takaishi was a bombed-out lot. Finally, Woodd got word that Takaishi was alive and living with friends at his old Ibaraki school in Osaka. He agreed to meet him at a department store in Yokohama that had been converted into an Allied military outpost.

Their reunion would have restored Coubertin's belief, something he had lost as the second war closed in. Despite the chaos around them, or maybe because of it, Takaishi and Woodd decided to meet again the next afternoon at Tokyo Imperial University. Remarkably, the pool was still open and maintained. They took a swim.

THREE FUNERALS
1966 – 1984

*"When people don't know me anymore or want
my autograph, then I'll think about retiring."*
—Johnny Weissmuller

KATSUO TAKAISHI'S LUNG CANCER came on quickly with nightly
seizures. Some friends thought his sudden illness was connected
to arduous and stressful work on behalf of Japan's swim team
during the 1964 Olympics. Bedridden in his final months and
struggling to talk, he still had a fierce interest in swimming.
Waseda athletes who came to donate blood for his transfusions
couldn't get away before he would start in with his coaching
tutorials for getting them faster.

On April 19, 1966, at 2:00 p.m., the first of 3,000 mourners arrived at a swimming pool in the city of Ashiya, outside
Osaka, for Takaishi's funeral. His friends and family were nervous about the unorthodox ceremony, his wife, Mineko, and
his six children making some concessions to accepted protocol

with a private ceremony the day before at the temple. The exception to the cautionary feeling surrounding the day was Den Sugimoto, who had arranged for a brass band from Tenri High School to begin the process of ushering his student into the beyond by playing "Toward a New Life," a theme song for the Los Angeles Games.

The enormous stadium pool, similar in design to Piscine de Tourelles in Paris, had a smattering of people in the upper grandstand, but most were seated on the deck, facing an altar of sorts with cherished photographs and flags and a raised platform for the many eulogists. Small white flowers like those on a lei — flowers were a favorite of Takaishi's — were everywhere, lining the diving board, the pool perimeter, the lane-dividing ropes. In the middle lane of the pool, the lane reserved in a race for the final's favorite, a large poster of Takaishi floated serenely. On the opposite end of the pool, two of his mentees, Tsuyoshi Yamanaka and Yoshihiko Osaki, both Waseda graduates and medal-winning Olympians, were poised to dive into the water, signaling an interlude of prayer as they swam the 100-meter crawl.

Friends remembered Takaishi's intensity but also his kindness and loyalty. During the war, when there was little food to be found, he delivered emergency supplies to a boyhood friend in Osaka. His only son, Katsu, spoke with emotion, wishing, he said, "we could have talked a lot more about life. He was a good, kind father." An Ibaraki friend fondly referred to him as Kappa, a mythological river monster that was small but mighty. He was a fantastic dancer who learned the English version of mah-jongg and taught it to teammates. Takaishi was laid to rest up the hill at the cemetery, facing the sea and the pool, the two mediums — one ancient and one modern — that he loved so well.

A few months later, Sugimoto, Takaishi's family, and an

intimate group of friends returned to the pool to install a large granite monument with a bronze plaque bearing his name. Sugimoto stood before it and seemed to feel the entirety of their journey together. They had their last swim the year before at the fiftieth anniversary celebration of the Ibaraki school pool. "Katsuo Takaishi," he said, "the king of water who pioneered the dawn of time. Your lifelong passion for water will continue to burn for as long as swimming in Japan continues."

In 2022 a senior researcher from Keio University who was studying Takaishi's legacy walked around the ruins of the house where the swimmer had lived with his family and many flowering plants. Quite improbably, the century plant — which typically blooms just once in its lifetime — had bloomed again.

AFTER A DEVASTATING STROKE in 1973, Johnny Weissmuller's health started a steep decline. Heart and stomach complications and multiple surgeries followed. Some people just lived too long, said one friend from the swimming world. Johnny was one of those. He was referencing the later-life indignities, like Weissmuller's eviction from the Motion Picture and Television Country Home and Hospital in Los Angeles because of disruptive antics. He was known to yodel at all hours, his son said. Toward the end of his life, he attended a Yale University tribute to his film career. The showing of his first motion picture, *Tarzan the Ape Man*, was interrupted and then stopped entirely when Black students protested the racist depictions of Africans. Shortly after Duke passed away in 1968, Weissmuller had told a reporter he didn't understand why American Black athletes might boycott the coming Olympics. "We never thought about it," he said about racial differences in his time.

He lived his final years in Acapulco, Mexico, the location for his last movie, with his wife, Maria, and his adopted daughter. The rental house had a pretty pool, but he could only sit by it, not swim.

When he passed away on January 20, 1984, it was international news, the stories about his spectacular Olympic stardom and athletic career a surprise to many who only knew him as a boy-toy Tarzan or his later role as Jungle Jim.

As much as Maria tried to arrange a funeral appropriate for one of the golden people of the twentieth century, she had trouble reaching the glittering who's who he had befriended as a younger athlete and actor. There was a time when he brought joy and wonder to his millions of fans – when he was the good-time instigator in Hollywood's first rat pack, made up of Weissmuller, John Wayne, Errol Flynn, and Humphrey Bogart. He graced the famous album cover of the Beatles' *Sgt. Pepper's Lonely Hearts Club Band*, alongside other twentieth-century giants such as Carl Jung, Lenny Bruce, George Bernard Shaw, Sonny Liston, and Marilyn Monroe. He's in the second row, just behind Ringo and Paul. But all the people who could have come didn't. Instead, most of the congregants were local to the community, most of them Mexican schoolchildren who created a long cortege that proceeded from the funeral home in downtown Acapulco to the cemetery some twelve miles away. The lone connections to his past, reported a syndicated wire-service reporter, seemed to be a body double, a Mexican actress from his last Tarzan movie, and a chimp named Samantha. The foreign location seemed incongruous. Neither his actor son, who was estranged from his stepmother, nor any other family members were in attendance. His white marble headstone was etched with his true birthdate, 1904. Per his wishes, his Tarzan yell was played three times as his coffin was lowered into the soft earth. Later, the family held another memorial service at the Church of the Good Shepherd in Beverly Hills, at which Senator Edward Kennedy arranged for a twenty-one-gun salute. Johnny Jr. didn't know how an honor customarily reserved for military or heads of state got approved but he was pretty sure his dad would have loved it.

————

THOUSANDS CROWDED the Waikiki waterfront despite the rain. Glistening outrigger canoes stood poised in the white sand. Schools were closed, government business at a standstill. Live radio carried the proceeding, etching Duke's send-off into the collective memory of haoles, native Hawaiians, and hundreds of Kahanamoku cousins and half cousins spread across the island chain. The grief was universal, the elements of it shaped by the ceremonies of the past, when kings and queens were put to rest.

He had died on January 22, 1968, a few months after the celebration of his seventy-seventh birthday, a joyous occasion attended by 6,000. Friends presented him with a sixteen-foot cake in the shape of a surfboard and a lustrous Silver Cloud Rolls-Royce. In a story in the *Los Angeles Times* a year earlier, the sports columnist Jim Murray had named Kahanamoku as one of the greatest athletes of the half century, and quipped, "Duke is the only guy in the world who can look overdressed in shoes."

Throughout 1967 the *Honolulu Advertiser* had excerpted Duke's authorized biography, helping to expose his story to younger generations of Hawaiians. He had just returned from a harbor swim and was digging into his pockets for his keys to the Rolls when he had a heart attack and fell to the ground. His brother Bill was with him. David Kahanamoku had also died of a heart attack, only five months earlier, as he skippered an outrigger canoe. Their father had died of a heart attack at forty-eight.

After the service at St. Andrew's Cathedral, Duke was given the traditional beach-boy funeral he asked for. The altar was a surfboard decorated in white carnation leis and laid atop Duke's red and white outrigger canoe. His fellow beach boys sang Hawaiian songs. The rain continued, and clouds lay close and dark. Pastor Abraham Akaka, in a plain white T-shirt and black swim trunks that evoked the Hui Nalu, said that God had given Duke as a gift from the sea, and "now we give him back from whence he came."

An armada of outrigger canoes paddled out, accompanied by 150 surfboards piloted, as the *Honolulu Star-Bulletin*'s Bob Krauss reported, by all types, some "mahogany beach boys, some businessmen with paunches." Sargent Kahanamoku steered the lead canoe carrying Duke's widow, Nadine, who held the plain bronze urn. The second crew was made up of the undefeated outrigger team Duke coached. The Kahanamoku brothers tried to draw the boats into a circle, but it felt as if they hit a wall at the reef; no one could maneuver forward. The boats stacked up in a line. Sargent looked over to Bill and said, "I guess this is where he wants to be."

Nadine kissed the urn and released Duke's ashes into the sea. Grief turned to celebration as boatmen and passengers peeled off their leis and flung them forward, the floating petals of plumeria, orchids, carnations, and pikake offering a new memory.

Some raced back to shore, per the beach-boy tradition, but Sargent and his crew went slowly, one of the last boats in. A newspaper photograph captured them, and when the brothers looked closely, they saw a shark fin cutting through the water near where Duke's ashes had been scattered. The family discussed the image many times. Sargent saw the shark as an *ʻaumakua* — a guide to bring their brother home. "Duke was never afraid of the blue water," he said.

AUTHOR'S NOTE

I AM AN UNLIKELY PERSON to write about swimming. I did grow up on the ocean, in a seaside town in northern Massachusetts. But interest in swimming was no more than transactional; I swam to get from point A to point B, usually in a rush to leave the bracingly cold Atlantic for the warm, sandy shore. That's it.

It all changed a few years ago after being diagnosed with a rare spine cancer. The surgery to save my life resulted in nerve damage that left one leg partly paralyzed. To make myself feel whole again, I turned to a wide sampling of adaptive sports. I tried a lot of them before I got to swimming in 2020. I hadn't liked water calisthenics. I decided I had to figure out how to swim with my bum leg so that I could start to string laps together in the pool.

A physical therapist told me about a shorty wetsuit with a built-in buoyancy device sometimes used by swimmers training for long-distance events. I photographed myself in it in the pool locker room and sent the image to my son. I identified myself as Steve Zissou, the Jacques Cousteau–like adventure diver played by Bill Murray in the Wes Anderson film *The Life Aquatic*. Funny thing, the suit worked. I wrote about my unexpected life aquatic in an essay for *The New York Times*.

I found joy I hadn't known before in the pool and ocean. I have since swam not only in the Atlantic but also in the Pacific, the Mediterranean, and with my then ninety-two-year-old mom at Steel Derrick, the deep, freshwater granite quarry of my boyhood hometown.

I read deeply about the sport, and one of the first books that wasn't a how-to was Bonnie Tsui's transporting bestseller, *Why We Swim*. One of the chapters that consumed me was about the remarkable history of swimming in Japan and the many strokes developed during the samurai era. Competitive swimming wasn't a priority in that age — warfare was — but Bonnie talked with master practitioners who are bringing the beautiful classical forms back to light. She also wrote about Japan's embrace of competitive swimming in the early 1900s, and the groundbreaking performances of several athletes in the United States and Europe who had trained themselves to learn the revolutionary crawl stroke, which has today become synonymous with freestyle.

Bonnie's pages about historic swim races in Hawaii in 1926 and 1927 inspired me to look deeper into the origin stories of several of the best swimmers of that time — America's Duke Kahanamoku and Johnny Weissmuller, and Japan's Katsuo Takaishi. Though Takaishi was far less well-known in this country, the three were forebearers to today's modern athlete. Stylish and photogenic, they drew audiences that filled the new swimming arenas being built worldwide. Almost insanely self-driven, they extricated the most from themselves and their sport. They pushed hard, like all the barrier-busting greats who came after them — the Jackie Robinsons, Billie Jean

Kings, Michael Jordans. Better yet, their paths first crossed at the 1924 Summer Olympics in Paris, where the Games finally came into their own.

Increasingly, I saw similarities with my 2008 book about Black cycling champion Marshall "Major" Taylor. Kahanamoku, Weissmuller, and Takaishi's journeys, like Taylor's, have all the things I adore in a sports story: rivalry, high-stakes performances, personal discovery, colorful coaches, cultural conflict, and racial reckoning. The idea of three champion swimmers of different cultures and ethnicities, each using their own variation of the fastest swim stroke to become world famous superstars, captivated me. I had to know more. One minute I was reading Bonnie's book and the next I was buried in a Japanese swimmer's technical treatise on the crawl and an unpublished 300-page dissertation on the most explosive murder case in Hawaii history, involving one of Kahanamoku's fellow native athletes. Things escalated quickly, ultimately leading to this book.

I attempted to explain my sudden passion for swimming to many, especially those in the Hawaiian and Japanese communities where I was asking permission to tell stories that were not my own. I was looking for contemporary perspectives in addition to existing archival material to better understand Kahanamoku and Takaishi's experiences living and competing in a time when eugenics, Jim Crow laws, and anti-immigration hysteria were on the upswing and chasing them.

I freely admitted I shouldn't feel a connection to either man — I'm an Easterner, a land athlete, a white guy — but my disability and ongoing battles with cancer gave me a better appreciation of their achievements. The obstacles I faced in learning how to swim again — an effort that consumed me during Covid and had me doing land exercises until the pools reopened — made Kahanamoku and Takaishi's travails, adaptations, and improbable triumphs more compelling still. I was moved by their struggle to belong and the prejudices each man endured. Sadly, struggles like theirs have not gone away and seem to be only getting worse as racism, sexism, and now social media ugliness continue to infect sports and those who play the game.

I wrote *Three Kings* with a keen interest in how things were then as compared with now. Late in life Kahanamoku was asked how swimming had changed since his time. "Swimming suit!" he responded. "Nowadays the swimmers wear nothing but diapers. In my time it seemed like they covered the whole body. When they got soaked, they weighed a ton." He said this in 1957, decades before performance suits that help to make swimmers even faster.

In 2024 things continued to evolve but there were also continuing nods to the past. The U.S. Olympic swim trials were again held in Indianapolis, only this time they weren't in what was then the world's biggest swimming pool, at Broad Ripple, but the 70,000-seat Lucas Oil Stadium. In Paris, the original Tourelles arena is still standing 100 years later, and the Seine River, site of the 1900 swim events but declared too dirty in 1924, was cleaned up and used for several Olympic swimming events, including the triathlon. A few years ago I swam in the recently restored, glass-domed sixth-floor swimming pool at the Los Angeles Athletic Club, where Duke and Johnny raced in the 1920s.

The cultural perspectives on what defines an Olympian remain distinct and are fascinatingly wide ranging. One perennial medal favorite, the Japanese swimmer Daiya Seto, a graduate of Waseda University like Takaishi, returned to the 2024 Games after being suspended from the 2020 season. His offense was unsportsmanlike behavior — specifically, an extra-marital affair. Seto was deeply contrite and fully accepted his extraordinary censure.

The rules about amateurism that forced Kahanamoku and many others to struggle to make a living have of course radically changed. As a freshman basketball player at USC, Bronny James (and son of LeBron) was a leading "amateur" money earner. When the 2023–2024 season was still weeks away and he had yet to play a single college game, he had an estimated worth of $5 million. Another top earner at USC, quarterback Caleb Williams, surprised the women's soccer team by gifting them all with Beats headphones.

While the competitive sport of swimming is still overwhelmingly white, the United States Olympic Committee announced in 2023 what would have been unthinkable in 1924: the hiring of Black head coach, Anthony Nesty. "It has to start somewhere," Nesty told *The New York Times*. "I was the first one . . . . Are we there yet? No, but I think we're getting there."

Finally, the men's U.S. swim team at Paris last year was no match for the Weissmuller/Kahanamoku-led one in 1924. They won a lone gold medal in individual competition and finished no better than 7th in the 100-meter freestyle.

SOURCE NOTES

Prologue: "Duke Kahanamoku, This Is Your Life!"

In the early years of the *This Is Your Life* program — a perennial Emmy candidate in the 1950s and a top-twenty-ranked radio broadcast — there were few celebrities. The show's conceit was to spotlight people nobody knew, such as "Man on the Street" Harry Steffel. One 1948 episode featured an elevator operator. The first athlete, baseball player Tris Speaker, appeared one year after the program debuted. But Hollywood stars and sports heroes soon became more common. Rock Hudson was featured in 1952, and then came Roy Rogers, Jayne Mansfield, Milton Berle, and many others. For a show that was struggling to come up with new and interesting profile subjects, celebrities were an obvious tack. The show would signal a new and now established popular preoccupation for TV viewers: the lives of famous people, those we think we know.

The first Olympian on *This Is Your Life* was Louis Silvie Zamperini, who was introduced as "Former Olympic Track Star and World War II Prisoner of War Turned Minister." Duke Kahanamoku was only the third Olympian on the program, and the first athlete of color. The next episode starred Arries Ann Ward, a ninety-five-year-old former slave. I don't know how 1957 America responded to large, proud, dark-skinned families on their TV sets, but the next person of color, baseball catcher Roy Campanella, paralyzed from a car accident, wouldn't be on until almost two years later.

How much Duke knew about the *This Is Your Life* surprise is hard to say, though it is hard to believe he wasn't suspicious. The show needed to secretly coordinate his brothers' and sisters' trips to Los Angeles and, in at least one instance, there was a near miss when a few of them went shopping downtown and nearly bumped into the honoree. The show's host, Ralph Edwards, said there were only four instances of the secret leaking out, resulting in cancellation of the segments. Duke's reticence to share his private life was well-known, but he seemed happy enough to go with the flow — perhaps more evidence he knew what was coming? Or more evidence of what a present-day admirer calls his "epic levels of chill." According to the *Honolulu Star-Bulletin*, he received an assortment of gifts for his appearance, including a radio phonograph, $1,000 worth of records, a speedboat, a movie camera and projection system, a gold bracelet for his wife, Nadine, and a gold-veneer hood ornament of a surfer to replace the one that was stolen from his Rolls-Royce.

Johnny Weissmuller's appearance on the segment begged the question, Why feature Duke but not Johnny? He would have been prime material, given the show's Hollywood bent, and perhaps the producers had contacted him to gauge his interest. But Weissmuller was a man bearing real secrets, not to mention a gossip-filled private life, so maybe it was a chance he wasn't willing to take. In 1957, his *Jungle Jim* TV series having been canceled, he was promoting a line of above-ground backyard swimming pools called the Johnny Weissmuller "All American."

At this time, Katsuo Takaishi was preparing for Japan's first-ever hosting of the Olympics. In 2014 Kumiko Suganuma, a senior researcher at Keio University, wrote a fascinating article on Takaishi's devotion to coaching in the 1940s and 1950s, and the development of his method for beginners, called "Takaishi style."

Chapter One: Paris, 1924

The media coverage at the 1924 Paris Games was vast. Hundreds of correspondents descended on the city from neighboring countries and, in numbers never approached, the U.S. I longed for one piece of source material above all else: the Radio Paris call of the 100-meter race. This was the first-ever radio broadcast of the Olympic Games, and though I came across a photograph of broadcasters in their tiny booth, and knew that one of them, the unstoppable Edmond Dehorter, had hovered in a hot air balloon basket to report on cycling and running events, my hunt for a radio file came up empty. When I emailed Hervé Manificat, perhaps the leading researcher of all things Duke Kahanamoku from the French perspective (he wrote an introduction to a French edition of *Waterman,* a 2016 biography of Duke), he confirmed that he hadn't found it, either. According to *Inathèque,* a French government archive of broadcast history, radio broadcasts before World War II were done live and rarely recorded on discs. An exception was a Paris boxing match on October 6, 1923, which Dehorter called from the historic Salle Wagram auditorium, earning the nickname *"Le Parleur Inconnu,"* the unknown speaker. At the 1924 Games the print press set the agenda, so much so that Olympic organizers originally banned Dehorter's live radio reportage because of their objections to what they considered unfair competition. After finally reaching a truce, Dehorter received credentials and likely called the 100-meter final from the pool deck.

Chapter Two: Queens Break, 1898 – 1912

The thematic focus of this chapter comes from interviews with Duke conducted in Hawaii in 1949 and 1950 by the intrepid broadcasting duo, Lowell Thomas and his son, Lowell Thomas Jr. The Marist College archive holds the audio files, which director John Ansley generously digitized for me. The files were transporting, from Sam Kahanamoku's deferential interruptions to boost Duke's storytelling to the brothers' charming ukulele playing and singing. Sam's brief mention of Duke swimming and surfing in the presence of the deposed Hawaiian queen consumed my thoughts and lent added meaning to the connection between past, present, and future. I sent the link to the tapes to Sam's granddaughter Elianne Vannatta (who was good enough to correspond with me); Pamai Tenn, longtime confidante of Nadine Kahanamoku and a gatekeeper to the family legacy; and Sarah Fairchild, the superb executive director of the Outrigger Duke Kahanamoku Foundation. I didn't hear back — I can imagine there might be some fatigue over mainland writers exulting over "finds" — but it wasn't for that reason I shared the link. I wanted to try to create an avenue where I gave as much as I received. I was keenly aware of sources in books skewed to white newspapers and observers. Ronald C. Williams, a writer and staff researcher at the Hawaii State Archives, which sits on the grounds of the historic royal palace, encouraged me to make a broader search of Hawaiian sources, which he said had been consistently ignored in books and media. The starting point was the database Papakilo, which contains hundreds of hits for

Duke Kahanamoku, and a blog called *Nupepa,* by an anonymous author who has translated many articles about Duke from historical Hawaiian newspapers.

During my 2022 research trip I talked with a range of young native Hawaiians who either directly or indirectly were influenced by Kahanamoku. His legacy remains vibrant for many. My thinking about Duke was heavily influenced by wide-ranging conversations with a number of people, including Kala Alexander, a fiery big wave surfer and activist (who couldn't help boasting of his toddler granddaughter's water talents); Keolu Fox, a doctor of genome science and a primary voice behind the Bishop Museum's pioneering re-exploration of the 1920s eugenics project in Hawaii; Duane DeSoto, the founder of the nonprofit school Nā Kama Kai, member of the Hawaii Waterman Hall of Fame, and actor who played Duke in two documentaries; and Cliff Kapono, an acclaimed surfer, journalist, and marine conservation scientist on the Big Island; and especially Isaiah Walker, author of *Waves of Resistance,* a book exploring how Duke and Hui Nalu found strength, agency, and renewal in the Waikiki surf, and projected it forward to succeeding generations. Walker's 2021 interview on the podcast *Waterpeople* was wonderfully engaging and insightful, and he was gracious with his time when I visited him at the Brigham Young University–Hawaii campus in Laie, where he is an academic vice president helping to shape the school's direction. He provides television commentary at one of Oahu's premier surfing events, the Hui o He'e Nalu Backdoor Shootout. During our conversation, he told me about a recent project that would have made the Hui Nalu, and presumably Duke, take notice. Arguing that Hawaii was a sovereign nation illegally overthrown, he and others were lobbying the International Olympic Committee to create an independent Hawaiian surf team to compete in the 2024 Olympics. They would wear the Hawaiian flag, not the U.S. flag. It reminded me of what DeSoto told me: "We are not anti-American," he said, "we're pro-Hawaiian."

Finally, anyone who writes about Hawaii or Duke Kahanamoku heads for the Bishop Museum, a sprawling institution on the historic property once owned by Charles Reed Bishop and Ke Ali'i Bernice Pauahi Bishop. The Bishop holds a fabulous photographic record of Kahanamoku's early career, comprising hundreds of prints as well as memorabilia books kept by his friends. Perhaps the best book, *Duke Kahanamoku's Swimming Trip*, was compiled by Lew Henderson, who accompanied Kahanamoku and fellow Hawaiian surfers as team manager on their trip to the mainland in 1912 and chronicled the cross-country stops.

The Outrigger Canoe Club's online archives have fantastic historical articles and oral histories that span Duke's life and times, including some from Nadine and his brothers. Marilyn Kali, a longtime member of the historical committee, has laboriously mined the club's vast collection and continues to scan new donations of scrapbooks. She is writing a book on Outrigger's competitive swimming years, from 1912 to 1936.

Chapter Three: The Olympic Age, 1896 – 1912

New journalistic attention is being paid to the life of Jim Thorpe and other pioneers like the indigenous and Black athletes who accompanied Kahanamoku to Stockholm in 1912. That class began the slow shift away from Olympic rosters comprised of privileged elites to selective representation from a broader pool of athletes. Only recently coming to light is how the emerging U.S. model spread to other countries. The Japanese had previously banned working-class laborers from Olympic rosters but changed to merit-based criteria in 1924, opening participation to all athletes with the potential to win medals.

James E. Sullivan was long suspected of knowing about Thorpe's minor-league professional career but elected to look the other way until the Carlisle School star was outed in a *Worcester Telegram* front-page story in January 1913. At the time, writes Kate Buford in *Native American Son,* the *Los Angeles Times* memorably described the controversial Sullivan as a "pompous little insect." Less well-known, then and now, is the eugenic experiment associated with the 1904 Olympics Sullivan directed. It might take some by surprise, especially the contemporary recipients of the award named for him and given each year to the nation's top amateur athlete. In 2023 the University of Iowa basketball star Caitlin Clark won the ninety-third James E. Sullivan Award at the New York Athletic Club. (Sullivan was also categorically opposed to female participation in elite sports.) Swimmers Mark Spitz and Michael Phelps, hurdler Edwin Moses, and Princeton basketball star Senator Bill Bradley are among the many past winners. Strong sources about the eugenics study Sullivan coordinated in St. Louis are not as hard to find as you might think. Erica X Eisen's 2019 article for the online magazine *The New Inquiry,* "Specimen Days: Human Zoos at the 1904 World's Fair," which relies on cultural anthropologist Susan Brownell's collection of original research essays focusing on the same subject, gives an excellent summary account of Sullivan's and anthropologist William J. McGee's deplorable side project.

Chapter Four: Hotbeds, 1905 – 1913

Bruce Wigo is a longtime historian and former president and executive director of the International Swimming Hall of Fame in Fort Lauderdale, where Johnny Weissmuller's collection of

Olympic and national medals, files, and ephemera resides. (Johnny's devotion to the Hall of Fame was such that it was written into his will.) His interest in historical topics runs the gamut from sports to politics, but he has been in the swimming game his entire life and probably is the person most familiar with the Weissmuller legacy and Johnny's living descendants. For a time, he was involved in a moribund documentary project focusing on Weissmuller's early life and swimming career. Wigo was extremely generous with his time and even hand-delivered to the hall of fame for my use a vintage Duke-related scrapbook he had recently won at auction. Johnny didn't leave behind any personal journals that he knew of, but Wigo, former COO Laurie Marchwinski, and collections specialist Todd Eller encouraged me to explore the Weissmuller papers and made available select scrapbooks compiled by Johnny's 1920s swimming contemporaries. In an unpublished transcript of an interview Wigo did for a scrapped documentary project, he movingly described the terrifying impact of the *General Slocum* fire within the German-American community, and how it motivated Elizabeth Weissmuller to take her young boy to Fullerton Avenue Beach in Chicago to learn how to swim. Johnny Weissmuller's son's memoir, *Tarzan, My Father*, is controversial within the family but the book includes invaluable original documents such as the physical abuse complaints listed in the 1925 divorce case "Elizabeth Weissmuller v. Peter Weissmuller."

Wigo also directed me to Lisa Maria Salb, Weissmuller's granddaughter, who has sought to bring his career back to prominence. Salb, based in the same Mexican city where her grandfather died, maintains a comprehensive website and is point person on several potential media projects about his life. She is a talented musician and compelling storyteller who shared fond memories of her grandfather and listed the biographies she has read about him. *Johnny Weissmuller: Twice the Hero* by David Fury is one of her favorites.

Perhaps the most useful and unbiased Weissmuller research item I came across is a comprehensive, citation-laden genealogical investigation of the Weissmuller family published in 2004 by GenealogyRO, based in Timişoara, Romania.

Much of the information on Japan's ancient swimming history and the country's contemporary turn to competitive international racing was a collaboration of sorts with Masaaki Imamura, the historian for the Japanese Swimming Federation and a master coach in the swimming martial art of *Nihon eiho*. Imamura provided me with multiple comprehensive Power-Point presentations on the history of swimming in Japan that contained images and data dating from the samurai era warfare swimming arts to the twentieth century turn to racing against the clock. He shared articles he had written about Japanese swimming technique, along with an electronic copy of a long essay Den Sugimoto composed on the fiftieth anniversary of the pool he and his students built. Midori Ishibiki, like Imamura a top practitioner, teacher, and preservationist of classical swimming methods, joined in all our Zoom meetings, each session agilely managed and translated by Ayane Miyashita, a student from Akita International University.

Chapter Five: Trouble, 1913 – 1915

Not much has been written about an alleged romantic affair Duke Kahanamoku had after his momentous gold-medal performance in Sweden. I was surprised by this, thinking that a sports hero's love life wasn't so much scandalous or an insult to his legacy, but humanizing. At the time there was minimal reporting on Duke after he was named as a co-respondent in the 1913 Deerr divorce proceeding, and no mentions in later biographies, but I found sources that lent credence to the affair, such as the guest registry at the hotel retreat in Hauula and the eyewitness observation published in the *Maui News* on October 11, 1913. That account added, "[Noël] Deerr says she has not been wife to him since November last year and, as a baby is alleged to be expected by Mrs. Deerr, the husband asks himself a question or two. Complexion may settle the question and a disagreeable matter set aside forever. Among the swimmers of the Hui Nalu there was a constant wish that Mrs. Deerr would fall off a pier . . . or do something really wicked that would forever rid Duke of her presence."

The lawsuit and the public airing of breakup details continued for months after the first news account. I found no mention of Duke after Rhoda Wilson Deerr's return to England, and no details about her baby. However, on February 13, 1914, Deerr's London lawyers claimed the unborn child to be her husband's and requested he pay expenses for her return to Honolulu so she could win back her good name and perhaps contest the divorce. Noël Deerr denied paternity but agreed to an immediate settlement and an alleged 200 pounds annual alimony payment.

Chapter Six: Nord Seite, 1917 – 1920

The horrifying 1919 race riot in Chicago would have been a momentous event for anyone in the city but especially for a teenager like Weissmuller, who came from a broken home and had flirted with the gang scene. The anti-German hysteria of a few years earlier proved equally compelling and provided some understanding of the hatred immigrant German families endured. It changed the way I thought about the young Weissmuller.

Biographies I read didn't give much consideration to the personal obstacles Weissmuller faced in this period. In his memoir, *Tarzan, My Father,* Johnny Jr. said his normally voluble dad didn't like talking about his adolescent years. I benefitted from several books documenting the era — from Douglas Bukowski's *Big Bill Thompson, Chicago, and the Politics of Image* to Cameron McWhirter's *Red Summer* — as well as archives from the *Chicago Tribune* and the Chicago History Museum. My visit to Chicago included an unsuccessful attempt to get past School of the Art Institute of Chicago security to view the still intact Illinois Athletic Club basement swimming pool at 112 South Michigan Avenue. (The School of the Art Institute purchased the former club in 1992.) By contrast, its rival a block away, the Chicago Athletic Club, survives with its trophies and memorabilia amply showcased. It is now a boutique hotel, with a cozy, speakeasy-feeling dining room and a sprawling game room with well-worn billiards tables.

During these years immediately following the Great War, Duke Kahanamoku was enjoying one of his best periods in Waikiki. Duke's happiness and comfort with himself was suggested by the openness of his relationship with Eleanor Snodgrass, a Berkeley student visiting the island with her mother. Historians were unaware of their relationship but in the summer of 2022, when I happened to be in Waikiki, her personalized scrapbook and a book of poems that Duke inscribed to her came to auction. The items are extraordinary, lending new insight into this time in Kahanamoku's life.

Then came the low point and the vicious Leonard Withington article in 1920. I relied on excellent summary reviews of Duke's subsequent libel case, *Kahanamoku v. Advertiser Publishing Company, Limited, a Hawaiian Company,* as well as the article "When 'Slacker' was a Dirty Word," written by lawyers at the Boston firm Foley Hoag LLP, which cites the Kahanamoku case.

Chapter Seven: Monsters from the West, 1920

A copy of the letter protesting the 1920 U.S. Olympic team's traveling conditions to the Antwerp Games is among the Duke Kahanamoku papers in the Hawaii State Archives. With that letter, amateur athletes united in a way they had never done before. Charles Paddock's 1932 book, *The Fastest Human,* is both entertaining and vivid in chronicling those colorful 1920 disputes and the later goings-on at the 1924 Paris Games. At the same time, there was the riveting story of another set of athlete-pioneers, the women's swimming and diving team. Ethelda Bleibtrey, Aileen Riggin, and company, led by manager Charlotte Epstein, forced the American Olympic Committee to drop its objection to female participation in 1920, allowing them to sail to Antwerp, where they dominated. Bleibtrey won three gold medals, and the tiny Riggin, age fourteen, won gold in fancy diving and inspired a wildly popular kids' fan club. In 1924, the top women swimmers ignored the American Olympic Committee's directive preventing them from going to Europe ahead of the Games to swim in exhibition races. By contrast, Bill Bachrach, who had scheduled lucrative European races for Weissmuller, decided to heed the ruling.

The birth of the Japanese crawl at the national meet in Heda in 1920 — through scrawny Ibaraki high schoolers like Katsuo Takaishi — happened at virtually the same time Japanese senior swimmers, using the old sidestrokes, were dying on the Olympic stage in Antwerp. The Japanese swimming historian Masaaki Imamura underlined the importance of Heda in multiple interviews, but even fuller details emerged in the writings of Den Sugimoto and Takaishi. Heda represented the beginning of a golden era in Ibaraki swimming that extended through the 1923 Far Eastern Games in Osaka and the 1924 Olympics in Paris. Sugimoto's 1965 book, *Swimming and Walking: 70th Anniversary of the Founding of Ibaraki High School and 50th Anniversary of the Founding of the Pool* was invaluable. His 1926 book, *Swimming Competition,* and the 300-page-plus biography *Remembering Mr. Takaishi* were also helpful, and contain photos about the program's evolution, including the journey to Paris. Later, when the crawl became celebrated in Japan, some contended that one of the 1920 Japanese Olympic swimmers, Kenkichi Saito, had led the charge to teach the younger generation. Takaishi didn't remember it that way. "Mr. Saito insisted on using one hand," says Takaishi in the biography. If he had adopted the crawl, Takaishi claimed, Saito would have been unbeatable and remembered for all time.

Chapter Eight: Comers, 1921

The Weissmuller discovery story was often told by his coach Bill Bachrach, first in interviews, then his syndicated instructional columns in 1923 and 1924, and, finally, in his 1924 book, *The Outline of Swimming.* Weissmuller kept to the script, saying that he showed up at the Illinois Athletic Club pool one day, where Bachrach recognized a raw but promising talent and immediately signed him up. Months later he was virtually unbeatable. In truth, Weissmuller had already been winning junior races for a couple of years and drawing notice and early instruction from another high-profile coach in Chicago, Harry Hazlehurst. The story of why Weissmuller switched from Hazlehurst's tutelage to Bachrach's interested me, but newspaper stories only recorded who Weissmuller swam for, not why. However, Bachrach seemed to always get the swimmer he wanted, except for Duke Kah-anamoku. Why that was so seemed related to his irresistible personality, his stable of champions, and, probably the IAC's deep pockets. Amateur racers were compensated, and everyone knew it. The sportswriter Paul Gallico spent many pages in his book *Farewell to Sport* detailing the hypocrisy of amateur sports and how the best managers and athletes got a steady stream of cash on the side. "Practically every athlete in the United States today is guilty of some breach of the amateur code, and the better known the athlete, the more certain the breach," he wrote.

The Bishop Museum in Honolulu supported the race science experiment in Hawaii that the New York anthropologist Louis R. Sullivan conducted. A hundred years later, the museum still holds the products of the fieldwork: reams of personal family data and photos. Even the sculptures produced for the American Society of Natural History eugenics exhibit remain. The life-sized David Kahanamoku sculptural centerpiece — one that surely would have been modeled on Duke had he not been at the Olympic Games in Antwerp — is in storage at the Bishop. In 2021, in a remarkably transformational event, the museum acknowledged the work of the long-discredited project with an exhibit and a series of speaker events called "(Re) Generations: Challenging Scientific Racism in Hawai'i." A principal objective of the exhibit was to repurpose the controversial Sullivan Collection, sharing the genealogical data and photos with native Hawaiians looking to research personal histories. I talked to two of the curators of the exhibition, Jillian Swift and Keolu Fox. They both expressed pride in taking something that in the 1920s was done *to* Hawaiians and turning it into something *for* Hawaiians. Fox, a native Hawaiian and an assistant professor at the University of California San Diego with a PhD in genome sciences says, "There is a lot of interest in decolonizing museums, and we were one of the first ones to turn inward and be reflective. Working within our community was gnarly, you are literally digging up all of this trauma. But overall, it was a really cathartic healing process."

Chapter Nine: Great White Hope, 1922

In hosting the championship meets starring Johnny Weiss-muller — one in the pool, one in open water — Hawaii saw itself reasserting its swimming dominance. In February 1922, the Elizabeth Waterhouse Memorial Pool was opened at Puna-hou prep school to considerable hoopla. It was modeled after the magnificent indoor pool at Yale University but was judged better because it was outdoors, backdropped by mountains and sky, and set into a lovely hillside. Yet when Weissmuller arrived, the story flipped to become about him and Bachrach. Photos of their visit are in scrapbooks at the Bishop Museum and the Outrigger Canoe Club, and in local newspaper archives. Their trip unfolded like an early preview of the Beatles invasion of America. The Liberty cinema showed film clips of opening races at Punahou; Weissmuller posed for photographers on surfboards and strummed a guitar; Bachrach sat cross-legged in a full suit in the hot sand. The impression was that while they had come for Weissmuller to set records, just as important was to show that a white celebrity visitor belonged in the local clime and maybe even in local waters, a place distinctly identified with native Hawaiians.

Alexander Hume Ford, the founder of the Outrigger Canoe Club and the mastermind of Hawaii's early 1900s tourism promo-tion, had begun the cultural appropriation process in 1907 when he introduced Jack London to surfing during the writer's famous sailing voyage in the South Pacific. London would later write in awe about the exotic local men and women riding the surf breaks, and how he rode some himself. Though his account would appear in his book *The Cruise of the Snark* (1911), it originally appeared as "Riding the South Sea Surf" in *Woman's Home Companion* in 1907. Several excellent scholarly articles have looked at this colonialist "discovery" period, including "Duke Kahanamoku's Body: Biography of Hawai'i," from the book *Sports Matters*. The author, Michael Nevin Willard, aptly describes "the racial gaze of tourism" and how London reinforced the notion of racial hierarchy. "[London] asserts an evolutionary narrative of civilized white progress by figuratively *taking the place* of the Native Hawaiian surfer," writes Willard. It was a trope played out repeatedly in Hawaii: the replacement of dark-skinned native Hawaiians and their water traditions with prominent Anglo-Americans who claimed to have discovered them.

The author James D. Nendel, in his superb dissertation about Kahanamoku's life (*Duke Kahanamoku: 20th Century Hawaiian Monarch*), argues that Duke's departure from Hawaii had been planned for months, but I arrived at a much different impression in reviewing the local coverage. The hasty-seeming decision to go when he did was influenced by a failed pitch to local businessmen to start a movie studio in Honolulu; a collapsed film deal to promote surfing in Scandinavia; and the frenetic media attention around Weissmuller's May arrival.

For this chapter, I talked to Cliff Kapono, a world-renowned surfer and marine scientist, who shared with me his anxiety about leaving the islands for a PhD scholarship in San Diego, California. It reminded me of the same wrenching decision Duke Kahanamoku faced about leaving Hawaii for a new life in Los Angeles. Kapono told me about hiking into the extreme island wilderness, hoping to get a sign of what to do. "I wanted to know I was doing right by my ancestors," he said. But it was quiet. No signs. He laughed a bit in the telling but the quiet, he thought, was his ancestors saying he was going to be lonely. Kapono moved to California to advance his career but described the experience as depressingly solitary. Racist abuse led to confrontations and some fights. He found himself in a dark place. There is no way to know what exactly Kahanamoku experienced in California and what the cumulative toll was, but Kapono gave me a lot to think about. He eventually returned to Hawaii, where he studies coral health at the University of Hawaii in Hilo.

Chapter Ten: Dreams, 1922 – 1923

This chapter is about two promoters: the IAC and Oscar Henning, each alluring and destructive in their way. Henning was the scam artist straight out of central casting, preying on a vulnerable mark. Kahanamoku was at a low ebb as Johnny Weissmuller set records in his Hawaiian waters, and Henning promised a golden future somewhere else. Their relationship was remarkably well chronicled in the Los Angeles and Honolulu papers. Duke wasn't the only one Henning fooled. During World War II Oscar Hellstrom (his real name) wowed journalist Walter Cronkite, who called him a "fabulous character" and "one hell of a valuable contact" in his book *Cronkite's War*. He added that Hellstrom was a multimillionaire and a "close friend of FDR." Eventually Hellstrom made his way to Seattle, where he ran the Big Four Inn and where he died in 1955.

The IAC was legitimate but equally exploitive of Weissmuller, insisting on nonstop travel and backbreaking record-chasing in the United States and overseas. The newspapers covered much of it, especially in Hawaii, but the best source was *Tri-Color* magazine, produced by the IAC and dripping with attitude and arrogance. Articles were sometimes written by the swimming stars themselves, like Norman Ross, other times by supportive journalists like Clarence A. Bush. The magazine boasted the work of some of Chicago's top illustrators; along with photographs, it enriched the superhero auras of Bachrach and Weissmuller. When the IAC's women's teams came to prominence, they were lavishly photographed to the point of objectification. When Weissmuller traveled to John Harvey Kellogg's Battle Creek Sanitarium, the magazine published a multipage story with photos and shadowgraphs. (In one of the rare non-swimming stories it published, a reporter visited a Ku Klux Klan recruitment event in Chicago. In an interview with the grand wizard, the reporter wonders about how many IAC members might sign up.) I found the complete run of *Tri-Color* at the Chicago History Museum. Top clubs, like the New York Athletic Club, also had their own magazines but none were as devoted as *Tri-Color* to boosting the careers of its leaders.

Chapter Eleven: Gone, 1922 – 1923

These years, 1922 to 1923, were full of change in Japan, as the country's young princes embraced the growing physical culture movement. At the same time, ambitious innovators like Sugimoto and Takaishi made themselves known. In the eccentric and enterprising communal project of building the Ibaraki pool, I saw echoes of Julie Checkoway's great book *The Three-Year Swim Club*, about the legendary Hawaiian coach Soichi Sakamoto and his use of irrigation ditches in sugar fields to train his Olympians. Much of the detail about the Ibaraki pool and Takaishi's improbable ascendance comes from Sugimoto's Japanese language books and *Remembering Mr. Takaishi*, an extraordinary book that was published in 1967, shortly after the swimmer's death, and includes recollections from Takaishi and surprisingly frank stories from his children and wife, and photographs of the thousands who gathered to memorialize him at his funeral.

Springfield College, which started as the YMCA Training School, has in its rare book archive a 224-page, fully illustrated compendium with the ponderous title *The Sixth Championship Games of the Far Eastern Athletic Association: Held in Osaka, May 21 – 26, 1923 Under the Patronage of His Imperial Highness Prince Chichibu and by the Sanction of the International Olympic Committee: Official Report*. It was "drawn up" by Franklin H. Brown, but was started by his late brother, Elwood S. Brown. It didn't disappoint, nor did the college museum, which features a who's who exhibit of early twentieth-century physical education and recreation pioneers, such as Luther Gulick and Amos Alonzo Stagg. In addition to the official report, I reviewed rare microfilm of back issues of *Osaka Mainichi*, an English-language Japanese daily paper that sponsored the 1923 Far Eastern Games.

Chapter Twelve: The Dance, 1923 – 1924

Johnny Weissmuller's secret — that he was born in Europe and altered his birth record to get his passport to swim for the U.S. in Paris — was kept for his entire life, not even shared with his children. The full story was finally told in an excellent 1984 piece in *Sports Illustrated* by Arlene Mueller titled "Johnny Weissmuller Made Olympian Efforts to Conceal His Birthplace." Mueller tells the story of the grand deception but also how the lie kept building, such as when Weissmuller accepted an invitation to Windber, Pennsylvania, in 1950 to be celebrated as a native son. In addition, she depicts the almost bemused point of view of the early 1900s diasporic community in Chicago and his countrymen in Romania, to whom Johnny's birthplace was no surprise. They kept the secret, too. When Mueller told Weissmuller's son, Johnny Jr., the tale of the secret, his response was: "I guess he was a better actor than any of the critics knew."

In David Davis's *Waterman*, a highly readable, excellently sourced biography of Duke Kahanamoku, there is mention of Congressman Henry Rathbone being friendly to the Weissmuller cause despite having requested an investigation. The motivation of a first-term, home-state congressman asking for an investigation of a local hero was perplexing. I requested the paperwork, supposedly filed through the Department of Labor, from the National Archives, but a detailed search turned up no references to Weissmuller. If the file ever existed, it seems to be no more. What does exist, however, are the multiple ship manifests from Johnny's trips to Hawaii in the 1920s, which list his birthplace as Hungary (after World War II border changes, the town became part Romania). The episode is emblematic of the wheeling and dealing to come from the United States Olympic Committee as it found ways to expedite and creatively manage citizenship cases of aspiring medal hopefuls in the lead-up to Olympic Games. Weissmuller and his team were pioneers in yet another way.

Chapter Thirteen: Spirit, 1923 – 1924

The U.S. anti-immigration legislation targeting Japan moved swiftly as the Olympic year approached. It had been discussed years earlier at the National Conference on Race Betterment in Battle Creek, where one of the lecturers worried about the hostility to Asians in America. Sidney Gulick, presenting on "Race Betterment and America's Oriental Problem," argued that the Japanese had lived for thousands of years in the North Temperate Zone, and had benefited from severe social discipline. "They are on the whole vigorous, brainy people," he said. He added that while intermarriage between Blacks and whites was considered bad, he couldn't say the same of white and Japanese coupling; the question needed further study. By 1924 that opinion was in the minority in Congress. The Immigration Act of 1924, which included the Asian Exclusion Act enacted months earlier, sent shock waves around Europe and especially Japan, where angry protests were chronicled in newspapers worldwide. Japan's small band of Olympic athletes had to survive the humanitarian catastrophe of the Great Kantō Earthquake in September, then the racist censure of the U.S., the country that would likely headline the Games in Paris.

In addition to an article written by Den Sugimoto — "Olympic Gift: Souvenirs from Paris" — my sources included the *Japan Times* archive, Waseda (University) Sports Museum, and the digital archives at hathitrust.org, which among other things, has the recorded proceedings of the major Race Betterment conferences held throughout the early 1900s. I also used a variety of American and British newspaper sources and the official reports of the French and American Olympic committees, available at LA84 Foundation Sports Library. The latter has a remarkable storehouse of historical reports, oral histories, scholarly works, and even early American Athletic Union meeting minutes.

Chapter Fourteen: The Race of the Century, 1924

In the Weissmuller file at the International Swimming Hall of Fame (ISHOF), I found a beautiful 1920s pamphlet of Indianapolis's Broad Ripple Park — a meaningful keepsake and perhaps a suggestion of the lasting weight of that first meeting between Johnny and Duke. The ISHOF put together a digital exhibit featuring its extensive cartoon collection from the era, several of them about Weissmuller and Kahanamoku. Photos from the Indy race revealed one surprise: starting blocks, an innovation that wouldn't be welcomed into the Olympics until 1936. Though I found rundowns of the two swimmers' measurements, and there was regular reference to their large "paddles" and feet in the press, detailed analysis of body physiology would come along much later, hitting a high point in the Michael Phelps era, when his body, mind, and nutrition were scrutinized across all media. (The Battle Creek lab assessment of Weissmuller — not of much interest to anyone except John Harvey Kellogg — was an interesting exception.) When I met Duke biographer Sandra Kimberley Hall for the first time, at the Waikiki Queen Kapiolani Hotel, she slid me a copy of an outline drawing of his hands, and encouraged me to press my own against them for comparison. Hall shared many resources and contacts, and had been a friend to Duke's late widow, Nadine. Her early-on reassurance that the connections between Duke and Johnny were worth exploring — particularly in the pre–Broad Ripple years, when they had yet to meet — counted for a lot.

Aaron Peirsol, a seven-time Olympic medalist (five gold), provided a crucial window into the psychology of high-stakes racing, given his well-known duels in the 2000s with the older American champion Lenny Krayzelburg. I was originally directed to Peirsol, a Californian who now lives in Oahu, because of his personal interest in Kahanamoku and his open, thoughtful manner. Peirsol's dominance in the 200-meter backstroke was analogous to Weissmuller's, and his world record, set in 2009, has yet to be broken. "There is an aura to Duke that maybe even Weissmuller doesn't have," he said. "Something more holistic, more grounded. The ocean is the beginning of it and the end of it." We talked for hours in Waikiki, in between his many duties associated with the annual, weeklong Duke Kahanamoku Ocean Festival. He also introduced me to Sonny Tanabe, legendary Hawaiian swimmer, waterman, and coach who invited me to lunch at the Elks Lodge, a historic waterfront property in Waikiki near the War Memorial Natatorium, where he once competed. Tanabe's wide-ranging memoir, *Once Upon a Time,* about growing up as a Japanese American in Hawaii during World War II, is excellent, and while it isn't overly focused on race, the theme is there. Peirsol also told me about going out to dinner with Tanabe during the Duke Festival in 2022. On their way to the exclusive Honolulu restaurant, Tanabe told Peirsol he remembered a time when he wasn't welcome there.

Chapter Fifteen: Citius, Altius, Fortius – Paris, 1924

Colorful oral histories were a boon to this chapter, such as those from 1924 U.S. Olympic athletes Norman Cleaveland (University of California Berkeley's Bancroft Library, 1995) and William Neufeld (LA84 Foundation Olympic Oral History Collection). Neufeld's interview in 1987 was a standout, with descriptions of the zany training setups aboard the boat headed for Paris, Weissmuller's swinging from the chandelier, and the wrestling matches between 1,500-meter-runner Joie Ray and medalist swimmer Gertrude Ederle. In the section on general team conduct in the Official Report on the Paris Games, American Olympic Committee President Robert M. Thompson expressed a wish to ban wives from going to future Olympic Games. And he might have had Weissmuller's comic antics in mind when he sternly wrote, "Some of the young men on the last team forgot this [the honor of participating in a great and solemn international event] and conducted themselves like children or like schoolboys out on a frolic."

The decision to do away with ad hoc vaudeville entertainment such as that performed by Weissmuller and his sidekick, Harold "Stubby" Kruger (team manager John Taylor wrote in the official report that the "French public couldn't get enough of it"), along with a crackdown on future boorish behavior, were topics at a vigorous meeting of the International Olympic Committee's jury d'honneur in Lausanne, Switzerland, in 1925. Baron Pierre de Coubertin, though supposedly retired, led the group.

David Bevan's "The Lost Generation and Olympian Man" (Dalhousie University, 1984) offered a comprehensive view of the world's infatuation with all things athletic in 1924 Paris. He writes that the fascination with sports during that summer was "unparalleled, to my knowledge, in any other country at any other time in history."

Chapter Sixteen: Golden People, 1927 – 1964

Waikiki's War Memorial Natatorium, which opened in 1927, has been out of use for years. Advocates for its restoration have mounted various efforts and helped produce a compelling 2015 documentary called *The Tank*. Others view its restoration as too expensive and see its seaside construction as misguided from the start. For now, the crumbling stadium is surrounded by high fencing and "no trespassing" signs. In a city where plaques and statues dedicated to Kahanamoku dot the shoreline and a celebration of Duke's birthday takes place each year at 7:00 a.m., this piece of his legacy remains in limbo. "How we respond to this challenge will mark the greatness or failure of who we are as a people," wrote Peter Apo in an opinion piece for *Ka Wai Ola,* a publication of the Office of Hawaiian Affairs.

I wondered if Weissmuller was influenced by eugenic ideologues such as John Harvey Kellogg. I found nothing to indicate he had formed any opinions on the subject, and certainly his admiration for Duke and their later friendship supports the argument that he was not in the race-betterment camp. Kellogg would find posthumous infamy with the 1993 novel *The Road to Wellville* by T. Coraghessan Boyle and the movie adaptation starring Anthony Hopkins. A 1994 *Washington Post* story about the movie and Kellogg's Battle Creek Sanitarium would be memorably headlined "An Enema of the People." The article and the film focused on Kellogg's health zealotry and less so on his other obsession, race purity. Weissmuller's 1927 visit to the sanitarium was covered in the *Battle Creek Enquirer* and *Tri-Color*, which reprinted a lengthy story on the visit that was originally published in *Good Health, the Battle Creek Journal of Health and Personal Hygiene*, edited by Kellogg.

Perhaps not much can be made of Duke's film work playing bit roles. But one glimpse of his comic potential is found in the 1925 short film *No Father to Guide Him*, in which he plays a cocky lifeguard who has to be rescued himself. He is brilliantly funny, and his performance points out the obvious: He was never able to get Hollywood leading parts because of the color of his skin.

The Takaishi legacy seems to have been diminished by his premature death at fifty-nine and the disappointing performance of the Japanese swimming team he directed at the 1964 Tokyo Olympics. After many months of trying, I finally made contact with his descendants — three surviving daughters in their eighties and nineties, including Yuriko Takaishi Kojima, the fourth of his five daughters, who lives in Ashiya City, near Osaka. When she was a young woman, she confessed to biographers that her strict father had once intimidated her. "When I married, he treated me as an independent person for the first time," she said. "It was a great sorrow he passed away when I just thought I finally wanted to try to get closer to him." That was almost sixty years ago. In a November 2023 Zoom conversation facilitated by Keio University's Kumiko Suganuma, Kojima recalled the time she and her father spent together teaching swimming, and his sense of service. He was a beautiful swimmer, she said, and he wanted everyone to feel a bit of what he did. "My father worked hard under the slogan, 'kokuminkaiei' (all people in Japan should be able to swim)," she said. "When he heard someone was drowning in the sea near the water training school he immediately ran to the sea, taking all the other instructors with him."

Epilogue: Three Funerals, 1966 – 1984

In the memorial book *Remembering Mr. Takaishi,* there are numerous photos from his extraordinary funeral, including ones of his sensei, Sugimoto; his children; and grandchildren. His daughter Yuriko vividly remembers that day, and the plaque dedication at the Osaka area pool shortly afterward. Still living not far from the old family homestead in Osaka, she confirmed the story of Takaishi's century plant and its unlikely awakening last year.

Much of Weissmuller's unusual funeral in Acapulco was reported by the Associated Press and United Press International. A UPI photo shows a chimp next to the coffin and dozens of mourners and tourists. Weissmuller's death, coming in an Olympic year (the Games in Los Angeles would be a huge success, especially for U.S. swimming), might have prompted a full-throated remembrance of Weissmuller's unbeatable days in the pool. But the one official tie-in event, a luncheon at his former house in Beverly Hills hosted by "Los Angeles Organizing Committee wives," received little notice. Asked about the venue, Ginny Ueberroth, wife of committee president Peter Ueberroth, told the *Los Angeles Times,* "We wanted the luncheon for the IOC wives there because first, it's a pretty home, and second, it gives them an idea of Beverly Hills." The Weissmuller family did hold an additional memorial service in Beverly Hills but apparently not Chicago, as was first announced.

The reporting on Duke's good-bye was extensive, richly chronicled in the Hawaiian newspapers. It was the lead story on the *Honolulu Advertiser* front page, more prominent than the news of the Apollo mission's successful test flight. A local friend who grew up in Oahu at the time (and whose affluent and prominent grandfather once drove a car with a gilded hood ornament of Duke surfing) remembers the community grief and emotional celebration of his life that peaked with his beach boy–style Waikiki funeral. One of the eulogists described Kahanamoku as "without a phony bone in his body." Ellen Fullard-Leo, the manager of the 1924 Hawaiian Olympic team, recalled his devastating loss to Weissmuller and how he was "great even in defeat." Oral histories collected in the Outrigger Canoe Club archives, specifically one from Sargent Kahanamoku, reflect on Duke's importance to Hawaiian sports and culture.

SELECTED BIBLIOGRAPHY

A Few Red Drops: The Chicago Race Riot of 1919, Claire Hartfield, Clarion Books, 2018.

All that Glitters Is Not Gold: The Olympic Game, William O. Johnson Jr., G. P. Putnam's Sons, 1972.

Ambassadors of Peace! Sport, Race, Cultural Diplomacy, and the 1927 Takaishi/Saito Swimming Tour of Australia, Sean Brawley, Fitness Information Technology, 2011.

American Museum of Natural History, Central Archives, letter from Henry Osborne to James Sullivan, July 7, 1920.

Bound for Freedom: Black Los Angeles in Jim Crow America, Douglas Flamming, University of California Press, 2005.

Contested Waters: A Social History of Swimming Pools in America, Jeff Wiltse, University of North Carolina Press, 2009.

"The Duke of France: Duke Kahanamoku's Parisian Stays, His Influence and His Representation in the French Press of the Time," Hervé Manificat, issues 107 and 108 of the French edition of The Surfers Journal, 2015.

Duke Kahanamoku: 20th Century Hawaiian Monarch, James D. Nendel, PhD thesis, Penn State, 2006.

Duke of Hawaii, Joseph L. Brennan, Ballantine, 1968.

Farewell to Sport, Paul Gallico, Alfred A. Knopf, 1938.

The Fastest Human, Charles W. Paddock autobiography, Paddock Family Estate, 1932.

Haunts of the Black Masseur: The Swimmer as Hero, Charles Sprawson, Pantheon Books, 1993.

Hawaiki Rising: Hokule'a, Nainoa Thompson, and the Hawaiian Renaissance, Sam Low, University of Hawai'i Press, 2013.

The History of Olympic Swimming, Volume 1: 1896–1936, Peter Daland, USA Swimming Press, 2009.

"How Japonisme Forever Changed the Course of Western Design," Nancy Hass, New York Times Magazine, February 11, 2021.

Japan at the Olympic Games, 1909–1938, The Emergence of an Athletic Power, Harold James Olson, unpublished master's thesis, California State Polytechnic, Pomona, California, 1991.

"Katsuo Takaishi: The Creator of Swimming in Japan," Kumiko Suganuma, Ashiya City magazine, 2014.

Lost Kingdom: Hawaii's Last Queen, the Sugar Kings, and America's First Imperial Adventure, Julia Flynn Siler, Atlantic Monthly Press, 2012.

Making the American Team: Sport, Culture, and the Olympic Experience, Mark Dyreson, University of Illinois Press, 1998.

Memories of Duke: The Legend Comes to Life, Sandra Kimberley Hall and Greg Ambrose, Bess Press, 1995.

Mid-Pacific Magazine, 1911–1922 (Hathi Trust digital collection, catalog.hathitrust.org).

"Modernization and Identity Creation (1868–1920): The Evolution of Competitive Swimming in Japan," Andreas Niehaus, The International Journal of the History of Sport, Vol. 27, No. 3, March 2010.

Native American Son: The Life and Sporting Legend of Jim Thorpe, Kate Buford, Alfred A. Knopf, 2010.

No Father to Guide Him, a Hal Roche silent comedy film featuring Duke Kahanamoku, 1925.

Our Town Ibaraki, published by Ibaraki City and Ibaraki Board of Education, 1985.

Raced to Death in 1920s Hawai'i, Jonathan Y. Okamura, University of Illinois Press, 2019.

Recreation in Japan, Seiichi Kishi, First International Recreation Congress Proceedings, July 23–29, 1932, National Recreation Association.

Remembering Mr. Takaishi, edited by the Japan Swimming Federation (Kansai Branch), National Diet Library collection, 1967.

Re-Viewing the Past: The Uses of History in Cinema of Imperial Japan, Sean D. O'Reilly, Bloomsbury Academic, 2018.

Shifting Currents, A World History of Swimming, Karen Eva Carr, Reaktion Books, 2022.

The Sixth Championship Games of the Far Eastern Athletic Association, Held in Osaka, May 21–26, 1923, Franklin H. Brown, The Far Eastern Athletic Association, 1924.

Sport, Race, and Ethnicity: Narratives of Difference and Diversity, edited by Daryl Adair, Fitness Information Technology, 2011.

Sports Matters: Race, Recreation, and Culture, edited by John Bloom and Michael Nevin Willard, New York University Press, 2002.

The Stadium Century: Sport, Spectatorship, and Mass Society in Modern France, Robert W. Lewis, Manchester University Press, 2016.

A Study of Amateurism of the Japan Athletic Association: Focusing on the Selection of the Japanese Delegates at the Games of the VIII Olympiad, Paris, Sou Nemoto, Hidenori Tomozoe, and Kazuyuki Nagashima, 2017.

That Summer at Boomerang, Phil Jarratt, Hardie Grant Books, 2014.

"The Greatest Olympiad," Elon Jessup, The Outlook, August 13, 1924.

Surfing in Hawai'i 1778–1930, Timothy Tovar DeLaVega, Arcadia Publishing, 2011.

Swimming and Walking: 70th Anniversary of the Founding of Ibaraki High School, 50th Anniversary of the Founding of the Pool, Den Sugimoto, 1965.

Swimming Competition, Den Sugimoto, Tokyo Sogensha, 1926; National Diet Library digital collection.

Swimming in Japan, International Young Women's and Children's Society, Tokyo, 1935.

"Exploring the Origins of Swimming in Japan," Masaaki Imamura, Japan Swimming Federation, Swimming magazine, February 2020.

Swimming the American Crawl, Johnny Weissmuller, Houghton Mifflin, 1930.

Tarzan, My Father, Johnny Weissmuller Jr. with William Reed and W. Craig Reed, ECW Press, 2002.

Johnny Weissmuller: Twice the Hero, David Fury, Artists Press, 2000.

Tri-Color magazine, Illinois Athletic Club, 1912–1929.

Viola: Diving Wonder & Aquatic Champion, Margery Voyer Cole, The Paragon Agency, 2001.

Waterman: The Life and Times of Duke Kahanamoku, David Davis, University of Nebraska Press, 2015.

Water, World & Weissmuller, Narda Onyx, Vion Publishing, 1964.

White Wash, a documentary film directed by Ted Woods, 2011.

Why We Swim, Bonnie Tsui, Algonquin Books, 2020.

Yokohama Burning: The Deadly 1923 Earthquake and Fire That Helped Forge the Path to World War II, Joshua Hammer, Free Press, 2006.

ACKNOWLEDGMENTS

THERE ARE SO MANY amazing people to thank for helping me along on this journey. Writing this book would not have been possible without my friend and longtime Chicago-based editor Laura Hohnhold. Through my health struggles and self-doubt that I could write what is perhaps my last book, she was unfailingly supportive and caring in all ways, and is the person singularly responsible for turning a draft into a book.

The blank spot on my research map was Japan and its early twentieth century swimming pioneers. Thanks to my friend and fellow author Bonnie Tsui, who shared her contacts in the classical swimming community — Masaaki Imamura and Midori Ishibiki — to get me going. I literally could not have talked with either of them without the standout assistance of Ayane Miyashita, a Global Studies major at Akita International University, who translated our many conversations and later independently found and translated works that were key to unfolding the personal story of Katsuo Takaishi and Den Sugimoto. Her last bit of sleuthing was phoning and interviewing Kumiko Suganuma, the author of a contemporary article which led to finally finding one of Takaishi's surviving daughters, Yuriko Kojima. Ayane started as an assistant with this project but became much more of a collaborator.

Many people generously offered their time and expertise as I researched the lives of Duke Kahanamoku, Johnny Weissmuller, and Katsuo Takaishi. I wish I had space to elaborate on the important roles each of them played, but please know my sincere thanks. They are Sean O'Reilly, Cory Hathaway, Sandra Kimberley Hall, Donald Love, Claire Sanford, Allen Anderson, Mickey Munoz, Pia Solywoda, Bruce Wigo, Laurie Marchwinski, Todd Eller, Brad Anderson, Dale Smith, Sonny Tanaka, Kala Alexander, Keolu Fox, Duane DeSoto, Cliff Kapono, Isaiah Walker, Jillian Swift, Aaron Peirsol, Kim Vandenberg, Lisa Maria Salb, John Cork, Michael Salmon, DeSoto Brown, Ron C. Williams, Jim Fulton, Sarah Fairchild, Earl Pamai Tenn, Elianne Vanetta, Marilyn Kali, John Ansley, Jeffrey Monseau, David Sterling, Jacqueline MacMullan Boyle, and Tim Creamer. Esmond Harmsworth, my agent for all my books beginning with *The Last River,* helped immensely with his constant encouragement and crucial hands-on crafting of my *Three Kings* proposal.

In addition to Laura Hohnhold, Mark Bryant, the editorial force behind Scribd's acclaimed Everand Originals series, is someone I have worked with for an almost incomprehensible thirty-five years, beginning with our time together at *Outside* magazine. He has supported me and my work ever since, and I can't say how lucky I've been because of it. I've only recently met Charlie Schroder, the publisher at Everand Originals, but she has been great, and worked furiously to partner with Blackstone, the print book publisher. To be the first Everand author to be published both digitally and in hardcover means a lot to me.

Lastly, my family, specifically my spouse, Patty Adams, but also my adult children, Celia and Henry, are responsible for me doing anything at all. We have been through so much the last couple of years but somehow, we have gotten through it. It's impossible not to have deep apprehension with metastatic cancer, but I also look forward with hope because of them. As the actor Michael J. Fox said recently about his daughter's upcoming wedding and the limitations of his illness: "There's something to be said for just pluck and optimism. I won't dance well [at the wedding], but I will dance."

ABOUT THE AUTHOR

Photograph by Stephen Sheffield

Todd Balf is a nonfiction writer known for his ability to identify little-known people and events in the worlds of adventure and sports and breathe new life into them. He is author of the bestselling, critically acclaimed adventure sagas *The Last River* and *The Darkest Jungle* and the biography *Major,* about the pioneering Black bicycle racer Marshall "Major" Taylor. Balf is also the author of the Scribd Original *Complications,* a memoir about how illness reshaped his own life as an athlete.

ABOUT EVERAND

Everand™ is a digital content subscription that offers millions of ebooks, audiobooks, magazines, news articles, podcasts, sheet music, and more. The app is a destination for stories and knowledge that constantly adds new and original content in partnership with the world's leading publishers, authors, and other storytelling partners. Everand recommends content that fits diverse lifestyles and reading habits — to make moments more interesting, entertaining, and meaningful. The app is available on iOS and Android devices — in addition to web browsers and Apple Watch.